FINLAND IN THE EUROPEAN UNION

T0373623

We would like to dedicate this work to our loved ones – Anni, Timo, Saska, and Jason – who have not only given us their support and love but have also reminded us of what really counts most in life.

FINLAND
in the
EUROPEAN UNION

Tapio Raunio
University of Tampere, Finland

and

Teija Tiilikainen
University of Helsinki, Finland

With a Foreword by
PAAVO LIPPONEN,
Prime Minister of Finland

Routledge
Taylor & Francis Group

LONDON AND NEW YORK

First Published in 2003 in Great Britain by
Routledge
2 Park Square, Milton Park, Abingdon, Oxon, OX14 4RN
270 Madison Ave, New York NY 10016

Transferred to Digital Printing 2010

Website: www.routledge.com

Copyright © 2003 Tapio Raunio and Teija Tiilikainen

British Library Cataloguing in Publication Data:

Raunio, Tapio
  Finland in the European Union
  1. European Union – Finland   2. Finland – Foreign relations –
  Europe   3. Europe – Foreign relations – Finland   4. Finland –
  Politics and government – 1981 –
  I. Title   II. Tiilikainen, Teija
  327.4'89704

          ISBN 0–7146–5375–6 (cloth)
          ISBN 0–7146–8309–4 (pbk)

Library of Congress Cataloging-in-Publication Data:

Raunio, Tapio.
  Finland in the European Union / Tapio Raunio and Teija
Tiilikainen.
    p. cm.
  Includes bibliographical references and index.
  ISBN 0-7146-5375-6 (cloth) – ISBN 0-7146-8309-4 (pbk.)
    1. European Union–Finland. I. Tiilikainen, Teija. II. Title.

  HC240.25.F5 R38 2003
  341.242'2'094897–dc21

                                            2002074077

*All rights reserved. No part of this publication may be reproduced in any form or by
any means, electronic, mechanical, photocopying, recording or otherwise, without
the prior written permission of routledge and Company Limited.*

Typeset in 10.5/12.5pt Classical Garamond by Vitaset, Paddock Wood, Kent

Publisher's Note
The publisher has gone to great lengths to ensure the quality of this reprint
but points out that some imperfections in the original may be apparent.

Contents

Tables and Illustrations

List of Abbreviations

CAP	Common Agricultural Policy
CFSP	Common Foreign and Security Policy
CoR	Committee of Regions
CSPEC	Confederation of Socialist Parties in the European Community
EC	European Community
ECB	European Central Bank
ECJ	European Court of Justice
EDU	European Democrat Union
EEA	European Economic Area
EEC	European Economic Community
EFGP	European Federation of Green Parties
EFTA	European Free Trade Association
ELDR	European Liberal, Democrat, and Reform Party
EMU	Economic and Monetary Union
EP	European Parliament
EPP	European People's Party
ERM	Exchange Rate Mechanism
ESC	Economic and Social Committee
ESDP	European Security and Defence Policy
EU	European Union
EUCD	European Union of Christian Democrats
EUL-NGL	Confederal Group of the European United Left/Nordic Green Left
EVA	Centre for Finnish Business and Policy Studies
FCMA	Treaty of Friendship, Cooperation and Mutual Assistance
G/EFA	Greens/European Free Alliance
IGC	Intergovernmental Conference
INC	International Network of Centre Parties
JHA	Justice and Home Affairs
KD	Christian Democratic Party
KESK	Centre Party

KOK	National Coalition
LFA	less favourable area
MEP	Member of the European Parliament
MP	Member of Parliament
MTK	Central Union of Agricultural Producers and Forest Owners
NATO	North Atlantic Treaty Organization
NDI	Northern Dimension Initiative
NELF	New European Left Forum
NUORS	Young Finns
OEEC	Organization for European Economic Cooperation
OSCE	Organization for Security and Cooperation in Europe
PES	Party of European Socialists
PS	True Finns
QMV	qualified majority voting
RKP	Swedish People's Party
SAK	Central Organization of Finnish Trade Unions
SDP	Social Democratic Party
SEA	Single European Act
SKDL	Finnish People's Democratic League
SKP	Communist Party of Finland
SMP	Rural Party
TEU	Treaty on European Union
UN	United Nations
VAS	Left Alliance
VIHR	Green League
WEU	Western European Union
WTO	World Trade Organization

Foreword

The accession of Finland to the European Union in 1995 was a logical and decisive step in Finland's long-standing policy of participation in European integration. Successive governments had pursued that policy with success since the time of the last war. By joining the Union Finland took her place in the new Europe emerging from Cold War division. Membership in the Union has strengthened Finland's international position and it is fair to say that it is now stronger than ever before.

In the referendum organised in October 1994, Finland's membership was approved by 57 per cent of voters. Since then support for membership has remained steady. As in many other member states, Finns don't always love the Union, which is at times seen as a distant bureaucracy meddling too much with issues considered primarily local, not European. But citizens put high value on the political and economic stability that membership in the European Union brings with it.

The broad aims and goals of Finland's EU-policy are widely supported across party-political lines at Eduskunta, the Finnish parliament. Right from the beginning of EU-membership Finland has relied on an advanced system of extensive consultation with the parliament on EU-policy. Aiming at full transparency and close interaction with the parliament, government ministers, including the Prime Minister, report on Council and the European Council meetings to the European Affairs Committee. This has done a great deal in enhancing democratic legitimacy and securing wide support for government's policy.

For a small country like Finland, the Union presents a unique opportunity to influence Europe's development and to strengthen positive interdependence in the Northern region with integration. The main feature of Finland's EU-policy has been active participation in strengthening and developing the Union. For Finland the Union is a tool in securing equal rights not only for the Member States but also for Europe's citizens and businesses. Finland has naturally strived to defend her own interests, for example in agriculture and regional policy, but has tried to do this by looking for the common good in the development of the Union's common policies. Making the Union stronger both internally and in its external policies has been a consistent aim of Finland's policy.

Equality can be pursued and defended only through common agreements and rules supported by strong institutions. A strong European Commission watching over the compliance with the common rules is ultimately the best guarantee against the domination of selfish and narrow national interest. In order to preserve democratic legitimacy, while being effective and responsive to new challenges, the Union needs to maintain a balance of power between the institutions while reforming its decision-making structures.

At the beginning of the twenty-first century the Union needs reforms. All institutions, including the Council, Commission and the European Parliament have the responsibility to make the Union's decision-making system more transparent and efficient. Citizens and businesses alike expect swift decisions, dialogue and accountability from the Union's institutions. In this respect, the Treaties of Amsterdam and Nice have meant a step in the right direction. But much more needs to be done and Finland is committed to continuation of reforms at the next Intergovernmental Conference due to take place in 2004.

It is first and foremost the responsibility of the Member States to make necessary economic and social reforms in order to stick to the commitments of the Growth and Stability Pact and the Lisbon strategy for boosting Europe's competitiveness. If big Member States start dragging their feet, as has often been the case, the small ones can only rely on powerful common institutions in order to make everyone live up to their commitments. The legitimacy of common institutions is therefore a crucial factor, and needs to be supported by accountability and efficiency.

One trademark of Finland's EU-policy has been our focus in making the Union a stronger actor in external relations. As a small and open economy relying on external trade, Finland has benefited from globalization. The rewards from opening up markets should and can be spread more evenly and the Union can continue to show global leadership with initiatives like granting full access to its markets for the least developed countries. Finland supports the Union in maintaining its strong role in opening up the world economy and developing the institutional arrangements needed for global governance.

Finland's contributions to enhancing Union's external role include the initiatives to build a crisis management capability for the Union (an initiative together with Sweden to the Intergovernmental Conference in 1996–97) and to expand the Community's competence in common trade policy (an initiative adopted in the IGC 2000). The Finnish initiative on the Northern Dimension of the European Union has become an established part of the Union's external relations.

The Northern Dimension has contributed both to the integration of all Baltic Sea States into the development of the Union's policy in the northern regions and to the strengthening of the Union's relations with Russia. Non-EU countries have been offered the possibility to participate in the development of a policy where the active contribution of partner countries is essential for concrete results in such diverse fields as energy, health, transport and the protection of the environment.

Early on in her membership of the European Union Finland concluded that the further widening and deepening of integration within the Union is decisive for all nations on the European continent. The bold decisions on enlargement – made in Luxemburg in 1997 and in Helsinki in 1999 – have proved the point. The most valuable achievement of integration is the peace and stability that has prevailed in the European Union. With enlargement the Union continues the elimination of old divisions in Europe. This process does not stop with the forthcoming accession of several new member states in 2004. After the present process of accession negotiations with 12 countries is completed, the Union will have to deal with the application of Turkey and face the challenges in the Western Balkans. The continent gradually unifies around the European Union.

This book fills a gap in the literature on national policy-making in the European Union. Comprehensive texts on Finland's policy on Europe have been scarce and it has been especially difficult to find an up-to-date analysis in English. The authors of this book have acquired a wide academic knowledge of Finland's policy and have mastered well the difficult task of presenting the main ingredients of the Finnish way of participating in the process of European integration.

I'm convinced that everyone looking for a good overview of Finland's policy in the European Union will find this book interesting and illuminating.

Paavo Lipponen
Prime Minister of Finland
September 2002

Introduction

Academic writings on Finland and Europe have normally approached the topic from the perspective of the international system, with scholars focusing on Finland's position given its geopolitical environment. Such emphasis is not surprising, as Finland shares a long border with Russia and during the Cold War had close political ties with the Soviet Union. During the past decade, Finland's international position has changed fundamentally from that of a 'neutral' Nordic country to that of a member state of the European Union (EU) with a firm commitment to further integration. Nevertheless, scholarly understanding of the Finnish political system and particularly of Finnish EU membership remains limited.

In view of the lack of studies on Finland, the purpose of this book is to analyse the impact of European integration on Finland and to examine the role of Finland as a new and small member state of the EU. Improved knowledge of Finnish politics is also important in terms of understanding politics in general at the European level. The division of labour reflects our fields of specialization. Tapio is responsible for Chapters 1, 3 and 4, while Teija wrote Chapters 2, 6, and 7. Chapters 5 and 8 were co-written. In 1998 we both came to work at the Centre for European Studies, located in the Department of Political Science at the University of Helsinki. For this opportunity, we thank Professor Tuomo Martikainen, who has provided us with an excellent and productive working environment. We owe a great debt to Hanna Wass, MSocSc, who read the entire manuscript and offered valuable comments and technical advice.

Tapio Raunio and Teija Tiilikainen
Helsinki
July 2002

1

National Politics and European Integration

The rapid constitutional transformation of the European Union (EU) since the mid-1980s, with five Intergovernmental Conferences (IGC) and substantial transfers of power from the national to the European level, has fundamentally changed the nature of European integration. While prior to the Maastricht Treaty (signed in 1992) scholars could still claim that member states would not delegate powers to the EU in so-called 'high politics' areas, these arguments now sound hollow, as the jurisdiction of the EU extends basically to all policy areas, ranging from funding cultural projects to the gradual development of common foreign and security policies, so that 'nearly every conceivable area of policy is now subject to shared national and EU competence'.[1]

The total size of the EU budget is admittedly small (maximum of 1.27 per cent of the total gross domestic product of EU member states until 2006), but the redistributive capacity of the EU should not be under-estimated, as its agricultural and regional policies (structural funds) have a profound impact on the farming sector and on the less wealthier areas of the Union. The EU is responsible for almost 80 per cent of legislation on the production, distribution, and exchange of goods, services, capital, and labour in the EU countries. It deregulates exchange by removing various barriers to trade while simultaneously regulating trade by setting up common standards that apply across the Union. More importantly, the introduction of the single currency with independent monetary policy decided by the European Central Bank (ECB), together with the increasing coordination of national fiscal and economic policies, means that the economic policies of member states are to a large extent tied to rules agreed at the European level.[2] Moreover, the decisions of the EU are enforceable by the European Commission and the EU court system, as European Community (EC) legislation is binding on member states and their citizens.

Despite the economic and political powers of the EU, its decision-making process is still dominated by national governments. Treaty amendment is subject to unanimous agreement by the member countries, while the EU institutions have no formal role in IGCs. Most important policy decisions, such as agreeing on the timetable of the Economic and Monetary Union (EMU) and the consecutive enlargements, are taken by heads of governments in the summits of the European Council, the real board of directors of the Union. Despite the extended application of the co-decision procedure, the Council still remains far ahead of the European Parliament (EP) in its legislative powers. The role of the European Commission in initiating and implementing legislation is controlled by national governments, whose civil servants participate in the hundreds of committees and working groups that draft the EU's legislative initiatives and oversee their eventual implementation.

The central role of national governments in the EU policy process makes it essential to study the behaviour and ideology of member states. But states are obviously not unitary actors, and the way national positions are arrived at varies among individual countries. Therefore, as the liberal intergovernmentalist approach of Moravcsik emphasizes, it is also essential to study the formulation of national preferences on integration: to identify the participants (government, parliament, state administration, economic and other interest groups, parties, and key individuals) in the game and their influence in the process. Thereby, we can answer the crucial question of *whose* interests are represented in national integration policy.[3]

The next section of this chapter reviews previous research on the impact of European integration on national political systems. Then the main features of the Finnish polity are introduced, starting with basic facts and a brief overview of recent history, and then outlining the evolution of Finnish integration policy. The final section explains the structure of the book.

EUROPEANIZATION AND DOMESTIC CHANGE

What are the consequences of European integration for national political systems? While scholars agree that the EU does matter and does produce domestic change, there is far less agreement on the scope of the change and on the role of European integration vis-à-vis other explanatory factors, domestic or international, in explaining that change. However, while understandably difficult, isolating the 'EU effect' is arguably easier in the case of the latecomers to the Union (Austria, Finland, and Sweden) for two reasons. First, they joined the Union in 1995, and therefore scholars do not have to rely on often less than reliable historical accounts. Second, the newcomers had to adapt to the challenges posed by EU membership very quickly, almost overnight, unlike older member states whose adaptation has been incremental and has occurred over several decades.[4]

Scholars have written extensively about the effect of the EU on national policies, with particularly the economic, environmental, and social policies of member states attracting much attention. Most of the literature on the impact of the EU on domestic political systems has understandably focused on governmental institutions (the executive branch, parliament, and the courts) and particularly on public administration. The overwhelming majority of these publications have been case studies of individual countries, notably of France, Germany, and the UK. As one would intuitively expect, there has been more convergence in national policies than in national institutions.[5]

Reviewing the literature on the balance of power among domestic institutions, we can identify two partially conflicting lines of argument. According to the liberal intergovernmentalist approach, the EU political system strengthens domestic governments because they, and not backbench parliamentarians or people outside the executive branch, participate in decision-making in the various EU institutions.[6] The main beneficiaries are the ministers in charge of most 'Europeanized' portfolios (notably prime ministers and finance ministers) and the civil servants within ministries responsible for EU matters. The key aspect behind these arguments is information. National parliaments have usually been described as the main losers in this process, with the informational advantage enjoyed by the executive branch limiting the ability of the members of parliament (MPs) to control their governments.[7]

According to the 'multilevel politics' scenario, however, the EU policy process can also weaken the position of the government, as societal groups can bypass the national government and use the new supranational channel to pursue their policy objectives. National executives are significant and probably the most important actors in EU decision-making, but they are not gatekeepers preventing access by domestic groups to the European level. This tendency is facilitated by EU institutions, most notably the Commission and the EP, which have consistently sought to establish and consolidate links with both European and national non-governmental organizations.[8] The introduction of structural funds has strengthened the regional level in several member states, with regional authorities, encouraged by the Commission, often circumventing national authorities and establishing direct contacts with the EU bodies. The

3

common standards of the EU are often more stringent than domestic legislation in some member states, and this has consequences for the relevant parties and interest groups in these countries. For example, EU environmental legislation can be much more 'progressive' than similar regulations in force at national level, and thus environmental groups can use the EU institutions to pursue their policy goals and achieve domestic, and even wider, change as they are marginalized in their own political system. Indeed, as indicated by the thousands of lobbyists working in Brussels, national interest groups make active use of the 'EU channel' to achieve their policy objectives. Political parties have also increased their activity at the European level, forming federations of parties known as 'Euro-parties'.

Another aspect of multilevel politics is that the process of integration, particularly the increasing interdependence of European and national agendas, reduces the autonomy of all actors, with national policy choices being constrained by the existing EU rules and legislation (*acquis communautaire*) and by what is politically feasible in light of the preferences of other member states and the EU institutions. Politics is also increasingly judicialized, with the decisions of both the European Court of Justice (ECJ) and national courts acting as another constraint on national parliaments and governments.

European integration can also lead to more deep-seated changes in the basic nature of the domestic policy process. For example, as most European legislation deals with the internal market and is highly technical, the preparation and implementation of laws are either formally or informally delegated downwards to middle-ranking civil servants or even semi-independent agencies.[9] This reinforces a style of governance and politics that favours technical policy expertise and pragmatism at the expense of more ideological partisan debates, a type of politics termed by Kohler-Koch the 'network mode of governance'.[10] On a yet broader level, the EU has played a crucial part in the economic development of certain member states (the Mediterranean countries and Ireland) and in helping Italy, Germany, Greece, Portugal, and Spain to distance themselves from their authoritarian past. These kinds of broader, incremental changes can be more difficult to detect, but in the long run they can also be more profound than other, more easily observable institutional or policy changes.

The research on the impact of the EU on member states is usually labelled as 'Europeanization', which is defined by Ladrech as 'an incremental process reorienting the direction and shape of politics to the degree that EC political and economic dynamics become part of the organizational logic of national politics and policy-making'.[11]

4

Europeanization is primarily a top-down concept, employed for analysing the impact of integration on developments at the national level. As our focus is on governmental institutions and on the formulation of Finnish integration policy, it is useful to examine in more detail some of the main findings of this research on the Europeanization of national institutions.

The comparative project led by Rometsch and Wessels defined 'Europeanization' as 'the shift of attention of all national institutions and their increasing participation – in terms of the number of actors and the intensity – in the EC/EU decision-making cycle'. They hypothesized that Europeanization would lead to fusion, 'the common sharing of responsibilities for the use of state instruments and the increasing influence of the EC arena on the vertical and horizontal interaction of national and European institutions', and that this would in turn produce constitutional and institutional convergence at the national level.[12] National institutions were increasingly involved in the EU policy process, and there was no clear division between national and European levels. In short, the picture they sketched was one of fairly strong interdependence. Regarding convergence, they detected certain similar patterns: the central role of the governments coupled with decentralization and flexibility in decision-making, the bureaucratization of public policy-making, high administrative coordination in national EU policy, and low involvement of parliaments.[13]

The volume edited by Kassim, Peters and Wright focused on national coordination of EU policy.[14] Heads of government have emerged as the true leaders of national integration policies, participating in the summits of the European Council and leading national delegations in the IGCs, at least during the final stages of the negotiations. Excluding Germany, foreign ministries provide the link between national policy formulation and the EU level, including both the permanent representation and the EU institutions. The position of foreign ministers has gradually eroded as prime ministers and sectoral ministers, notably finance ministers, have strengthened their positions. Member states have established interdepartmental units or committees for EU policy coordination, the most famous being the General Secretariat of the Interministerial Committee on European Questions (SGCI, *Secrétariat Général du Comité Interministériel*) in France. At the highest political level, coordination is often carried out in specific EU ministerial committees. Spain has an Interministerial Committee, Denmark a Foreign Policy Committee, the UK a Subcommittee for European Affairs, Greece an Interministerial Committee, Belgium an Interministerial Conference for Foreign Policy, and Germany a Cabinet Committee for European Affairs. Individual ministries have established new procedures or organizational structures for EU matters, both within and between ministries. Parliamentary input across the Union is relatively limited, regardless of the formal powers of the MPs to 'mandate' their governments.[15]

The convergence or at least similar patterns are explained mainly by adaptational pressure: 'In common, member states confront pressures and procedures at the European level that determine in which forums and under which decision rules, in what sequence and by which actors, business is to be transacted.'[16] Member states also learn from each other, adopting good practices from their colleagues. But, there are also significant differences, not least those due to the different policy styles and organizational structures and cultures found across the member states. States can have either impositional or consensual approaches to decision-making, with highly inclusive or narrow consultation of societal groups. Certain countries are proactive, seeking to influence agenda-setting, while others mainly react to developments at the European level.[17] Some member states have placed great emphasis on policy coordination, while other countries simply focus on ensuring the consistency of national positions on certain essential questions, such as structural funds in the case of Mediterranean member countries. France, the UK, and Denmark have highly centralized coordination structures and aim at coordinating national positions in a broad range of matters handled at the EU level, with centralization at least partially explained by 'suspicion of integration and the desire to preserve national sovereignty'.[18] However, centralization does not necessarily imply quality or success in EU negotiations, as success depends on overall resources and the expertise of civil servants and elected politicians, and, of course, on whether national integration policy and more concrete policy goals find support among EU institutions and other national governments.[19] Furthermore, while coordination is important, the sectorization of the EU policy process makes policy coordination rather difficult, as policy communities with considerable technical expertise, informational advantages, and special interests are constructed and will probably resist intervention by other ministries.[20]

This brief overview of recent literature on the Europeanization of political systems shows that there are certain important similarities among the 15 EU member states. The executive has strengthened its position, with particularly the status and visibility of prime ministers being reinforced through the summits of the European Council and through their leading role in the coordination of national EU policy. The sectorization of EU decision-making puts a premium on policy-specific technical expertise, and this regulatory or managerial style of politics empowers civil servants at the expense of democratically elected office-holders. National parliaments have gradually started to improve their involvement in the EU policy process, but, arguably, only certain parliaments are really able to influence the direction of national integration policies. Finally, a broad range of national agents from courts to interest groups have increasingly shifted their attention to the European level, with strong interdependence between EU and national politics. Moreover, the Austrian case illustrates how strong and pervasive the impact of EU membership can be. While the Austrian national authorities were aware of the institutional implications of EU membership for national political systems and took precautionary measures in order to safeguard the roles of the parliament, the Länder, and interest groups, their positions were nevertheless weakened as a result of the political dynamics of the EU policy process.[21]

However, does size explain any variation among member states? Comparative studies on national adaptation to integration suggest that generally it does not. Small countries do not behave in the Council in a similar fashion. Their integration policies differ, and so do their organizational solutions at the national level. However, this should not lead us to disregard too hastily the impact of size. In policy influence, smallness may well bring benefits that at least partly compensate for the greater numerical weight of the larger member states. For example, while wisely warning against simplistic generalizations, Arter has suggested that smallness might confer certain advantages. Small member states may be better positioned to push particular issues onto the EU agenda, especially when the initiative is presented as being in the interests of the Union as a whole. Larger member states, which, on average are more influential, may find it more difficult to get similar proposals accepted, as they are more likely be perceived as simply pursuing their own interests at the expense of the larger community. Secondly, small member states may be better placed to build compromises between competing sides, acting as neutral brokers between larger countries. Thirdly, their smallness may allow them to be more fluid in their coalition behaviour.[22]

Regarding national adaptation and the management of domestic integration policy, Hanf and Soetendorp argue that the influence of small states in international negotiations requires effective organization at the national level. Thus, they should have centralized systems for formulating national EU policies, with the political leadership, and particularly the prime minister, being directly involved in the management of EU affairs.[23] At least the three Nordic EU countries, all of which are small member states, seem to have followed this pattern: 'To maximize national influence, the ideal is thought to be that representatives of national governments speak with one voice on European affairs. Their positions are to be based, as far as possible, on national consensus or compromise worked out between interested parties. National policies in various policy areas are not supposed to contradict each other.'[24] Describing the strategy adopted by Sweden, Ekengren and Sundelius note the importance of prioritization: 'National coordination of prioritized policy positions is presented as a substitute for material resources and political weight for a small but ambitious member state.'[25] Smaller member states therefore pay special attention to presenting unitary, cohesive national positions at the European level: 'The presentation of one homogeneous position in the negotiations in the Council and its preparatory fora was considered to be a satisfactory instrument for effective behaviour in Brussels.'[26] However, the goal of speaking with one voice is not limited to small member states:

> As well as coordinating their internal policy-making activities, govern-
> ments must be prepared to defend more coherent programmes at
> the EU level and also to ensure that their proposals in Brussels and
> their actions in the national capital are compatible. Further, given
> that there are economic and political resources to be gained from
> Brussels, national governments may believe that they need to present
> the best possible cases for their country in that arena, and that this
> can best be done through presenting a unified front against Brussels
> bureaucrats and the demands from other countries.[27]

Table 1
Distribution of Seats Among Member States in the EU Institutions (2001)

Member state	Council (votes)	Commission	European Parliament	European Court of Justice	Economic and Social Committee	Committee of Regions
Germany	10	2	99	1	24	24
France	10	2	87	1	24	24
Italy	10	2	87	1	24	24
UK	10	2	87	1	24	24
Spain	8	2	64	1	21	21
The Netherlands	5	1	31	1	12	12
Belgium	5	1	25	1	12	12
Greece	5	1	25	1	12	12
Portugal	5	1	25	1	12	12
Sweden	4	1	22	1	12	12
Austria	4	1	21	1	12	12
Denmark	3	1	16	1	9	9
Finland	3	1	16	1	9	9
Ireland	3	1	15	1	9	9
Luxembourg	2	1	6	1	6	6
Total	87	20	626	15	222	222

Nevertheless, size can matter here in three respects. First, small countries are normally more dependent on trade and a narrow range of export industries than large countries, and thus they probably have, on average, fewer and more clearly defined national interests to defend. Second, as Thorhallsson emphasizes, size has consequences for state administration. As smallness means fewer staff, this scarcity of resources forces small member states to adopt more flexible and pragmatic approaches to EU policy-making, with more power delegated downwards to civil servants than in larger member states. Third, and more significantly, small states need to prioritize: they cannot focus on everything with the same intensity. While, in most issues, small member states will mainly be reactive and flexible, in selected prioritized areas, they will be proactive and even inflexible, defending their special interests with vigour.[28]

These considerations are relevant here, as Finland can undoubtedly be classified as a small member state. In 1998, Finns constituted approximately 1.4 per cent of all EU citizens. Table 1 shows the distribution of seats among member states in the various EU institutions in 2001. Finland has one commissioner and one judge in the ECJ. In the Council under qualified majority voting (QMV), Finland has three votes out of 87; that is, about 3.4 per cent of all votes. The 16 Finnish members of the EP (MEPs) form 2.5 per cent of all 626 Europarliamentarians. The consultative Committee of Regions (CoR) and the Economic and Social Committee (ESC) both have 222 members, nine of whom come from Finland.

The next two sections outline the main features of Finland and her integration policy.

BASIC FACTS ABOUT FINLAND

Box 1 presents some basic facts about Finland and a brief chronology of her main historical milestones since the nineteenth century. In 2000, the population of Finland was just under 5.2 million, and the total population is projected to stay at current levels in the near future. The eastern and northern regions are sparsely populated; most people live in the more urbanized southern parts of the country. The capital Helsinki together with its surrounding area has approximately one million inhabitants. The official languages are Finnish, spoken by 92 per cent of the population, and Swedish, the first language of just below six per cent of the citizens. Approximately 85 per cent of Finns are Lutheran. Culturally, Finland is very homogeneous, and the foreigners residing in the country in 2000, approximately one-third of whom were Russians and Estonians, made up 1.7 per cent of the total population.

Box 1
Basic Facts About Finland

Basic facts

Population	5.2 million (2000)
Official languages	Finnish (92 per cent), Swedish (6 per cent)
Religion	Lutheran (85 per cent), no religious affiliation (13 per cent)
Area	338,145 km² (68 per cent forest, 10 per cent lakes)
Land boundaries	Russia (1,269 km), Norway (727 km), Sweden (586 km)

A brief chronology of modern Finnish history

1809	Finland becomes an autonomous Grand Duchy of the Russian Empire
1906	The old four-estate assembly replaced by a unicameral national parliament, the Eduskunta, with universal suffrage established, the first country in Europe to enact this. First parliamentary elections are held in 1907
1917	Declaration of independence
1918	Civil war between the Reds and the Whites
1939–45	Second World War: Finland fights two wars against the Soviet Union, the Winter War (1939–40) and the Continuation War (1941–44). After the armistice with the Soviet Union, Finnish forces drive the German army out of Lapland in 1944–45
1948	Treaty of Friendship, Cooperation, and Mutual Assistance signed with the Soviet Union; the pact eventually lapses in 1991
1995	Finland joins the European Union

In area, Finland covers 338,145 km², 68 per cent of which is forest, ten per cent lakes, and six per cent cultivated land, thus making her the fourth largest EU member state after France, Spain, and Sweden. Finland shares borders with Russia (1,269 km), Norway (727 km), and Sweden (586 km), with, in addition, about 1,100 kilometres of coastline. Finland is divided into five provinces (Southern Finland, Western Finland, Eastern Finland, Oulu, and Lapland). The autonomous Swedish-speaking province of Åland has approximately 25,000 inhabitants. At the start of 2001, the country was divided into 448 municipalities, over 300 of which were, in terms of population, very small rural municipalities.[29]

Having formed a part of the Swedish Empire since the thirteenth century, Finland became, in 1809, an autonomous Grand Duchy of the Russian Empire. In 1860, Finland acquired her own currency, the *markka,* or Finnish mark. The constitution adopted in 1906 established – the first European country to do so – universal suffrage. At the same time,

10

the old four-estate assembly was replaced by a unicameral national parliament, the Eduskunta, with the first parliamentary elections being held in 1907. Finland declared independence from Russia on 6 December 1917. A short but bitter civil war between the Reds and the Whites followed in 1918, and it was won by the government's forces led by General Mannerheim. The constitution adopted in 1919 gave Finland a republican form of government combined with strong powers for the president.[30]

During the Second World War, Finland fought two wars against the Soviet Union, the Winter War (1939–40) and the Continuation War (1941–44), and in accordance with the armistice agreement with the Soviet Union, Finland fought German forces in Lapland in 1944–45. As part of the peace settlement, Finland was forced to concede a significant amount of territory, mainly from the Karelia region, to the Soviet Union. The peace settlement also led to close economic and political ties with her eastern neighbour, consolidated in the Treaty of Friendship, Co-operation, and Mutual Assistance (FCMA) signed in 1948. During the Cold War, Finland stressed the maintaining of cordial relations with the Soviet Union. While the direct interference of the Soviet leadership in Finnish politics has often been exaggerated, the Finnish political elite nevertheless was always forced to anticipate reactions from Moscow, and this set firm limits to Finland's cooperation with the western European and other Nordic countries. Following instructions from Moscow, Finland was forced to reject Marshall Plan aid in 1947. In 1955, Finland joined the United Nations (UN) and the Nordic Council. In 1961, Finland became an associate member of the European Free Trade Association (EFTA), as the Kremlin ruled out full EFTA membership.

FINLAND AND EUROPEAN INTEGRATION

Studies on Finland's place in Europe have usually focused on foreign and security policy aspects. Even Finnish integration policy is normally analysed from the perspective of the changing international power structure, with other policy sectors or the institutional consequences of EU membership receiving much less attention. Such emphasis is under-standable given Finland's geopolitical location 'between east and west', but it also means that scholarly knowledge of the overall Finnish integration policy remains underdeveloped, particularly among foreign observers.

The significance of EU membership for Finland should not be under-estimated, for it has constituted a key element in the 'process of wholesale re-identification on the international stage'.[31] While the pro-EU camp argued before the membership referendum held in October 1994 that by joining the Union Finland would merely be maintaining or consolidating its place among western European countries, there is little doubt that, especially among foreign observers, the 'western' identity of Finland was far less clear. After all, Finland shares a long border with Russia and had during the Cold War very close economic and political relations with the Soviet Union (see Chapter 2).

Box 2 contains a brief chronology of Finnish integration policy. In 1973, Finland signed a free trade agreement with the European Economic Community (EEC). Finland became a full member of the EFTA in 1986 and joined the Council of Europe in 1989. The debate on possible EC/EU membership began in 1990/91 when three parties, the conservative National Coalition (KOK), the Social Democratic Party (SDP), and the Swedish People's Party (RKP), came out in favour of membership. Finland became a member of the European Economic Area (EEA) from the start of 1994. A consultative referendum on EU membership was held in October 1994, with 57.1 per cent of voters supporting membership. Turnout was 74 per cent.

Finland joined the EU in January 1995, only just over a year after the entering into force of the Maastricht Treaty, which had quite fundamentally changed the nature of the EU. The tight schedules and the importance of issues on the EU agenda left precious little time for

---

Box 2
A Chronology of Finnish Integration Policy

1961	Finland becomes an associate member of the EFTA
1973	Free trade agreement with the EEC
1986	Full member of the EFTA
1989	Joins the Council of Europe
1990/91	Debate on possible EC/EU membership begins. The National Coalition, the Social Democrats and the Swedish People's Party advocate membership
1992	Finland applies for EU membership
1994	Finland becomes a member of the EEA. A consultative referendum on EU membership is held in October; 57 per cent vote in favour of joining the Union
1995	Finland joins the EU
1999	Finland joins the third stage of the EMU and holds the EU presidency from July until December
2002	Finland begins use of single currency

12

adjustment. Fulfilling the convergence criteria of the EMU meant that the government had to impose a strict budgetary discipline, a politically less than easy task in a country still recovering from a particularly severe economic recession. The IGC leading to the Treaty of Amsterdam (signed in 1997) was scheduled to begin in the spring of 1996. Moreover, it would be Finland's turn to hold the rotating EU presidency in the latter half of 1999. Nevertheless, commentators throughout the EU have generally agreed that Finland has adapted successfully to the challenges posed by EU membership. Perhaps the most glowing evaluation of Finland's attitude was provided by *The Economist* in March 1999:

> Since joining the EU in 1995, and despite coming from its most distant edge, they have displayed an almost uncanny mastery of its workings. Many point to them as the very model of how a 'small country' (vast in land mass, but with only 5.2m people) should operate within the EU's institutions: not preachy like the Swedes, not difficult like the Danes, not over-ambitious like the Austrians, merely modest and purposeful, matching a sense of principle with a sense of proportion.[32]

The Finnish approach is usually described as pragmatic and constructive, and Finnish civil servants and politicians are normally portrayed as cooperative and committed to integration.[33] When the three Nordic states, Finland, Norway, and Sweden, applied for EU membership, several commentators expected that they would pursue rather similar integration policies, with emphasis on pragmatic intergovernmental cooperation between formally sovereign member states. For example, Miles argued that neither Finland nor Sweden 'has a federalist tradition and hence they are likely to resist future extensions of EU power, once full members. They will strengthen the trend towards intergovernmentalism that has been apparent since the problems with the Maastricht Treaty. As they are relatively small states in terms of population size, they will also resist any institutional reform which would reduce the powers of small states.'[34] Such predictions proved wrong.

The Finnish approach to integration stands in rather striking contrast to the integration policies of her two Nordic neighbours, Denmark and Sweden, both of which have been far less supportive of further integration.[35] Indeed, Finnish European policy has been consistently pro-integrationist. In membership negotiations, the centre-right government led by Prime Minister Esko Aho of the Centre Party (KESK), 36 per cent of whose supporters voted for EU membership in the 1994 referendum, accepted the Maastricht Treaty without any major opt-out clauses or policy exemptions. In the two IGCs held during Finland's membership, the governments headed by Paavo Lipponen have supported further transfers of competencies from the national level to the EU, together with the extension of QMV in the Council and a (cautiously) stronger role for the Commission and the EP. Moreover, Finland joined the third stage of EMU among the first countries and has adopted an active role in the development of Justice and Home Affairs (JHA) policies and the Common Foreign and Security Policy (CFSP), with the common initiative by Swedish and Finnish governments resulting in the inclusion of a new article in the Amsterdam Treaty on crisis management. Finland can therefore with good reason be categorized as an 'integrationist' member state.[36]

THE STRUCTURE OF THE BOOK

The purpose of this book is threefold: to introduce the main features of the Finnish political system, to examine the impact of EU membership on the domestic political system, and to explain the pro-integrationist policies of Finnish governments. In particular, we are interested in the interaction between the two levels of decision-making, European and national, and in the ways in which the process of European integration influences the domestic policy process and the roles of the leading political actors: parties, parliament, the executive branch, and the president. The main research questions that we answer in this book are the following. How is national integration policy formulated in Finland? What impact has EU membership had on the Finnish political system? What explains the integrationist approach of Finland in the EU?

We focus on governmental institutions and on decision-making processes, because previous research has shown that the configuration of domestic institutions plays a key role: institutional choices can have both intentional and unintended consequences, and these organizational arrangements structure the way in which national integration policy is formulated. To quote Aspinwall: 'Even if institutions are not the product of conscious choice, but rather evolve through practice, the effect of *regularized behaviour* tends to make some options (or 'paths') more likely than others.'[37] Therefore, we not only analyse the impact of EU membership on the balance of power between domestic institutions, but also explain the interaction between Finnish integration policy and the system established for formulating and coordinating national EU positions. However, we also discuss the cultural dimension of adapting to integration, notably how EU membership and integration in general are perceived among the political decision-makers and in the state adminis-tration.[38] Our analysis incorporates therefore also the domestic discourse on Europe: to what extent and from what perspective is integration debated, and have EU membership and the deepening of integration changed traditional national values (such as sovereignty)?

The rest of the book is structured as follows. In the following chapter, we examine the reasons that led Finland to apply for EU membership, and the level of support among the citizens for membership and further integration both before and after Finland joined the Union. When making the decision to apply for EU membership, all potential member states weigh the probable benefits and disadvantages of membership. The primary economic gains include access to larger markets, reduction of transaction costs, and perceived overall economic stability. Political benefits include the improvement of external security and the enhanced status the membership brings for the country. Naturally, these factors can also be seen as drawbacks, particularly as membership entails the diminution of sovereignty. We argue that the relatively broad elite consensus behind Finland's membership needs to be understood in the context of her geopolitical situation and economic dependence on western markets.

The next three chapters examine the positions of the key domestic actors. In Chapter 3, we analyse the European policies of parties rep-resented in the Eduskunta, and the impact of integration on their organization and ideology. While basically all the main Finnish parties are cautiously or strongly pro-integrationist, the same consensus is not replicated among the voters. The lack of effective partisan competition is largely explained by the consensual system of formulating national integration policy.

Chapter 4 analyses the role of the parliament. The parliamentarization of the Finnish political system is in no small measure connected to EU membership. In comparison with other member state legislatures, the Eduskunta has developed a fairly effective system for controlling the government in EU affairs. While decision-making on routine European legislation is rather strongly decentralized, with much ministerial auton-omy, the overall direction of national EU policy and key policy choices are coordinated within the Cabinet EU Committee and among parties, including the opposition, in the Eduskunta. This domestic consensus-building is at least partially driven by the need to achieve consistency and cohesion when negotiating with other member states and the EU institu-tions. The multi-party coalition governments, together with the role accorded to the opposition in the process, facilitate broad backing for governmental action at the European level.

Chapter 5 explores the changing positions of the government and the president, and the coordination of national EU policy within the executive branch. The constitutional changes implemented since the early 1990s have substantially strengthened the role of the government and reduced that of the president. The government has dictated national integration policy, with the president intervening mainly when second-pillar (CFSP) questions are on the EU agenda. Within government, Paavo Lipponen, the prime minister since the March 1995 elections, has played a big part in guiding Finland into the EMU and the inner core of the EU. Nevertheless, the system of dual executive may cause problems in the future, particularly when the prime minister and the president represent different parties, or when they have strongly different views over integration.

The Finnish EU presidency is analysed in detail in Chapter 6. The presidency of the Council presents a particular challenge for policy coordination and arguably is particularly challenging for small member states. The handling of the rotating presidency is a good example of the basic substance of Finnish EU policy, with emphasis on compromise, flexibility, and cooperative behaviour in negotiations. The presidency was regarded as Finland's greatest international challenge since achieving independence (1917) and preparations for it began already in 1996.

Chapter 7 looks at Finnish adaptation to the CFSP. This policy area is particularly interesting because of its central role in Finnish integration debates both before and after the membership referendum. Despite the continuous political rhetorics about neutrality and military non-alignment and the strong historical attachment to national sovereignty and her own credible armed forces, Finland has not only adjusted to the CFSP without any real problems but has also succeeded in contributing to its development. We examine the government's position on the institutional structure of the CFSP and assess its priorities in the future evolution of the EU's military structure.

The concluding chapter summarizes the key findings of the book and discusses the main challenges facing Finland in an integrative Europe.

NOTES

1. See M.A. Pollack, 'The End of Creeping Competence? EU Policy-Making Since Maastricht', *Journal of Common Market Studies* 38:3 (2000), p. 524.
2. See S. Hix and K. Goetz, 'Introduction: European Integration and National Political Systems', *West European Politics* 23:4 (2000), pp. 1–26; and S. Hix, *The Political System of the European Union* (Basingstoke: Macmillan, 1999).
3. See A. Moravcsik, *The Choice for Europe* (Ithaca, NY: Cornell University

Press, 1998); A. Moravcsik, 'Preferences and Power in the European Community: A Liberal Intergovernmentalist Approach', *Journal of Common Market Studies* 31:4 (1993), pp. 473–524; A. Moravcsik, 'Taking Preferences Seriously: A Liberal Theory of International Politics', *International Organization* 51:4 (1997), pp. 513–53; and A. Moravcsik, 'A New Statecraft? Supranational Entrepreneurs and International Co-Operation', *International Organization* 53:2 (1999), pp. 267–306.
4. G. Falkner, 'How Pervasive Are Euro-Politics? Effects of EU Membership on a New Member State', *Journal of Common Market Studies* 38:2 (2000), p. 224.
5. See the references in M. Green Cowles, J. Caporaso and T. Risse (eds) *Transforming Europe: Europeanization and Domestic Change* (Ithaca, NY: Cornell University Press, 2001); Hix and Goetz, 'Introduction: European Integration and National Political Systems'; S. Bulmer and C. Lequesne, 'New Perspectives on EU-Member State Relationships', paper presented at the ECSA Biennial Conference, 31 May–2 June 2001, Madison, Wisconsin; C.M. Radaelli, 'Whither Europeanization? Concept Stretching and Substantive Change', *European Integration Online Papers* 4:8 (2000) (*http://eiop.or.at/eiop/texte/2000-008a.htm*); A. Héritier, D. Kerwer, C. Knill, D. Lehmkuhl, M. Teutsch and A.-C. Douillet, *Differential Europe: The European Union Impact on National Policymaking* (Lanham, MD: Rowman & Littlefield, 2001); and T.A. Börzel, 'Towards Convergence in Europe? Institutional Adaptation to Europeanization in Germany and Spain', *Journal of Common Market Studies* 37:4 (1999), pp. 573–96; and other works mentioned in this chapter.
6. A. Moravcsik, 'Why the European Community Strengthens the State: International Cooperation and Domestic Politics' (*Centre for European Studies Working Paper Series* 52, Harvard University, 1994).
7. See T. Raunio and S. Hix, 'Backbenchers Learn to Fight Back: European Integration and Parliamentary Government', *West European Politics* 23:4 (2000), pp. 142–68, and the list of references in that article.
8. See L. Hooghe and G. Marks, *Multi-Level Governance and European Integration* (Lanham, MD: Rowman & Littlefield, 2001); and W. Sandholtz, 'Membership Matters: Limits of the Functional Approach to European Institutions', *Journal of Common Market Studies* 34:3 (1996), pp. 403–29.
9. See particularly G. Majone, *Regulating Europe* (London: Routledge, 1996).
10. See B. Kohler-Koch and R. Eising (eds) *The Transformation of Governance in the European Union* (London: Routledge, 1999).
11. R. Ladrech, 'Europeanization of Domestic Politics and Institutions: The Case of France', *Journal of Common Market Studies* 32:1 (1994), p. 69.
12. W. Wessels and D. Rometsch, 'Conclusion: European Union and National Institutions', in D. Rometsch and W. Wessels (eds) *The European Union and Member States: Towards Institutional Fusion?* (Manchester: Manchester University Press, 1996), p. 328.
13. See D. Rometsch and W. Wessels (eds) *The European Union and Member States: Towards Institutional Fusion?* (Manchester: Manchester University Press, 1996).
14. H. Kassim, B.G. Peters and V. Wright (eds) *The National Coordination of EU Policy: The Domestic Level* (Oxford: Oxford University Press, 2000). The companion volume, focusing on national coordination at the EU level, was

not yet published at the time of writing this book.

15. H. Kassim, 'Conclusion: The National Co-ordination of EU Policy: Confronting the Challenge', in H. Kassim et al., *The National Coordination of EU Policy*, pp. 237–41.
16. Ibid., p. 241.
17. Ibid., p. 250.
18. On France, see A. Guyomarch, H. Machin and E. Ritchie, *France in the European Union* (Basingstoke: Macmillan, 1998), pp. 43–72; and A. Menon, 'France', in H. Kassim, et al., *The National Coordination of EU Policy*, pp. 79–98. On the Danish system, see T. Pedersen, 'Denmark', in H. Kassim et al., *The National Coordination of EU Policy*, pp. 219–34.
19. See the discussion in V. Wright, 'The National Co-ordination of European Policy-Making: Negotiating the Quagmire', in J. Richardson (ed.) *European Union: Power and Policy-Making* (London: Routledge, 1996), pp. 148–69, particularly pp. 163–4.
20. On sectorization and EU decision-making in the various policy sectors, see J. Peterson and E. Bomberg, *Decision-Making in the European Union* (Basingstoke: Macmillan, 1999).
21. See Falkner, 'How Pervasive Are Euro-Politics?'; and G. Falkner and W.C. Müller (eds) *Österreich im europäischen Mehrebenensystem: Konsequenzen der EU-Mitgliedschaft für Politiknetzwerke und Entscheidungsprozesse* (Wien: Signum, 1998).
22. See D. Arter, 'Small State Influence Within the EU: The Case of Finland's "Northern Dimension Initiative"', *Journal of Common Market Studies* 38:5 (2000), pp. 679, 691–5.
23. K. Hanf and B. Soetendorp, 'Small States and the Europeanization of Public Policy', in K. Hanf and B. Soetendorp (eds) *Adapting to European Integration: Small States and the European Union* (Harlow: Longman, 1998), pp. 4–5, 9.
24. E. Damgaard, 'Conclusion: The Impact of European Integration on Nordic Parliamentary Democracies', in T. Bergman and E. Damgaard (eds) *Delegation and Accountability in European Integration: The Nordic Parliamentary Democracies and the European Union* (London: Frank Cass, 2000), p. 162. The chapters in the volume edited by Bergman and Damgaard were first published as a Special Issue of *Journal of Legislative Studies* 6:1 (2000).
25. M. Ekengren and B. Sundelius, 'Sweden: The State Joins the European Union', in Hanf and Soetendorp (eds) *Adapting to European Integration*, p. 137.
26. B. Soetendorp and K. Hanf, 'Conclusion: The Nature of National Adaptation to European Integration', in Hanf and Soetendorp (eds) *Adapting to European Integration*, p. 192.
27. H. Kassim, B.G. Peters and V. Wright, 'Introduction', in H. Kassim et al., *The National Coordination of EU Policy*, p. 1.
28. See B. Thorhallsson, *The Role of Small States in the European Union* (Aldershot: Ashgate, 2000); and B. Thorhallsson, 'The Administrative Working Procedures of Smaller States in the Decision-Making Process of the EU', paper presented at the ECPR Joint Sessions of Workshops, Copenhagen, 14–19 April 2000.
29. This information was taken from the website of Statistics Finland (*www.tilastokeskus.fi*). The website offers time series data on various aspects

of Finnish society in Finnish, Swedish, English, French and German. Another useful website for finding basic information about Finland is *virtual. finland.fi*, operated by the Ministry for Foreign Affairs.

30. The presidential system was adopted after plans to import a monarch from Germany. In June 1918 the government introduced in the parliament a proposal for a monarchical constitution. While the Eduskunta approved the initiative, a minority of republicans were able to defer the matter over the next elections (according to the constitutional deferment rule, one-sixth of MPs could prevent constitutional amendments from being declared urgent and adopted during the lifetime of one parliament). The monarchists then changed their strategy, arguing that the parliament itself should elect a monarch for the country. In October 1918, the Eduskunta elected the Prince of Hessen, Friedrick Karl, as the King of Finland. However, the monarchists' hopes were destroyed by Germany's defeat in the First World War. See D. Arter, 'Finland', in R. Elgie (ed.) *Semi-Presidentialism in Europe* (Oxford: Oxford University Press, 1999), p. 51.

31. Arter, 'Small State Influence Within the EU', p. 691. See also C. Ingebritsen and S. Larson, 'Interest and Identity: Finland, Norway and European Union', *Cooperation and Conflict* 32:2 (1997), pp. 207–22; and D. Arter, 'The EU Referendum in Finland on 16 October 1994: A Vote for the West, Not for Maastricht', *Journal of Common Market Studies* 33:3 (1995), pp. 361–87.

32. Sauli Niinistö, 'On Europe's edge', *The Economist*, 13 March 1999, p. 41.

33. See, for example, N. Petersen, 'The Nordic Trio and the Future of the EU', in G. Edwards and A. Pijpers (eds) *The Politics of European Treaty Reform: The 1996 Intergovernmental Conference and Beyond* (London: Pinter, 1997), pp. 159–87.

34. L. Miles, 'Sweden and Finland: From EFTA Neutrals to EU Members?', in J. Redmond (ed.) *Prospective Europeans: New Members for the European Union* (Hemel Hempstead: Harvester Wheatsheaf, 1994), p. 84. See also S. Gstöhl, 'The Nordic Countries and the European Economic Area (EEA)', in L. Miles (ed.) *The European Union and the Nordic Countries* (London: Routledge, 1996), p. 61; L. Miles, 'Conclusion', in L. Miles (ed.) *The European Union*, p. 280; and L. Miles and J. Redmond, 'Enlarging the European Union: The Erosion of Federalism?', *Cooperation and Conflict* 31:3 (1996), pp. 295–8. For a contrary interpretation, see C. Ingebritsen, 'Coming Out of the Cold: Nordic Responses to European Union', in A.W. Cafruny and C. Lankowski (eds) *Europe's Ambiguous Unity: Conflict and Consensus in the Post-Maastricht Era* (Boulder, CO: Lynne Rienner, 1997), pp. 239–56. Ingebritsen argues (p. 253) that Sweden and Finland are 'enthusiastic members'.

35. See K.M. Johansson (ed.) *Sverige i EU* (Stockholm: SNS Förlag, 1999); L. Miles (ed.) *The European Union and the Nordic Countries* (London: Routledge, 1996); L. Miles, *Sweden and European Integration* (Aldershot: Ashgate, 1997); L. Miles (ed.) *Sweden and the European Union Evaluated* (London: Continuum, 2000); and N. Petersen, 'National Strategies in the Integration Dilemma: An Adaptation Approach', *Journal of Common Market Studies* 36:1 (1998), pp. 33–54.

36. See A. Stubb, H. Kaila and T. Ranta, 'Finland: An Integrationist Member State', in E.E. Zeff and E.B. Pirro (eds) *The European Union and the Member States: Cooperation,Coordination, and Compromise* (Boulder, CO: Lynne

19

Rienner, 2001), pp. 305–16.

37. M. Aspinwall, 'Structuring Europe: Power-Sharing Institutions and British Preferences on European Integration', *Political Studies* 48:3 (2000), p. 426. Emphasis added.

38. Discussing the adaptation of British central administration to integration, Bulmer and Burch argue that 'the *cultural* dimension has been influenced by persistent political dispute over British sovereignty within the EU. On the one hand, there has been a gradual emergence of a substantial cadre of EU-aware officials who have been brought together through sharing a common task and, through training and practical experience, have developed appropriate skills and to some extent shared values about the nature and handling of European policy. . . . On the other hand, the political climate has made a positive engagement with integration very intermittent. As a consequence, the defining attitudes have been less concerned with adapting Whitehall to the EU than with adapting EU business to fit traditional Whitehall methods of operation.' S. Bulmer and M. Burch, 'The "European-isation" of Central Government: the UK and Germany in Historical Institutionalist Perspective', in G. Schneider and M. Aspinwall (eds) *The Rules of Integration: Institutionalist Approaches to the Study of Europe* (Manchester: Manchester University Press, 2001), p. 85.

2

Finland Joins the European Union

Finland joined the EU together with Austria and Sweden in the beginning of 1995. At first sight, Finnish membership might appear to reflect a rapid change of political orientation, given the firm and inflexible policy of neutrality the country had been conducting until the first years of the 1990s. In spite of the brevity of the national discussion, the decision to follow Sweden and submit an application for EU membership was based upon an overwhelming political consensus. All the major political elites, including the party and interest organization leaderships, and the media, in addition to key players in the private sector, were in favour of Finnish membership. In the national referendum on this issue held in October 1994, 57 per cent of the people supported the elite and voted in favour of the membership option.

The purpose of this chapter is to analyse the domestic debate on Finland's membership in the EU and the alignment of agents taking place before the referendum of 1994. What were the reasons for the overwhelming support given to the reorientation of national foreign policy? The chapter starts by examining the historical starting points of Finland's integration policy, followed by an evaluation of the most notable opinions on the issue among the key political and social players. Finally, the development of public opinion regarding EU membership will be assessed, first in the context of the referendum and then during the first years of Finnish EU membership.

COLD WAR NEUTRALITY POLICY AND EUROPEAN INTEGRATION

Post-war Finnish foreign policy had its roots in the outcome of the Second World War. As an ally of Germany, Finland was considered to have lost the war and was required to accept the terms of peace dictated by the winners. For Finland, the terms of peace led into a special relationship with the Soviet Union.[1] The core of this relationship was a treaty on military cooperation that Finland – like the central and eastern European states – in the aftermath of the war had to conclude with the Soviet Union. The Finnish treaty (Treaty of Friendship, Cooperation, and Mutual Assistance [FCMA]) differed from the corresponding treaties of the others in the sense that military cooperation with the Soviet Union was limited to one particular case (Germany or one of its allies attacking the Soviet Union through Finland). Cooperation in this case would also be based on the mutual agreement of the two parties.

The special relationship meant that Finland had to take into account the interests of the Soviet Union – or 'the facts' – as this was expressed by the first post-war president, Juho Kusti Paasikivi. The other dominant characteristic of Finnish foreign policy, the policy of neutrality, was launched in the 1950s in order to counterbalance the special relationship and to give Finland more international room of manoeuvre while still maintaining good relations with the Soviet Union. Nevertheless, irrespective of its political – and not legal – character, Finnish neutrality became known as a very strict policy line, the purpose of which was to keep Finland out of superpower conflicts. As the possibility of superpower conflict was strong, Finland's policy of neutrality became very comprehensive, necessitating compliance in many policy sectors outside a purely security policy.

Neutrality and its demands, domestic and foreign, led to a cautious attitude vis-à-vis Western political and economic cooperation.[2] Consequently, Finland did not accept the offer of Marshall Plan aid in the late 1940s, but did open her foreign trade to the countries of the Organization for European Economic Cooperation (OEEC) through the 1957 Helsinki protocol.[3] Finland joined the Nordic Council in 1955, three years after the organization was established, but with the reservation that her membership would not include security policy matters or relations between the superpowers.[4] In addition, Finland initially participated in the EFTA only as an associate member, thus enabling her to claim that her membership excluded features of political cooperation. After an arduous domestic debate, Finland finally also concluded a free trade agreement with the European Economic Community (EEC) in 1973. However, in contrast to the treaties signed by the other EFTA members, the Finnish treaty was more limited, lacking, among other things, a development clause.

At least until the mid-1980s, Finnish foreign policy enjoyed virtually unanimous political and public approval. During Urho Kekkonen's long presidency (1956–81), foreign policy was personally identified with the president, who was visibly supported by political elites within the Soviet Union. Political debate and open conflict on foreign policy issues were rare, as most domestic political key players acquiesced in the idea that foreign policy was the privilege of the president. Annual public opinion surveys indicated that the Finnish people also supported the official foreign policy line. Around 90 per cent of the population considered that foreign policy had been conducted effectively up until the late 1980s.[5]

In this somewhat unhealthy political climate, the political debate on the Finnish EEC treaty in the early 1970s was exceptional. However, even during this period, the most significant political players were still careful not to exceed the limits of the official policy line. Full EC membership was not seriously proposed by anyone, and the political debate was limited to the question of whether Finland should conclude a free-trade agreement with the EC. Indeed, the strongest opposition to the agreement came from the extreme left, and even the president's own Agrarian Party opposed the agreement on the grounds that it deviated from the traditional foreign policy. Nevertheless, most criticism of the free trade agreement was neutralized by the fact that the policy of neutrality was balanced by the offering of identical trade privileges to the Soviet Union. Almost two decades were to pass before the issue of European integration re-emerged in Finland when the Finnish government's policy on European integration changed in the early 1990s.

FROM NEUTRALITY TO EU MEMBERSHIP

Even in the very beginning of the 1990s, the argument that EC membership would be incompatible with the policy of neutrality still proved to be the final obstacle to a more extensive Finnish integration policy. The changes in the international system in the late 1980s, including the liberation of eastern and central Europe from communist power, partly contributed to a more active Finnish integration policy, but these changes did not lead to fundamental revision of it. The European Economic Area (EEA) appeared to be a natural step in the pragmatic Finnish policy, and, consequently, Finland supported that concept from the start. The EEA treaty never became a major political issue in Finland, especially as the country was experiencing domestic adjustment to a more open political culture after the long incumbency of President Kekkonen. The economic advantages of the EEA were generally accepted by all parties, and the concept was seen to be compatible with Finland's policy of neutrality.[6] Nevertheless, the official Finnish position on EC membership remained unchanged until the end of 1990. Full membership was viewed as impossible because of its infringement of the independence of foreign policy and, in particular, in Finland's policy of neutrality.[7]

Although notable figures representing Finnish academia had been proposing closer Finnish–EC relations since the early 1980s, the first to diverge from this long-standing integration policy were figures from industry and commerce.[8] The argument of the economic figures was that although Finland would be provided with the economic advantages of integration through the EEA, she would be left in a secondary position in terms of influence without full membership. Despite their intensification, the demands for a policy change were modest, and the debate started only after the Swedish intention to apply for membership was announced in October 1990.[9]

From this time onwards, the political elites in Finland started to perceive full EC membership as a possibility. This revised attitude surfaced within the internal party debates during 1990. It became a major force once the March 1991 parliamentary elections were completed.[10] Unqualified support for full EC membership came from the National Coalition (KOK), the Swedish People's Party (RKP), and the Social Democratic Party (SDP). Of these parties, the first two were represented in the new cabinet and had to support the official policy prioritizing the EEA project, a fact which made the position of their leadership somewhat difficult. The other major participant in the cabinet, the agrarian Centre Party (KESK) – holding the posts of prime minister and foreign minister – adopted a more cautious approach to full membership. Its main support came from the farming and rural communities, which, in general, had a negative attitude towards membership because of the heavy loss of national subsidies the EU's Common Agricultural Policy (CAP) would imply. The Left Alliance (VAS), representing the radical left, and the Green League (VIHR) were clearly divided on the question, including even the leadership.

Full politicization of the membership issue did not take place until the Finnish government had applied for membership in March 1992. Without doubt, one of the reasons for this slow start was the novelty in Finland of the whole concept of European integration, and the fact that the issue had traditionally been cloaked in economic terms within Finnish political debate. However, the negotiations on the EEA were actually in progress, making the situation problematic for the cabinet parties. The parliament got involved in the membership issue through the two-step national application procedure. The government first presented an extensive report to the parliament in February 1992 and then, in March, a proposal that was put to a vote in the parliament.[11] The parliament accepted the proposal with 108 votes for and 55 against. There were, however, some technical peculiarities connected with this vote, and a more correct division of the parliament in this matter would be 133 votes in favour and 60 against membership.[12]

The parliament's consent had been given to the submission of the membership application, and the government was cautious enough not to tie itself to the membership option before the negotiations on membership were completed and the details of Finnish membership agreed. During the negotiations, the government even promised to submit the result to a referendum.[13]

MEMBERSHIP NEGOTIATIONS

The Finnish application for EC membership was presented in March 1992. The next interesting stage in the membership procedure was the Commission opinion that was given in November of the same year.[14] The opinion was very positive, giving a firm political starting point for negotiations on Finland's accession to the EC. The negotiations started in March 1993 and were completed very smoothly in 12 months. For Finland, the organization for the accession negotiations has been characterized as the biggest ever for international negotiations.[15] The negotiating delegation was headed by the minister for foreign trade, Pertti Salolainen, and the minister for foreign affairs, first Paavo Väyrynen and then Heikki Haavisto. The delegation, which consisted of high-ranking civil servants, was supported by working groups; all in all, around 500 experts were involved in the organization.

The negotiations on Finland's accession were facilitated by the fact that in the recent negotiations on the EEA, Finland had already adopted the entire internal market legislation of the EC. The major difficulties in negotiations were related to agriculture and regional and structural policies.[16] In addition to these areas, some individual issues related to competition policy (the state alcohol monopoly) and taxation (traveller's duty-free allowances) proved complicated. Two additional fields, where more particular problems arose, were the common foreign and security policy and the position of the Åland Islands. All in all, as can be judged from their brevity, the negotiations lacked any overwhelming political difficulties.

The conditions for joining the CAP were a key issue in Finnish domestic politics. With farmers as the main social group opposing membership and their own representative, the KESK, as the leading party in the cabinet, the details of this part of the debate attracted much of the domestic attention paid to the negotiations. The difficulties in this area emanated from disagreements between Finland and the EC concerning

25

the compensation that Finnish agriculture would receive for the losses resulting from becoming a part of the CAP. Finland's main objective was to get northern support in the form of having all of Finland designated as a mountain LFA (less favourable area). This was not acceptable to the EC because it would have established a precedent for giving LFA support to an entire country. After long and complicated negotiations, Finland achieved LFA support for 85 per cent of its arable land. North of the 62nd parallel of latitude, this would take the form of 'mountain region' support. Finland was even made eligible for certain forms of national support in order to balance the special circumstances for farming. Finland, however, failed to gain a transitional period for agriculture and was required to shift to EC producer prices directly upon achieving membership.[17]

As far as structural and regional policies are concerned, Finland wanted to make sure that she would receive the same treatment as the existing EC members in terms of Community support. Finland even tried to prevent decisions being taken on the basis of the economic parameters of the time preceding the country's deep economic recession at the beginning of the 1990s. Many controversies had to be resolved in the process of applying the structural and regional policies to the newcomer, but finally, a solution was achieved.

The questions of the state alcohol monopoly and the duty-free traveller's allowance of alcoholic beverages are among the very long-term issues related to Finnish EU membership. The key reason for this can be found in the Finnish (or Nordic) conception of alcoholic beverages as, in addition to their market value, an important instrument of social and health policy. The control of access to alcohol by high prices is seen as a way to restrict the consumption of alcoholic beverages. All Nordic candidate states, consequently, had state alcohol monopolies. The Finnish monopoly was extremely comprehensive, covering imports, exports, and wholesale and retail sales, and this meant that it was in many respects in violation of the rules of the EC competition policy. A compromise solution was achieved during the negotiations, to the effect that Finland should dismantle the export, import, and production monopolies of alcohol immediately and gradually even the wholesale monopoly. The monopoly of the retail sale of alcohol was thus retained. Another point in the EC system that contradicted the Finnish alcohol policy concerned the traveller's duty-free import allowance. The Finnish aspiration to limit the quantity of duty-free allowances, and allowances on alcohol in general, could not be accepted by either the Commission or other member states. After a long process of negotiation, Finland had to consent to a compromise model by which she was supposed to adopt the EC system after a short transitional period of slightly tighter restrictions.

The Common Foreign and Security Policy (CFSP) was an area where unusual problems arose during the negotiation process. The shift from neutrality to the new type of foreign policy activism and commitment that EU membership implied had taken place very rapidly in Finland. At this stage, Finland, consequently, wanted to limit the scope of changes to the political dimension of her security policy, emphasizing her military non-alignment as a starting point for her EU membership.[18] The non-alignment policy of the three new candidates, Austria, Finland, and Sweden, appeared, to some member states to restrict the efficacy and further development of the CFSP. This led to a situation where Finland tried to close the CFSP chapter without any further negotiations, whereas the Belgian presidency proposed that the non-aligned candidates answer a set of questions in order to confirm their commitment to the CFSP. The result – a common declaration given by Austria, Finland, and Sweden – represented a compromise.

Another special problem in the negotiations was the issue of the Åland Islands. In this case, the Finnish government mediated between two parties, the EC on the one hand and the autonomous government of Åland on the other. For historical reasons, the Åland Islands has a special status both as a part of Finland and in international law. The political autonomy of the Åland Islands is confirmed in the Finnish constitution, which guarantees Åland's right to its own language (Swedish) and culture. However, Åland's status as a demilitarized area is confirmed by international treaties.[19] In the negotiations on admission to the EC, Finland asked the EC to confirm these two principles. A third demand concerned a reservation for Åland in internal market legislation. Åland's economy is heavily dependent on the duty-free sales made in the ferry traffic between Sweden and Finland. If a specific status had not been given in this respect, the duty-free sales would have had to cease upon Finland's admission to the EC. The Åland Islands did not become a lengthy issue in negotiations because of political disagreements related to the Finnish demands. Instead, the controversies were related to the procedure to fit Finland's request into the legal framework. It was suggested that the Åland Islands be excluded from the EC; this, however, would not have been possible without the exclusion of Åland from all three pillars of the EU. Finally, the situation was resolved by attaching to the treaty on Finland's EU membership a particular declaration on the applicability of the EC Treaty to the Åland Islands.

The treaty on Finland's admission to the EU was completed in April 1994. The EP gave its consent to Finnish membership in May, enabling the parties to sign the treaty in June. The last hurdle was the national referendum to which the government had committed itself when submitting the application.

REFERENDUM CAMPAIGN

Once the application had been submitted, the battle lines for the ensuing domestic political contest started to be drawn.[20] In general, though, the main political elites seemed to be almost unanimously in favour of EU membership, with the notable exception of the KESK. The pro-membership campaign was boosted when President Mauno Koivisto gave his support to EU membership during the opening session of the Eduskunta in 1992.

Opposition cut across all the traditional political divisions and in many ways can be regarded as proof that civic activism – which many believed had totally disappeared – still existed within Finnish political culture. Organized opposition to EU membership started in 1992, although it remained heterogeneous in terms of social and political groups. Its main constituents came from the nationalist right and the extreme left, while another more unified group were the environmentalists. Opposition also remained strong among women who feared that membership would lead to the deterioration of their social and employment rights. Opposition to EU membership was strongly represented by key figures, who even functioned as the leaders of ad hoc movements established for this purpose. One of the most visible figures in the anti-EU camp was Keijo Korhonen, a former professor and foreign service diplomat, who had first campaigned in his own party, the KESK, against membership and then ran for nomination as that party's candidate in the 1994 presidential election. However, in the face of probable failure, he bolted into the Front of Independence of the Finnish People, established for this particular purpose. Another key opposition figure was Jan-Magnus Jansson, a former professor and editor. He was one of the leaders of the Society for Finnish Independence, and, together with Korhonen, a favourite of the Finnish media during the entire membership campaign. The one opposition movement that was to retain some visibility even after Finland joined the EU was Alternative to the EU (see Chapter 3).

In addition to this rather ad hoc opposition, one socio-economic group was almost universally against EU membership, the farmers. Despite their relatively small number, representing only six per cent of the population, the farmers have traditionally maintained a prominent and influential position within Finnish politics. They seized upon every possible means

to prevent Finland from joining the EU, and, in addition to their professional organization, the Central Union of Agricultural Producers and
Forest Owners (MTK), their interests were championed by the leading
cabinet party, the KESK.

The ways in which the issue of EU membership became politicized in
Finland, and in which it divided the political field, covered all conceivable
arguments, starting with a cautious economic logic before involving
security and defence. It was typical of the state-centric political culture of
Finland, however, that both sides approached European integration from
a state-centric perspective, with the pro-EU and anti-EU camps rational-
izing their arguments in terms of the potential impact on the Finnish
nation state. A broader European perspective, implying that the significance of integration should be defined from a European point of view,
was extremely rare. The same can be said of all the other alternative
political perspectives.

Political debate generally focused on issues of economy, identity, and
security. The first main conflict between the two camps centred on the
potential economic benefits of EU membership for Finland, given that
access to the single European market had already been granted to the
Finnish economy when Finland joined the EEA. The issue concerned
whether it was necessary for Finland to move from the EEA to full EU
membership. The supporters of full membership argued that as influential
decisions affecting the European nation states were to be taken at the EU
level, it was essential for Finland to 'be part of where decisions are made'.[21]
It was simultaneously argued that continued EEA participation would
result in a direct loss of Finnish influence, given that the EEA countries
enjoyed only limited rights in shaping single-market legislation. This
argument was extensively used by EU membership supporters, who added
that, irrespective of the Finnish choice in the question of membership,
decisions having a direct impact upon the Finnish economy would
increasingly be taken by the EU.

In contrast, the 'decision-making' argument of the EU supporters was
often countered by the 'independence' argument of the 'No' camp. The
argument stressed the potential loss of Finnish independence and became
one of the tenets of anti-EU opposition. National independence and state
sovereignty used to be the key values in Finnish politics. They have
constituted the starting point for Finland's neutrality policy and its
reserved attitude towards European integration.[22] These values were
stressed by the 'No' camp. In essence, the core of the 'independence'
argument was that EU membership would imply a renunciation of Finnish
independence; for example, during the campaign, a parallel was drawn
between EU membership and the subordination of Finland within the

Russian Empire after 1809.[23] Support for the 'independence' argument
was sought both in political and juridical considerations. In political
terms, it was argued that the loss of independence would be reflected by
the fact that Finland would be of only minor political importance in
comparison to other EU member states, and her influence within the EU
would thus be minimal. In juridical terms, it was also argued that
membership would infringe the legislative and juridical powers of the
Finnish parliament and courts, and could therefore be viewed as a
violation of the Finnish constitution.

Somewhat later in the membership debate, a new pair of arguments
emerged that could be loosely defined as the 'Finnish identity'
arguments.[24] EU membership supporters tried to prove that membership
was a logical step for Finnish foreign policy, as Finland had, in fact, always
been associated with western values, including those of democracy and
market economy. Therefore, Finland was merely maintaining its place
within the community of western European states. The 'identity' arguments, like those of 'independence', were based upon a rhetoric whose
primary objective was to ignite the passions of the Finnish public, rather
than using analytical reasoning as a method of persuasion.

In particular, the benefits of European integration in fostering closer
relations between Finland and other EU member states were rarely
discussed in detail. The same can be said about the impact of EU membership upon the Nordic welfare state, which was one of the main arguments
of the opposition in terms of 'identity'. Indeed, concerns over the implications of EU membership for the welfare state were central to the
referendum debate. There were widespread fears among the Finnish
public that the high levels of social and political equality, in terms of both
welfare provision and civil rights, would be undermined and even reduced
as a result of EU membership. These concerns were especially evident
among women. Indeed, the belief that EU membership would lead to a
deterioration in the position of women in Finnish society was claimed to
be the main reason for such a large number of women opposing EU
membership.

The last phases of the Finnish referendum campaigns were
characterized by the fact that the security arguments began to work in
favour of EU membership. The issue of security, including the future of
neutrality policy and bilateral relations with Russia, at first appeared to
support the argument that EU membership was inappropriate for Finland.
One of the first challenges that EU advocates had to face was the need to
persuade the Finnish public that full membership was now compatible
with security policy. Although there were many reasons for this abrupt
change in political attitudes, most of which can be identified with

alterations at both the Finnish domestic and international level, it seems that the increasing openness and self-criticism in Finnish political culture and the continuing instability in Russia were central elements.

By the summer of 1993, Finnish foreign policy thinking had been revised, as members of the Finnish cabinet started to emphasize security as an argument in favour of EU membership.[25] This argument was couched in cautious terms and focused upon the general impact of the EU on European security in general and northern European security in particular. Gradually, however, the terms became more daring, and the impact that EU membership was seen to have upon Finnish security began to be thought of also in terms of the protection that membership would bring about vis-à-vis Russia.[26] Suddenly, the whole idea of a Finnish membership had been brought into a new light, as the focus was put on the new options of security policy that would be opened through it.[27] This also had a significant impact upon the results of the Finnish referendum as, ironically, the security argument turned from being one of the most powerful weapons against membership into one of the most important rationales in favour of it.

PUBLIC OPINION BEFORE THE REFERENDUM

Until the late 1980s, Finnish opinion polls reflected the general political climate regarding the question of European integration. For the most part, the public supported the official foreign policy, with very little pressure for redirecting Finnish policy towards European integration. The specific attitudes were, however, mostly unknown, as there were very few public opinion surveys which questioned the details of official foreign policy. Consequently, very little accurate data is available on Finnish views on EC membership before 1987. Nevertheless, the annual surveys measuring the popularity of foreign policy produced high scores in support of existing policy, but, to a large extent, these surveys did not test the popularity of potential alternative policy lines. There is, however, one early opinion survey on the EC question that measured Finnish opinion, even though the questions were limited to just the official foreign policy.[28]

When, in 1970, the Finns were asked to define their attitude towards the EC, their opinions expressed ignorance and uncertainty. The question posed at that time concerned the merits of the free trade agreement only. Half of the Finnish population supported the signing of the free trade treaty, while one in three Finns felt unable to take a stand in the question. The results indicate that there was limited support for European integration, although this may have partly been buoyed by the comparatively recent failure of the Nordek project that had aimed at establishing a common market among the Nordic states, which at that time led to an increased interest in closer relations with the EC among the Nordic governments. It can be assumed that Finnish public opinion remained homogeneous and stable until the late 1980s. Thus, when the time came to consider EC membership seriously, there was a high level of ignorance among the Finnish public. Regular opinion surveys began in 1987, even though the existing foreign policy remained intact. Half of the Finns who were consulted on the EC membership issue in 1987 were simply unable to answer the question (see Figure 1). Of the other half, 40 per cent claimed to support EC membership while 11 per cent opposed it. There were no significant differences between various political or socio-economic groups with respect to how public opinion was divided. Supporters of the small RKP and entrepreneurs and white-collar workers tended to be more positive towards the EC than other groups.

If the first 1987 public opinion survey is taken as the point of departure, public opinion can be analysed as to the extent to which it changed due to the fact that a major change took place in the government's policy.

Figure 1
The Development of Finnish EC Opinions (1987–1994) (percentage)

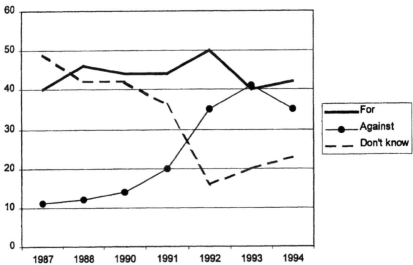

Sources: Suomen Gallup Oy, Euroopan yhteisö 1987; EVA Report on Finnish
  Opinions 1991, 1993; Finnish EC opinions 1992, 1993 spring and autumn,
  1994 spring.

Curiously, during the whole period preceding the referendum in October 1994, support for EU membership never greatly surpassed that reached in the very first survey. In other words, the change in official foreign policy did not really influence levels of public opinion in favour of Finnish membership. However, the most apparent change that did take place in public opinion was linked to the increasing politicization of the issue after 1991. It was only then that the Finnish people started to formulate their own views on the question, leading to a huge growth in negative opinion and a decrease in levels of ignorance. Nevertheless, this trend stabilized as the referendum drew closer, and on the eve of the referendum, public opinion was, according to the polls, evenly split between those in support of membership and those opposing it (40 per cent each), while some 20 per cent were still undecided.[29]

As the issue became more politicized, people's socio-political background clearly played a larger role in determining their opinion than in the beginning of the survey period (Table 2). Certain socio-political variables were important while others remained surprisingly insignificant. The correlation between political party allegiances and declared viewpoints in the surveys was especially noticeable in the case of two parties. Supporters of the right-wing KOK seemed to constitute the most coherent group in terms of following the party line, with EU support averaging around 80 per cent. The next most cohesive group were the supporters of the Left Alliance, who consistently opposed EU membership at around 70 per cent after 1992. However, supporters of the other political parties were not nearly as unified as far as EU opinion was concerned. The main party in the cabinet, the KESK, was deeply divided. Its large constituencies and residual voting base within the farming communities restricted party allegiance on the EU issue. Supporters of the major party outside the cabinet, the SDP, also remained divided, in spite of the positive stance taken by the party leadership. The Green League, as well as the Left Alliance, proved to be the exception, as they declined to take a stand at the party level on the EU question (see Chapter 3).

If party loyalty is replaced by socio-economic background as the main criterion, similar incoherence is also evident, although there was one social group whose internal opinion on EU membership was united. The farmers displayed virtually complete unity in opposing EU membership. Differences in age or gender played only a minor role as far as variations in Finnish EU opinion were concerned. In general, though, young people, tended to be less critical of EU membership than older age groups within the population. Women were also inclined to take a more negative view and to deliberate longer on the matter. For example, it was estimated that

33

Finland in the European Union

Table 2

The Percentage of Voters in Favour of EU Membership in the 1994 Referendum

Groups	Yes	No
Gender		
Men	61	39
Women	54	46
Age		
15–24 years	54	46
25–49 years	58	42
50≧ years	56	44
Education		
Primary school	46	54
Comprehensive or vocational school	55	45
A-levels/higher school examination	66	34
University degree	72	28
Profession		
Farmer	6	94
Blue-collar workers	53	47
White-collar workers	65	35
Management, entrepreneurs	73	27
Party affiliation		
Left Alliance	24	76
Social Democratic Party	75	25
Centre Party	36	64
National Coalition	89	11
Swedish People's Party	85	15
Green League	55	45
Christian Democrats	10	90
Rural Party/True Finns	20	80
Region		
South	62	38
Central	55	45
North	42	58
All	57	43

Sources: H. Paloheimo, 'Pohjoismaiden EU-kansanäänestykset: puolueiden peruslinjat ja kansalaisten mielipiteet Suomessa, Ruotsissa ja Norjassa', *Politiikka*, 37:2 (1995), p. 117. Party affiliation figures are from H. Paloheimo, 'Vaaliohjelmat ja ehdokkaiden mielipiteet', in P. Pesonen (ed.) *Suomen europarlamenttivaalit* (Tampere: Tampere University Press, 2000), p. 58.

on the eve of the referendum one-third of Finnish women were still undecided on the membership question, as opposed to only one-fifth of the men.[30]

There were also some general geographical variations in public opinion. The main geographical division can be drawn between northern (mainly opposed) and southern (mostly in favour) Finland, with the metropolitan areas in the south being the regions most enthusiastic about the prospect of EU membership. The north/south divide was also closely connected with the sources of livelihood in Finland. Farming is more important in central and northern Finland, while the occupations are more diverse in urban southern Finland. However, this is not the only factor behind the geographical variations in public opinion, as the rural areas of eastern Finland have tended to be less critical of EU membership than the western parts of the country, where the number of urban communities is greater. One possible explanation is the proximity of the Russian border, which increases the merits of the security dimension of EU membership for the eastern regions.

All in all, the issue of Finnish EU membership has contributed to the formulation of new types of political divisions among the political key players in Finland (see Chapter 3). Their respective stances on the EU membership issue seem to have consistently been the only common factor in maintaining rather diverse coalitions either for or against membership. Rather than traditional political or even socio-economic perspectives dividing the Finns, they have instead been split on geographical lines or on the lines of much narrower political and sectoral interests.

A REFERENDUM WITHOUT SURPRISES

Two further heated debates associated with the referendum stirred up emotions before the Finnish referendum held on 16 October 1994. Without doubt, they had an impact upon the final result. First, a controversy arose over the order in which the referendums were to be held in the three Nordic applicant countries.[31] Many groups opposing Finnish membership demanded that the Finnish referendum should be held either simultaneously or after the corresponding Swedish referendum, and not prior to it, as planned. Towards the end of the campaign, events in Sweden appeared to be quite influential, especially among those Finns who were still undecided on how to vote.

The second debate struck at the heart of the referendum and concerned its role in relation to parliamentary decision-making. The central question was whether the referendum, which according to the constitution was merely consultative, should be of a binding character politically, and, under this scenario, what would constitute a sufficiently large threshold for approval. Some anti-EU groups emphasized the supremacy of parliament with respect to the decision on EU admission, and several Finnish MPs declared their intention to vote against membership irrespective of the referendum result. As the campaign drew to an end, these concerns increased the uncertainty of the Finnish public over the constitutional significance of the referendum and their votes.

These rather unique circumstances in Finland were reflected in the relatively low turnout (74 per cent) in the referendum. According to studies conducted on the referendum, two of the most frequent reasons for not voting seemed to be, first, an inability to decide upon the EU question and, second, suspicions about the significance of the referendum.[32] Finns voted for EU membership by 57 per cent to 43 per cent in the referendum. The result was sufficient to advise the parliament even if the victory of the 'Yes' camp was not as large as had been predicted by the opinion polls. Indeed, there was only a difference of 400,000 votes between the 'Yes' and 'No' positions, and the geographical voting patterns further emphasized this modest majority.[33]

In the referendum, Finland was geographically split between the northern provinces, which opposed membership, and the southern ones, which supported it (see Table 2). However, the division was much sharper than anyone had expected, with opposition to membership exceeding 50 per cent in several northern provinces. In the larger cities and towns, there were clear majorities for membership, while there were even larger majorities in the rural municipalities of, in some cases, over 80 per cent against Finnish EU membership. The supporters of EU membership gained their largest victories in the metropolitan areas, where an average of 74 per cent voted in favour of membership. The highest figures against membership were achieved in Ostrobothnia.

A study conducted after the referendum did not reveal any considerable variations from the predictions and the results of the public opinion surveys.[34] Positive attitudes towards membership correlated directly with higher levels of income and education; indeed, income seemed to have been one of the strongest explanatory factors with respect to Finnish voting behaviour, being valid for both sexes and for all geographical areas. There were no considerable variations among different age groups with the exception of young men (aged 18–25), who voted for membership in particularly high numbers (79 per cent). The prediction concerning party loyalties also held, although the supporters of the leading cabinet party, the Centre Party, took a slightly more positive stance towards membership than had been expected. This was probably a result of the leading position adopted by the party on the issue (see Chapter 3). Four main factors seem to have encouraged support for EU membership.[35] A majority of Finns mentioned 'economic reasons' as the most important factor behind a positive stance, followed by 'influence', 'culture', and 'security'. A large number of those who were against Finnish membership could not give a reason for their opposition.

PUBLIC OPINION AFTER THE REFERENDUM

After the necessary decisions concerning Finnish EU membership had been taken and Finland had joined the EU in 1995, the divisions of the referendum campaign gradually faded away. The two pro-European parties, the SDP and the KOK, won the 1995 general election and formed the cabinet together with three smaller parties (see Chapters 3 and 4). Having posts in the cabinet was apt to reduce criticism of the EU by at least the Green League and the Left Alliance. The movements opposing Finnish membership took part in the 1996 EP elections, but have been left in a very marginal position.

Public opinion concerning EU membership has proved relatively stable ever since Finland joined the EU. The regular surveys conducted both by the European Commission (Eurobarometer) and by the Centre for Finnish Business and Policy Studies (EVA) have indicated a level of support averaging around 40 per cent, while the share of the population that is opposed to EU membership has varied around 30 per cent.[36] Among all EU member states, Finland is well under the average in its support of the EU. A relatively high level of 'neutral' opinions has been more characteristic of Finland than of the other EU members. This corresponds rather well with the low level of interest shown in EU issues by the Finnish people.

However, another regular survey on public opinion (Figure 2) indicates that criticism of EU membership might be constantly increasing in Finland. When people have been asked how they would vote if a referendum on EU were held now, the number of 'No' votes seems to have constantly increased since Finland joined the EU.[37] There is a clear discrepancy, however, between this trend of rising criticism and the level of support given to the very pro-European government led by Prime Minister Paavo Lipponen (SDP). The parties that formed the cabinet in the very year of Finnish entrance into the EU were even able to renew their mandate in the 1999 general election. Nor are there any signs that this criticism is leading to reinforcement of the anti-EU movements.

Rather than interpreting the increasing level of criticism as growing

Figure 2
Support for European Union in Finland (1996–2000) (percentage)

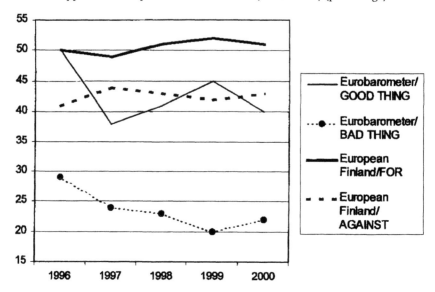

Eurobarometer: 1996–97 percentage 'don't know' not shown; 1998–2000 percentage 'don't know' and 'neither good nor bad' shown.
European Finland: 1996–2000 percentage 'don't know' not shown.

opposition to Finnish EU membership, we could interpret it as a sign that the gap is widening between the people and the elites on the EU issue and, consequently, as a sign of growing uninterest among the people. The whole phenomenon of European integration seems distant to ordinary people, an attitude which is also reflected in the distrust shown of its main forms of development.[38] The extremely low turnout (31 per cent) in the 1999 EP elections is further proof of this distrust.

SUMMARY

On 1 January 1995, Finland became a full member of the EU, after experiencing a new and revised form of political debate. First, the Finns had to become accustomed to the fact that the Paasikivi–Kekkonen line was neither holy nor everlasting, and that open discussion and disagreement on foreign policy matters were permitted. In practice, Finland has been through a learning process in which new concepts and political thinking have entered into Finnish politics.

Once the dominant political elite had almost unanimously decided to advocate membership, the revised integration policy was strongly recommended to the Finnish people. Compared to the high-ranking pro-EU supporters, the opponents of membership seemed outdated and anachronistic, often referring to traditional political concepts, which many Finns no longer identified with. If Finnish public opinion is evaluated overall, the influence of the political elite appears to be only moderate. Even though support for membership has remained constant since the first opinion survey in 1987, the fate of Finland was decisively held in the hands of those Finns who ultimately made up their minds at the very end of the referendum campaign.

Still, the Finnish referendum caused no great surprises. The Finnish people consented to EU membership by a relatively slim majority, and powerful social interests opposed full membership. The most significant of these were the farmers, who had dominated the issue of integration in Finland since the end of the negotiations for membership. The unified and hostile reaction of the farmers was reflected by the sharp geographical division of the country in the referendum. Membership in the EU constitutes a substantial challenge to Finnish agriculture – something that farmers had successfully avoided thus far. The social and political clashes caused by the membership issue have not continued to play a dominant role in Finnish politics. The government – with a very broad party base – has balanced attitudes towards integration in some parties, and the movements that had been established to prevent Finnish membership have had only a marginal position. However, the increasing criticism of the EU among the Finnish people indicates that during the initial years of membership the EU has remained distant to ordinary people.

NOTES

1. In the Paris Peace Treaty of 1947, Finland was required to return the province of Petsamo to the Soviet Union as well as to grant the area of Porkkala-udd on the basis of a 50-year lease. The size of the Finnish armed forces was confirmed by the treaty (including the demilitarization of Åland Islands and a ban on the possession of atomic weapons), and Finland was required to pay reparation worth $300,000,000 in commodities. See T. Polvinen, *Between East and West, Finland in International Politics 1944–1947* (Helsinki: WSOY, 1986), pp. 299–309.
2. David Arter has characterized Finland as a 'belated European'. See D. Arter, 'The EU Referendum in Finland on 16 October 1994: A Vote for the West, Not for Maastricht', *Journal of Common Market Studies* 33:3 (1995), p. 364.
3. See E. Antola and O. Tuusvuori, *Länsi-Euroopan integraatio ja Suomi* (Helsinki: Finnish Institute of International Affairs, 1983), p. 128.

4. See O. Apunen, *Paasikiven-Kekkosen linja* (Helsinki: Tammi, 1977), p. 121.
5. The annual surveys were conducted by The Planning Commission for Information on National Defence; see P. Alanen and T. Forsberg, 'The Evolution of Opinion about Foreign Policy in Finland from the 1960s till the 1980s', *Yearbook of Finnish Foreign Policy 1988–89* (1989), pp. 29–33.
6. According to Raimo Väyrynen, the Finnish consensus on the EEA can even be explained by the fact that the treaty excluded the two most sensitive areas, agriculture and foreign policy. See R. Väyrynen, 'Finland and the European Community: Changing Elite Bargains', *Cooperation and Conflict* 28:1 (1993), p. 39.
7. This position was held by Prime Minister Harri Holkeri (KOK) until late 1990. In his speech of 27 November 1990, Holkeri used a phrase that was to become famous where he equated Finnish EC membership with squaring the circle. H. Holkeri, 'Suomi hakee tietään', *Ulkopoliittisia lausuntoja ja asiakirjoja 1990* (Helsinki: Ministry of Foreign Affairs, 1990) pp. 161–5.
8. Professor Esko Antola was one of the first Finnish academics to propose closer relations between Finland and the EC, whereas associations such as the Finnish Foreign Trade Association and the EVA (maintained by the key business organizations in Finland) were the first collective voices of the same message.
9. In October 1990, the main party of the government, the Social Democrats, adopted the objective of bringing Sweden as close to the EC as possible. The decision to apply for membership was taken by the Swedish Parliament in December 1990. The Finnish strategy was another proof that the Finnish foreign policy was 'acquiescent adaptation'. See Väyrynen, 'Finland and the European Community', p. 42.
10. See O. Rehn, 'Odottavasta ennakoivaan integraatiopolitiikkaan', in T. Forsberg and T. Vaahtoranta (eds) *Johdatus Suomen ulkopolitiikkaan* (Helsinki: Gaudeamus, 1993), pp. 166–231.
11. The report is entitled *Suomi ja Euroopan yhteisön jäsenyys*. Report to the Parliament by the Council of State, 28.2.1992.
12. The way of voting on communications led to a situation in which two proposals – the government's and the opposition's – opposed each other, although both of them favoured the application. The numbers (108 for, 55 against) express the support given to the government's proposal – thus, they do not reflect the opposition's support of membership, whereas the numbers 133 for and 60 against show the membership's support in its entirety. See A. Kuosmanen, *Finland's Journey to the European Union* (Maastricht: EIPA, 2001), p. 9.
13. See Rehn, 'Odottavasta ennakoivaan', p. 208.
14. This analysis of the negotiations on Finland's accession is based upon Antti Kuosmanen's description of the process (*Finland's Journey to the European Union*). Kuosmanen participated in the negotiations as a member of the Finnish delegation.
15. See Kuosmanen, *Finland's Journey to the European Union*, p. 34.
16. Eighty per cent of the problems in the negotiations are said to have been related to agriculture. See T. Kivimäki, 'Transnationalisaatio, ryhmäintressit ja Suomen EU-neuvottelut', *Politiikka* 39:1 (1997), p. 31.
17. Arter, 'The EU Referendum in Finland', p. 374.
18. Ibid., p. 372, which even refers to the apparent strength of the public

attachment to the concept of neutrality as a reason for this conservatism.

19. Convention on the Demilitarization and Neutralization of the Åland Islands (1921), bilateral treaty between Finland and the Soviet Union on the Åland Islands (1940), Paris Peace Treaty (1947).
20. A shift in terminology has to be taken into account here. After the Treaty on Political Union had been agreed upon in Maastricht in December 1991, the political debate thus dealt with Finnish EU membership. In the governmental documents, 'the European Community' was still the concept used.
21. See, for example, J. Laine (the Director of the National Board of Customs in Finland), 'Suomi ja EY', *Ulkopolitiikka* 28:1 (1991), pp. 68–9.
22. See T. Tiilikainen, *Europe and Finland: Defining the Political Identity of Finland in Western Europe* (Aldershot: Ashgate, 1998), pp. 141–57.
23. K. Korhonen, *Meidän on uudesta luotava maa* (Helsinki: Otava, 1994), p. 150.
24. According to Arter, 'The EU Referendum in Finland', p. 378, the 'identity argument' had a strong attraction for the young generation.
25. See J. Salovaara, 'Finnish Integration Policy – from an Economic to a Security Motivation', *Yearbook of Finnish Foreign Policy 1993* (1994), pp. 16–23. For instance, on 23 August 1993, Foreign Minister Heikki Haavisto stated that in addition to its economic role the EC was important for Finland as a factor creating security.
26. According to Olli Rehn (then MP for the KESK), 'EU membership implies, though, additional value even to the national security of Finland. The EU is a political community based upon common European values. They create a political unity that does not provide military guarantees but avoids decisions taken on Finnish security without our own impact. . . . Probably, it even puts a constraint on exerting political pressure.' See O. Rehn, 'Pienen valtion legitiimi turvallisuusintressi', *Ulkopolitiikka* 28:1 (1991), pp. 34–41.
27. An important starting point for this debate was that Finland, in acknowledging the Maastricht Treaty as the basis for negotiations, stated its 'open attitude' towards all the options of security policy included by that treaty. This stand was taken both by President Mauno Koivisto and by Prime Minister Esko Aho in various connections in the year 1992.
28. The results of the survey were published in the daily newspaper *Helsingin Sanomat*, on 8 March 1970.
29. Elinkeinoelämän valtuuskunta, *Suomalaisten EU-kannanotot* (Helsinki: EVA, 1994), pp. 8–9.
30. See P. Pesonen, 'Äänestäjäin EU-päätösten synty', in P. Pesonen (ed.) *Suomen EU-kansanäänestys 1994: Raportti äänestäjien kannanotoista* (Helsinki: Ulkoasiainministeriö, Eurooppa-tiedotus, ja Painatuskeskus, 1994) pp. 76–8.
31. On the importance of the order of referendums in practice, see D. Jahn and A-S. Storsved, 'Legitimacy through Referendum? The Nearly Successful Strategy of the EU Referendums in Austria, Finland, Sweden and Norway', *West European Politics* 18:4 (1995), pp. 18–37.
32. See Pesonen, 'Äänestäjäin EU-päätösten synty', p. 79.
33. Ibid., p. 77.
34. See R. Sänkiaho, 'Jako kahteen: ketkä puolesta, ketkä vastaan', in Pesonen (ed.) *Suomen EU- kansanäänestys 1994*, pp. 64–73.
35. See P. Pesonen, 'EU-kannan pohja ja perusteet', in Pesonen (ed.) *Suomen EU-kansanäänestys 1994*, pp.84–95.

36. Both Eurobarometer and the opinion surveys conducted by the EVA have included three alternative responses (positive/neutral/negative) to the question, 'What is your conception of your country's membership in the EU?' The share of Finns adopting a neutral position has varied between 20 and 30 per cent. An analysis of the results can be found in T. Raunio, 'Valitsijoiden EU-tavoitteet', in P. Pesonen (ed.) *Suomen europarlamenttivaalit* (Tampere: Tampere University Press, 2000), pp. 83–6.
37. See '*Eurooppalainen Suomi*' (*http://www.eurooppalainensuomi.fi*), mieli-pidemittaukset.
38. Finns, for instance, are critical of eastern enlargement and of the deepening of integration towards a federal state. People seem to be longing for the strengthening of the citizen dimension, and this is reflected in the strong support given to the Charter on Fundamental Rights and even the constitution of the EU.

3

Parties and Elections

Since the majority of the main political parties in EU member states were established before the start of the integration process, the European issue has introduced a new dimension to their politics, both behaviourally and ideologically. Ideologically, parties both shape European integration by pursuing policy objectives in national and EU levels and adapt to integration by operating in an environment increasingly influenced by legislation and treaties decided by the member states and the EU institutions. Organizationally, through Euro-parties and their EP delegations, parties have a permanent presence at the European level, while at the same time the political dynamics of the EU policy process can have consequences for balance of power within parties.

National parties have been remarkably solid in their support for integration. Outright opposition to integration is mainly limited to ideologically extremist or populist parties; that is, virtually the same group of parties that are excluded from government in their member states.[1] However, this broad pro-European partisan consensus may be challenged by the increased salience of the EU for parties. As Europe is now more relevant to the parties, and as no party or member state can alone dictate the policies adopted by the EU, parties simply must pay more attention to European matters. But, perhaps most significantly, European integration has been a destabilizing and divisive factor for parties. The penetration of EU issues into domestic party competition has led to electoral defeats, backbench rebellions, intense factionalism, and leadership resignations, particularly in Denmark, France, Great Britain, and Norway.[2]

This chapter examines the impact of EU membership on Finnish political parties, their electoral performance, ideology, cohesion and organization. The data consists of party documents, parliamentary records, and in-depth interviews with the European or international secretaries of six parties carried out in April and May 2000.[3] The following section introduces the main features of the Finnish party

system. The European policies of the parties represented in the Eduskunta
are analysed below under the heading 'Ideological Convergence', with
emphasis on the role of integration in facilitating this convergence among
the parties. The impact of the EU on party cohesion is then examined
under the heading 'Cohesion and Factionalism'. Next the section headed
'Party Organization' examines whether participation in EU decision-
making has altered the balance of power within parties. Then the role of
EP elections in Finnish politics is analysed. The concluding discussion
highlights the main problems facing Finnish parties in their adaptation to
integration.

Measured by the effective number of parliamentary parties, Finland's
party system is relatively highly fragmented.[5] Partly as a result of the
proportional electoral system, no party has ever alone controlled the
majority of seats in the Eduskunta.[6] The core of the Finnish party system
consists of three parties: the Social Democratic Party (SDP), the agrarian
Centre Party (KESK), and the conservative National Coalition (KOK),
which among them have captured between 57 and 68 per cent of the votes
in national parliamentary elections since 1945.[7] While electoral volatility
has increased and the party system has become more fragmented, the
three core parties have consolidated their positions during recent decades,
especially as the vote share of the radical left or former communist parties
has declined rapidly since the 1970s. The main cleavage has been the
left–right division,[8] but, since the early 1990s, the rural–urban or
centre–periphery divide has become the second main cleavage, partly
because integration and foreign policy issues have entered internal party
debates, having previously been the almost exclusive domain of the
president.[9] Table 3 shows the distribution of votes between parties in
national parliamentary elections held in the 1990s.

Recent governments have been broad coalitions, including two of the
three main parties, the SDP, the KESK, and the KOK, and uniting parties
across the ideological spectrum (the composition of Finnish governments
is analysed in more detail in Chapter 4). Such cooperation is facilitated
by a convergence in party ideologies, notably so regarding economic
policy. A five-party, oversized coalition government, bringing together the
SDP, the KOK, the Left Alliance (VAS), the Swedish People's Party (RKP),
and the Green League (VIHR), took office after the 1995 elections, and
this 'rainbow government' renewed its mandate in the March 1999 elections. According to Nousiainen, the formation of the five-party coalition

Parties and Elections

Table 3
Distribution of Votes in National Parliamentary and European Elections in the
1990s (percentage)

Party	1991	1995	1996 EP	1999	1999 EP
Centre Party (KESK)	24.8	19.8	24.4	22.4	21.3
Social Democratic Party (SDP)	22.1	28.3	21.5	22.9	17.8
National Coalition (KOK)	19.3	17.9	20.2	21.0	25.3
Left Alliance (VAS)	10.1	11.2	10.5	10.9	9.1
Swedish People's Party (RKP)	5.5	5.1	5.8	5.1	6.8
Green League (VIHR)	6.8	6.5	7.6	7.3	13.4
Christian Democrats (KD)	3.1	3.0	2.8	4.2	2.4
Rural Party (SMP)	4.8	1.3			
Young Finns (NUORS)		2.8	3.0	1.0	
True Finns (PS)			0.7	1.0	0.8
Others	3.5	4.1	3.5	4.2	3.1
Total	100	100	100	100	100

The autonomous Åland region has one MP. This representative is not formally a representative of the RKP, but, in practice, sits with the RKP group.
Source: *Statistics Finland.*

indicates that 'the traditional bloc boundary of the party system has lost much of its importance.'[10] Indeed, the one feature causing bewilderment in Finnish politics, at least among foreign commentators, is the bargaining and ideological moderation involved in building broad, oversized coalition governments.

The history of the SDP dates back to 1899, with the current name being adopted in 1903. The SDP has won, on average, 25 per cent of votes in parliamentary elections held since the Second World War, making it the biggest party in Finland. The KESK was founded in 1906 as the Agrarian Party to defend the interests of smallholders against the impending urbanization and industrialization. Throughout its history, the KESK has drawn most of its support from the countryside, and support in the urban areas remains modest. With the exception of the 1995 Eduskunta elections, it has won over 20 per cent of votes in elections held since the early 1990s. The KESK has traditionally occupied the median position on the left–right spectrum, and this ideological centrism primarily explains its strong position in government formation. The centre–right KOK was founded in 1918. The party advertises itself as a 'moderate conservative' force, and the description is largely accurate. Excluded from government for foreign policy reasons (Moscow's influence) between 1966 and 1987, the party has been in the government continuously since 1987.

45

The radical left or communist bloc has traditionally been very strong in Finland, and the Finnish People's Democratic League (SKDL) won over 20 per cent of the votes in elections held between 1945 and 1966. From the 1970s onwards, however, the seat share of the SKDL started to decline and, reflecting the fate of communist parties in several European countries, the party experienced internal splits in the 1980s. In the 1990s, its successor, the Left Alliance, founded in 1990, polled around ten per cent of the votes. The Left Alliance brings together a variety of leftists and former communists, and the party has become considerably more pro-market since the early 1990s. The RKP, founded in 1906, is primarily an ethnoregionalist language party, representing the interests of the Swedish-speaking minority that live along the coastline. The RKP can also be classified as a liberal party, with its moderately right-wing economic policy and a strong emphasis on human rights and minority issues. Its vote share has normally reflected the size of the Swedish-speaking minority; since the early 1990s, the RKP has won five to six per cent of the votes. Despite its minor seat share, the RKP has traditionally been in the government, with only the KESK having been included in more cabinets than the RKP. Moreover, the RKP has been in every cabinet formed since 1979.[11] The Green League gained its first MPs in 1983, and, since the early 1990s, its electoral support has remained between six and eight per cent. In 1995, the Green League became the first western European green party to gain government status. In comparison with most European green parties, the Green League is ideologically moderate and definitely belongs to the pragmatic wing of the green movement.[12]

As for the smaller parties, the Christian Democratic Party (KD) was founded in 1958. The party draws most of its support from rural areas. It changed its name from Christian Union to Christian Democrats at the party congress held in May 2001 (see below). The right-wing Young Finns was formed in 1994, and the party won two seats in the 1995 elections. Four years later, the Young Finns failed to win any seats, and the party was subsequently disbanded. The right-wing True Finns (PS) are virtually a successor to the Rural Party (SMP), albeit with less populist tendencies. The SMP was effectively a family enterprise, founded by Veikko Vennamo in 1959 as the Smallholders' Party. Vennamo senior passed the party leadership on to his son Pekka, but the party was disbanded after its meagre showing in the 1995 elections.

Examining the impact of European integration on national party systems, Mair concluded that out of over 120 parties established in EU member states (excluding Greece, Portugal, and Spain) to contest national parliamentary elections after the first direct EP elections held in each country, only three were formed 'with the explicit and primary intention of mobilising support for or against the EU'.[13] Party members, at least on the elite level, have therefore decided not to defect to other parties despite the differences of opinion over Europe. The same applies to Finland. The existing national parties have successfully absorbed the new EU dimension into their policy profiles without suffering any major vote losses or defections to other parties. To be sure, integration matters have produced heated debates within most parties, but the basic shape of the Finnish party system has not been altered as a result of European integration.

IDEOLOGICAL CONVERGENCE

While European integration has not directly led to the formation of new parties in Finland, it has nevertheless had an impact on the cohesion and ideology of parties. This section outlines the EU policies of parties represented in the Eduskunta after the 1999 elections, and examines to what extent adaptation to integration has produced changes in the ideological orientation of Finnish parties. The data consists of party programmes adopted between the early 1990s and 2001, with emphasis on election manifestos used in the Eduskunta and EP elections.[14]

The 1994 membership referendum was a clear indication that European issues would prove to be problematic for Finnish parties.[15] Table 4 shows party positions on membership before the referendum and the share of party supporters voting in favour of Finland's joining the EU. The only party in which the voting behaviour of its supporters contradicted the official party line was the KESK, with just above one-third (36 per cent) of party supporters favouring membership. Two parties, the Left Alliance and the Green League, were so divided internally that they deliberately left their position open in order not to antagonize their supporters. The only Eduskunta parties that officially resisted membership were the KD and the now defunct Rural Party. In both parties, the leadership and the rank and file were almost unanimously against membership.

In autumn 1991, the executive committee of the then main opposition party, the SDP, demanded that Finland should apply for EC membership. The party's electorate was more sceptical, as only 75 per cent of the SDP voters were in favour of membership in the referendum. The elite opinion was highly influential in mobilizing party supporters behind the official party line:

> Still in September SDP supporters were almost evenly divided into three camps: 'Yes', 'No', and those yet to make up their minds. This

47

Table 4
Party Positions in the 1994 Membership Referendum

Parties	Official party line	Voters supporting membership (per cent)
Social Democratic Party	Yes	75
Centre Party	Yes	36
National Coalition	Yes	89
Left Alliance	No position	24
Swedish People's Party	Yes	85
Green League	No position	55
Christian Democrats	No	10
Rural Party/True Finns	No	20

Sources: Party documents, voters' figures from H. Paloheimo, 'Vaaliohjelmat ja ehdokkaiden mielipiteet', in P. Pesonen (ed.) *Suomen europarlamenttivaalit* (Tampere: Tampere University Press, 2000), p. 58.

was problematic for the party elite as the chairman Paavo Lipponen had been one of the first to publicly speak in favour of membership. Also the leading party organs had unanimously favoured membership, but the rank and file were much more hesitant. In the actual referendum those social democrats that a month earlier had not yet formed an opinion voted 'Yes'. Thus the party leadership influenced the voting behaviour of the SDP electorate.[16]

The European programme of the SDP reflects the views of its fellow social democrats in the Party of European Socialists (PES). The policy is primarily explained by the party leadership's unequivocal support for integration, and the moderate welfare state ideology of the party. In particular, the prime minister and party chairman, Paavo Lipponen, has from the beginning of his premiership been determined to lead Finland into the inner circle of the EU. While a section of the party elite has been much more reserved, the party leader has not met any strong resistance as the Euro-sceptics have not organized themselves. The SDP's goals include increasing the scope of Council majority voting, strengthening the EU's competence in social and environmental issues, and reducing the EU's control over agricultural policy. The near unanimous party council decided in September 1997 in favour of Finland's participation in the third stage of the EMU from the start of 1999. The SDP wants to develop the CFSP, particularly through increasing the EU's involvement in crisis management, but argues that the Union should not develop a common defence policy.

As the leading governing party in 1991–95, the KESK was a key player in making the decision to apply for membership. The party itself, both the elite and the supporters, was far from united. The actual membership application met resistance within the party, with 22 out of 55 KESK MPs voting against the application in the Eduskunta in 1992. On 18 June 1994, the party congress decided to support membership. The atmosphere in the meeting was heated, and it was only after the prime minister and party chairman, Esko Aho, had threatened to resign were the KESK to oppose membership that a favourable decision was reached by 1,607 votes to 834. In the referendum, 36 per cent of party supporters favoured membership. The majority of the leadership and voters living in the southern cities voted 'Yes', while those in the countryside voted 'No'. The party leadership, in particular Esko Aho, were able to persuade some of the opponents to change their opinion:

> The supporters of the main governing party, the Centre [KESK], were in September clearly against membership. A large part of these persons voted 'No' in the referendum, but a much bigger share than in other parties changed their opinion from opposing membership to favouring it. Surprisingly those yet to decide were split evenly between 'Yes' and 'No' camps in the referendum. Thus the official line of the party converted part of the opponents. A crucial role in this 'shepherding' was performed by Prime Minister Esko Aho who ... according to the survey was the only person that widely influenced people's European opinion.[17]

Party leader Aho has faced a tough challenge in balancing the often uncompromising anti-integrationism of the party electorate and the need to maintain his party's credibility as a potential governing party. The Euro-critics have not formed their own organization, and the opposition has mainly centred around Paavo Väyrynen, an MEP and former party chairman and foreign minister. The main agricultural interest group closely attached to the party, the MTK, has been critical of integration. This is not surprising considering the destructive impact of the CAP on the farming sector.

Like other European agrarian parties, the KESK emphasizes the intergovernmental nature of the EU. Even though the party is a member of the strongly pro-integrationist European Liberal, Democrat, and Reform Party (ELDR), the Centre Party has very little in common with the Euro-liberals' vision of Europe. It explicitly rejects a federal Europe and argues that the EU should be developed as an association of independent member states. The party favours the maintenance of institutional status quo and wants to balance the introduction of European-level environmental taxation by reducing the EU's competence in agricultural and regional policy. An additional party congress held in September 1997 decided against Finland's EMU membership. However, the party indicated in spring 1998 that it respects the outcome of the Eduskunta vote, and will not seek to withdraw from the EMU in the future. The party favours the continuation of Finland's traditional foreign policy of military non-alignment.

The National Coalition (KOK) decided in June 1991 that Finland should apply for EC membership. Eighty-nine per cent of party supporters voted in favour of membership in the referendum. The KOK has been the most united of the core parties on integration. No central party figure has openly criticized the party line. This internal coherence is mainly explained by the moderate right-wing ideology of the party. While the party ideology emphasizes traditional conservative values, including national sovereignty, the overwhelming majority of the party supporters favour EU membership and developing closer links with the West.

In line with other conservative parties in the European People's Party (EPP), the KOK does not support a federal Europe. The party argues that, with the exception of a common immigration policy and improved legal rights for citizens and companies, the EU does not need any substantial new powers ('less but better'), and places strong emphasis on a clearer delineation of powers between the Union and its member states, and particularly on the smooth and efficient functioning of the single market, which requires closer coordination of national economic and employment policies. In institutional questions, the party supports increased use of the co-decision procedure and majority voting in the Council, while underlining the importance of maintaining the current balance of power among the EU institutions. The KOK was strongly in favour of the EMU, and approves the development of a common foreign and security policy, as outlined in the Amsterdam Treaty.

Integration matters have stimulated fierce debates within the Left Alliance. The party did not adopt an official position on membership prior to the referendum, and only 24 per cent of its supporters voted 'Yes'. The contrasting opinions of the leading party figures have attracted much media attention. The rival opinions have been expressed by the successive party chairpersons Claes Andersson (1990–98) and Suvi-Anne Siimes (1998–) and the MEP Esko Seppänen, the last being very critical of integration. The Euro-sceptics have not organized themselves. The party supporters and trade unions close to the party are internally divided over integration. This ambivalence is mainly explained by ideology: the market-driven logic of integration is rather distant from the world-view of the average Left Alliance voter. The party has been in government since the 1995 elections and has been forced to balance the Euro-scepticism of its electorate with the responsibility of being a junior partner in a government committed to further integration.

The Left Alliance emphasizes the importance of international co-operation in the fight against market forces. Enlargements and the need to confront unemployment and social exclusion throughout the continent are prioritized. The party favours extended use of majority voting; the holding of referenda on important integration questions; and cautious strengthening of the EP's powers, increasing the EU's competence in social, environmental, and taxation policies, and reducing it in agricultural matters. With the exception of crisis-management capacity, the party opposes moves to develop the EU's military dimension. The party did an ideological U-turn on the EMU. Against EMU membership in its Euro-election manifesto adopted in April 1996, the party leadership took a bold step in November–December 1997 by organizing an internal party caucus on whether Finland should join the EMU. The wording of the question aroused much controversy, as the party executive linked the issue to whether the party should continue in the government. The turnout was 67.1 per cent, with 9,253 out of 13,790 enfranchised party members casting votes. The results showed that 52.4 per cent were in favour, 41.5 per cent were against, and 5.9 per cent left the decision to the party leadership.

The RKP came out in favour of membership in 1991. In the referendum, 85 per cent of RKP voters were in favour of membership. However, there was a geographical and urban–rural split within the party: farmers, in particular those from the Ostrobothnia region, opposed membership, while those residing in southern Finland were in favour. The party supports increased use of majority voting, especially in environmental issues; the application of the co-decision procedure whenever the Council decides by majority voting; a partial transfer of agricultural powers back to the member states; and making the Charter of Fundamental Rights part of the EU's constitution. The June 1997 party congress approved Finland's EMU membership. In relation to the CFSP, the party stresses the development of a credible foreign and security policy, concentrating on conflict prevention and crisis management.

The Green League did not take a decision on membership before the referendum. The elite disagreement was reflected at the voter level, with 55 per cent favouring membership. While the Green League has remained divided over integration, the party has avoided factionalization and open leadership disputes. Its European policy has within a short time become strongly pro-integrationist, a change which owes much to the former

51

party chairperson, Heidi Hautala, MEP, and to active transnational co-operation in the context of the European Federation of Green Parties (EFGP). Of the Finnish parties, the Green League has probably been most influenced by such transnational party activities.

The Green League argues that the priorities of the EU do not reflect the needs of the citizens and the environment. The cure is increasing the EU's powers and making its decision-making structures more democratic. According to the Green League, third-pillar (JHA) issues should be included under the first pillar, the CAP needs to be reformed by transferring powers back to the national level, and environmental and social policies should become central areas of EU competence with common minimum environmental and energy taxes. Democratization involves the holding of binding referenda on the most important decisions and increased use of QMV together with strengthening the EP's role through widening the scope of the co-decision procedure. The Green League is against a common defence policy. On EMU, the Green League was in the same position as the Left Alliance. Supporters and the party elite were divided over the issue, but the party was a junior member in a government committed to entering the third stage from the start of 1999. The party first favoured the postponement of EMU, but a joint meeting of the party council and its MPs, in January 1998, decided in favour of Finland's participation. The voting result was 31 in favour and 13 against, with the party chairperson Satu Hassi on the losing side. At its party congress in May 2001, the Green League became the first party in Finland to adopt a statement in favour of a federal Europe. The Green League's vision was one of decentralized federalism, that is, 'a strong Europe of regions', with the Charter of Fundamental Rights incorporated as the first section of the EU's new constitution.

The KD favours a Europe in which independent nation states practise wide-ranging cooperation. The party does not want to increase the EU's powers, environmental and minimum taxation regulations excluded. The June 1997 party congress decided against EMU membership despite the proposal by the party chairman Bjarne Kallis to postpone the issue. The party wants the CFSP to remain as intergovernmental cooperation. European integration acted as a stimulus for reshaping the name and identity of the KD. Encouraged by the electoral success of its sister Christian parties in Norway and Sweden, and in order to emphasize its European links, the party changed its name from the Christian Union to the Christian Democrats at the party congress in May 2001. Adopting the name 'Christian Democrats' was a key move in the attempt by the party leadership to modernize the party's image and thereby broaden its electoral appeal.[18]

The True Finns (PS) is the most Euro-critical Eduskunta party. The party ideology is rather nationalistic, and the party was against EU membership in 1994, then as its predecessor, the Rural Party. The PS wants the EU to be an association of independent nations and is against the deepening of integration.[19]

Finnish parties are in broad agreement over several dimensions of European integration: enlargement, simplifying existing decision-making structures mainly through extending the application of the co-decision procedure and QMV in the Council, replacing the existing treaties with a more easily understandable document, producing a clearer division of powers between the EU and its member states, making the EU policy process more open and transparent, improving the involvement of national parliaments in the EU decision-making system, developing the EU's crisis management capacity, and, in general, bringing the EU 'closer to the people'. In line with the principle of subsidiarity, parties and individual politicians often demand that decisions are taken closer to the citizens. However, apart from the CAP and regional policy, parties have not really put forward any concrete proposals for reducing the EU's powers. Rather predictably, parties focus in their European programmes and statements on issues closest to them: leftist parties (the SDP, the Left Alliance, and the Green League) emphasize the EU's role in improving social and environmental standards, and in safeguarding employment and the welfare state in an increasingly globalized economy. The KESK has focused on agriculture and regional matters, the KOK stresses the stability provided by EMU and the single market, and the RKP emphasizes human rights policies. However, reflecting the overall status of security issues on the Finnish political agenda, and Finland's proactive role in second-pillar questions (see Chapter 7), the development of the CFSP has attracted much attention among parties.[20]

When we examine the terminology used by parties and the nature of the integration debate, it is notable how rapidly Finnish parties adjusted to life in the EU. All Eduskunta parties support membership, and no party winning seats in the parliament has at any point since the referendum publicly called for Finland's withdrawal from the EU. This does not imply that in the early years of membership Finnish parties would have been notably proactive in their EU policies. On the contrary, parties have mainly reacted to policy initiatives from the European level. In a sense, this is only natural, as the agenda of the EU has been quite full since 1995, with two IGCs and the introduction of the single currency. At least on the rhetorical level, partisan support for integration is to a large extent defended in instrumental terms, focusing on the importance of the EU in protecting national economic and security interests. Therefore, the federalist programme adopted by the Green League in May 2001, and particularly the speech by Prime Minister Lipponen in Bruges in November 2000, in which he called for a federal union without actually explicitly calling it federal, represent potentially significant departures in the rhetoric of Finnish integration.[21]

But which factors explain the positions adopted by Finnish parties? The strongest explanatory factors are party competition, especially government formation; the influence of party elites; and overall ideological convergence. The geopolitical and economic context is also highly relevant, as all parties see the EU as a way to consolidate Finland's place in the West. Party leaders have been particularly decisive in parties whose supporters have been critical of or against integration: the Left Alliance, the Green League, the SDP, and the KESK. The pro-membership views of the SDP and the KESK leaders were crucial in converting a section of their parties' supporters to the 'Yes' camp in the 1994 referendum. Indeed, party elites have taken a gamble on European issues by adopting positions that have conflicted with the mood of the voters. For example, EMU membership was approved by the Eduskunta in April 1998 with 135 MPs for, 61 against, one abstaining, and two absent. At the same time, public opinion surveys reported that only around 40 per cent of the citizens were in favour of the project. Such behaviour is mainly explained by the elites' desire not to exclude their parties from future government negotiations.

Government formation contributes to ideological convergence, namely the clustering of parties towards the centre of the left–right spectrum, which remains the main structure of competition in all western European societies. Ideological distances between parties have arguably diminished, and individual parties and party groups have moved gradually towards the political centre, or, in the case of left and green parties, to the right, a development occurring also among the Euro-parties.[22] Nearly all established parties, excluding some radical left, extreme right, and populist parties, are now potential government partners. Such ideological convergence results mainly from the dominance of neo-liberal economic policies throughout Europe, with international agreements further narrowing the policy options available to individual countries. According to Mair, ideology has vanished from party activity to the point where 'partisan purpose is itself more difficult to discern'.[23]

The shape of the Finnish party system, with no party as a rule winning more than 25 per cent of votes in parliamentary elections, together with the rather corporatist nature of the polity, facilitates ideological convergence among all parties aspiring to enter the government. In the Left Alliance, the Green League, and, to a certain extent, the SDP, the policy moderation and ideological compromise, certainly not least in integration matters, implied by multi-party coalition governments, have gradually reduced the influence of the more radical left-wing sections that also were against EU membership and remain more sceptical of the benefits of integration. The programmatic adaptation and ideological moderation implied by government formation, short- and long-term interests in maintaining government status, and mutual commitments agreed between the parties in the cabinet largely explain why Finnish parties supported EMU and are in broad agreement on national integration policy.[24]

COHESION AND FACTIONALISM

The ideological convergence necessitated by adaptation to European integration, together with the introduction of a completely new (EU) issue dimension, must naturally have consequences for the cohesion of parties. Moreover, as outlined in the introductory section of this chapter, European integration has indeed destabilized party systems and led to intense factionalism and divisions within parties. Interestingly, the retrospective expert survey carried out by Ray showed that 'record levels of internal dissent are found primarily in nations which have had referenda, and occur in parties across the political spectrum'.[25] While the 1994 referendum revealed significant differences within parties, this section shows that EU issues have not led to organized factionalism in Finnish parties, a fact largely explained by the strongly candidate-centred electoral system.

Factionalism can take many forms: 'Factionalism can be the result of a prominent figure publicly breaking off from the overall party position. Other indicators of factionalism lie in organization and identity: whether there is actually a degree of cooperation between activists on this issue and whether they have identified themselves under a particular rubric.'[26] In fact, in the context of European integration, it might be better to speak of issue-groups instead of factions. According to Hine, factions are 'solidly organised, disciplined, self-aware groups, enjoying a relatively stable and cohesive personnel over time'. Issue-groups instead try to 'influence the way in which power is exercised (by others) on given questions'.[27]

Applying these definitions to Finland, we note that EU matters have not produced any organized factions within parties. Euro-criticism has so far been based on prominent individual MPs or MEPs. Such lack of organized factions is at least partially explained by the Finnish electoral system. The candidate selection process is decentralized and voters choose between individual candidates in both national and EP elections. This mechanism facilitates intraparty protest based around individual persons and reduces the probability of establishing organized factions. The same features apply naturally in domestic politics, with the national-level party executive having only limited means to control the candidate selection process carried out by district branches.

But how do parties manage and contain factionalism over Europe? We can distinguish between three main strategies: giving a free hand or issue avoidance, accommodating the opposition, and persuasion or sanctions. In the first strategy, the party leadership allows internal dissent without even trying to make MPs or ordinary party members toe the party line. Afraid of alienating sections of their voters, parties can also leave the issue open and not take a stand at all or be conspicuously ambivalent in their position-taking. Such behaviour was evident in Denmark, France, and Ireland in the run-up to the referendums on the Maastricht Treaty.[28] Aylott reports similar behaviour in the case of the Swedish Social Democrats before the membership referendum in 1994. Initially, the party leadership agreed to refrain from making any recommendation to the party members and supporters before the conclusion of membership negotiations. The anti-EU section of the party was organized with approval and money from the party, and, after the pro-membership decision taken by the party congress, party members were assured that they could continue to oppose Swedish membership from within the party and contradict their leaders' advice with a clear conscience. Legitimizing intraparty opposition was a crucial factor in successful party management, as a less accommodative approach might have led to open rebellion or even defections to the two other leftist parties that were against the EU.[29]

Accommodating the opposition is the second alternative. The individuals or sections of the party elite are pacified through co-optation, offering them representation in leading party organs, or even offering them government portfolios. An example of this strategy is the accommodative tactics of the Swedish Social Democrats. Having won the general elections in September 1994, Prime Minister Carlsson appointed two anti-accessionists to his cabinet. In the 1995 and 1999 Euro-elections, two social democratic lists were offered to voters in each of the five regions. The top 12 names on all the lists were the same, but their order was different in each region, one list giving higher placing to candidates who were more positive towards the EU, while the other gave priority to those of a more sceptical disposition.[30] In the third strategy, the party leaders persuade, with or without the threat of sanctions, party members to support the official party line. For example, in countries using closed lists, the leadership can threaten troublesome MPs with exclusion from party lists. A gentler method is to invest resources in 'educating' party members about the rationale and motives behind party policies, either through arranging seminars or distributing information.

Finnish parties have resorted to all three strategies in dealing with internal EU opposition. The Left Alliance and the Green League left their position open on membership prior to the referendum in order not to alienate the anti-EU voters, with individual senior party figures campaigning both for and against membership. Immediately after the referendum, the party secretaries of the KESK and the Left Alliance made it clear that opponents of the EU would be welcome to their ranks.[31] More broadly speaking, nearly all parties have deliberately kept a low profile in EU matters before both EP and Eduskunta elections. With the exception of some behind-the-scenes manoeuvres, party leaders have refrained from applying any sanctions against the Euro-sceptics. For example, no party members have been prevented by party leaders from standing as candidates in EP or Eduskunta elections due to their EU stances. In fact, the situation is largely the opposite. In the hope of maximizing their vote share, parties have deliberately included in their pool of candidates people with divergent views on integration, notably in the KESK, the Left Alliance, and the Green League. Parties have left individual candidates to run their own campaigns, with little if any interference from the party leadership. Elections to the EP have in a way provided the parties with a convenient outlet for releasing tensions within parties.

The third strategy has been most pronounced among the SDP. Despite some qualified resistance both before and after the membership referendum, the party leadership has not strayed from its course of taking Finland into the inner core of the EU. Together with the leading trade union organization, the Central Organization of Finnish Trade Unions (SAK), the SDP has, since the early 1990s, invested significant resources in distributing information to their members about the consequences of integration, and especially about the single currency. Perhaps the only clear example of sanctions or threats was when the KESK adopted its pro-EU position in 1994 only after the prime minister and party chairperson, Aho, had threatened to resign were his party to oppose membership.

If we look forward into the future, cleavage theory is helpful in predicting both the integration policies of parties and particularly their internal cohesion in European matters. Applying the social cleavage theory of Lipset and Rokkan, we can expect that internal party conflict over integration will increase when the party position on integration is different from that predicted on the basis of the cleavage theory.[32] Euro-scepticism will continue to be most pronounced and intransigent within the KESK. According to the expert survey conducted by Ray, the KESK was, in 1996, one of the most conflict-ridden parties in the EU in integration matters, with only the Social Democrats and the Socialist People's Party in Denmark, the Social Democrats and the Centre Party in Sweden, and the Conservative Party in Great Britain also evenly split on the issue of integration.[33] The negative attitude of Centre Party supporters towards integration is both instrumental, with the CAP and the single market having a negative impact on primary producers, and more ideological due to the conservative nationalism typical of agrarian parties. For the Left Alliance and the Green League, internal divisions are likely to continue to trouble the party leadership as sections of party voters view the EU as too exclusive and market-friendly. The level of internal cohesion on integration within the SDP and the KOK will depend largely on the economic policies – neo-liberal versus regulated capitalism – of the EU.

Institutional questions have so far proven more controversial than the division of powers between the EU and member states. This is understandable, for strengthening the powers of supranational institutions (the European Commission, the EP, the ECJ) at the expense of intergovernmental decision-making will, at least numerically, further limit national independence and sovereignty, two hard-won core values in Finnish society.

PARTY ORGANIZATION

When we turn to the balance of power inside parties, we find that measuring power in party organizations is a complex task. According to research on national party systems, parties have arguably become more centralized, with the party leaders being fairly autonomous between elections and party congresses of the ordinary members. To summarize briefly the main findings of this literature, two findings warrant special attention. First, the increasing personification of politics, especially electoral campaigns, has concentrated power in the party leaders and their team of advisers. Second, parliamentary groups have strengthened their position vis-à-vis the extra-parliamentary party organization. The parliamentary group is, through increased staffing and committee specialization, better equipped to deal with most policy issues. Therefore, party group influence is particularly pronounced in day-to-day decision-making, as MPs need to react quickly to new issues, which often are technical and very detailed, while the central office focuses primarily on more long-term developments.[34]

As outlined in the introductory chapter, there is a strong argument that systemic features of the EU policy process exacerbate centralization inside parties. Informational advantage is a key factor behind these arguments, according to which European integration consolidates centralization and top-down decision-making by providing the party leadership (as cabinet members) with an arena (EU) where the party organization exercises little if any control over the party representatives. As a partial counterbalance of this executive dominance, the increasing relevance of European matters should also tip the scales in favour of the parliamentary group, because MPs, through their legislative work, acquire EU-related policy expertise lacking among the ordinary members and in the central office. Apart from members of the government, MPs are therefore best placed to learn about Europe within parties.

While Finnish parties can be characterized as rather centralized between elections, the decentralized candidate selection process limits the disciplinary powers of party leaders vis-à-vis MPs. The national level party organization includes the party congress, the party executive, the party council, various working committees, and the organizations for youth, women, and students. Some right-wing parties also have an executive committee whose task is mainly to prepare the meetings of the party executive. The chairperson is selected by the party congress, with no formal limits on the number of terms, except in the Green League, where the same person can be the chairperson for no more than two consecutive terms. The party congress convenes usually every second year in the larger parties and every year in the smaller parties. While the party congress is the main forum for approving political programmes, internal decision-making within parties is otherwise fairly centralized.[35]

In Finland, the extent of leadership autonomy has been limited by two factors. First, the active scrutiny by the Eduskunta of the government on EU affairs has provided the ordinary backbenchers – and not just ministers, MEPs, and the parties' international/European secretaries – with the opportunity to familiarize themselves with integration matters (see Chapter 4). Second, the divisive nature of EU has forced the party leaders to listen carefully to MPs' opinions on Europe. Nevertheless, it is fair to conclude that party leaders have been central figures in shaping parties' European policies, particularly in the three largest parties.

The status of European matters inside the party clearly reflects the personal priorities of party leaders, and not just the divisiveness of the EU dimension. In this sense, the situation has arguably been 'best' in the SDP, the KOK, and the Green League. Lipponen's European credentials are well-known in the EU, while the finance minister and the former chairperson of the KOK, Sauli Niinistö, was elected chairperson of the European Democrat Union (EDU) in 1999. Several leading figures of the Green League have held leadership positions in the EFGP. The former party chairman, Pekka Sauri, co-chaired the EFGP for three years from January 1994 onwards, and Pekka Haavisto was elected to the same position in 2000, while Heidi Hautala became the co-chairperson of the green group in the EP after the 1999 elections.

Examining next the structure of party organization, we note two developments: the establishment of new party organs or offices and the participation in Euro-parties. All Finnish parties have established EU working groups or committees to formulate and coordinate their inte-gration policies. Between them, parties have appointed only a few new officials as a result of integration. This is partially explained by the rising costs of election campaigns that have forced Finnish parties to main-tain fairly strict budgetary discipline. The work of parties' international secretaries is now strongly focused on integration matters. Moreover, the officials of the EP's party groups working for the Finnish member parties and MEPs' personal assistants, both financed from the EP's budget, have provided an additional workforce for the parties. Even minor sums of extra money can make a difference; thus, the additional staff and funding available from the EP's budget have been important, particularly for the smaller parties. Nevertheless, parties recognize the need to hire new staff in order to improve the scrutiny of EU initiatives and to process them more efficiently.[36]

A direct impact, and arguably a rough indicator of the salience of European matters for parties, is the time reserved for debating EU issues in the various party bodies. Parties' European or international secretaries were asked in April–May 2000 how much time national-level party organs annually spend in processing EU matters. The response categories were less than ten per cent of available time, 10–25 per cent, 25–50 per cent, 50–75 per cent, and 75 per cent or more. In five parties, the party congress spent less than ten per cent and in one party 10–25 per cent of its time on EU questions. Regarding party councils, the responses were less than ten per cent in three parties and 10–25 per cent in the other three parties. Turning to the party executive, integration matters in three parties took up less than ten per cent of the time, and in three parties between 10 and 25 per cent. Finally, EU matters play a more important role in the work of parties' parlia-mentary groups: five parties replied that these matters take 10–25 per cent of the time and only one less than ten per cent.[37] The fact that parliamentary groups spend more of their time on European matters than the other national party organs is largely explained by the fact that the Eduskunta has a rather extensive and decentralized mechanism for controlling the government in European affairs, and party groups debate EU issues in their own meetings prior to the meetings of the Grand Committee.

Membership in Euro-parties and their EP groups offers national parties a new forum through which to influence public policy in a Europe characterized by increasing interdependence between national and EU levels. National parties can utilize Euro-parties for pursuing their own policy objectives, while simultaneously learning and getting information from their sister parties. Considering the range of meetings taking place every year between national parties, and particularly their leaders, it would be wrong to discount the possibility of policy diffusion through mutual exchange of information and ideas. Participation in Euro-parties can also shape the ideology of national parties, particularly their European policies.[38]

Table 5 shows the Euro-party memberships of Finnish parties. The SDP became an affiliated member of the Confederation of Socialist Parties in the European Community (CSPEC) in 1990 and an observer member two years later. The CSPEC was turned into the Party of European Socialists in November 1992, and at the same meeting the SDP was accepted as a member of the new Euro-party. The KESK became an observer member of the Federation of Liberal, Democratic, and Reform Parties of the EC in 1992 and a member of the ELDR from the start of 1995. The KESK sits rather uneasily in the strongly pro-integrationist Liberal group. The KESK delegation voted against the ELDR Euro-election manifesto in the Liberals' party congress in Berlin in April 1999.[39] In the 1995–98 EP, the KESK MEPs, together with the Left Alliance representatives, voted against their group more often than other Finnish party delegations.[40] However, the numerically strong position of the KESK in the ELDR group has enabled the party to influence group objectives, notably on the CFSP and agricultural policy. The KESK has also participated in the work of the International Network of Centre Parties (INC), a loose cooperation network of agrarian parties. The KOK became a member of the EPP in 1995, having been an observer member since 1993. The KOK is considerably less pro-integrationist than the median national party in the EPP. According to the rules of the EPP and the ELDR, full membership is open only to parties from EU member states.

Radical left parties have no European-level party, but the Left Alliance is a founding member of the New European Left Forum (NELF), an

Table 5
The European-Level Party Affiliations of Finnish Parties

Party	Europarty (full membership)	EP group
Social Democrats	PES (1992)	PES
Centre Party	ELDR (1995)	ELDR
National Coalition	EPP (1995)	EPP
Left Alliance		EUL–NGL
Swedish People's Party	ELDR (1995)	ELDR
Green League	EFGP (1993)	G/EFA
Christian Democrats		EPP

informal network of various left-socialist parties. The Left Alliance MEPs sit in the Conferederal Group of the European United Left/Nordic Green Left (EUL-NGL) group in the EP. In fact, the subtitle NGL was added to the group name at the insistence of Finnish and Swedish MEPs, who wanted to emphasize their separate identity within the otherwise largely Mediterranean group. The RKP joined the ELDR federation as an observer member in 1992 and became a full member in 1995. The Green League joined the EFGP in the constitutive meeting of the federation held in Helsinki in 1993. As one of its founding members, the Green League has played an important role in shaping the identity and goals of the EFGP. The Green League MEPs are members of the Greens/European Free Alliance (G/EFA) group in the EP. The KD was an observer member of the now defunct European Union of Christian Democrats (EUCD) in 1990–99, and the party's MEP sits in the EPP group.

The status of MEPs within parties has caused problems, particularly in parties where, for ideological or personal reasons, the Euro-parliamentarians have strained relations with the party leaders. MEPs or the leaders of parties' EP delegations are in every party represented in leading party organs. However, according to the MEPs themselves, the parties back home, especially MPs, have not appreciated their work or made full use of their informational expertise. Therefore, the influence and status of MEPs inside parties depends primarily on the contacts individual Euro-parliamentarians have with party leaders.[41] Furthermore, during Euro-election campaigns, MEPs have received little if any support from their party leaders, a topic to which we now turn in the next section.

EURO-ELECTIONS

Two findings from this and the preceding chapter are particularly relevant to elections to the EP. First, parties are divided over integration, with particularly institutional questions, such as the powers of the European Parliament, being problematic for Finnish parties. The fairly broad elite-level partisan consensus on the EU is not replicated among voters, with citizens remaining far less supportive of integration than their elected representatives. Second, the state-centric political culture influences electoral campaigns and citizens' voting decisions.[42]

The first Euro-elections in Finland were held in October 1996. The turnout was 60.3 per cent. Several factors contributed to getting people out to vote. The elections were held in conjunction with municipal elections, the parties were able to attract high-profile candidates, and the Finnish *markka* was tied to the Exchange Rate Mechanism (ERM) a week before the election, with the impending EMU membership therefore high on the political agenda. Moreover, as shown by comparative analyses on factors affecting turnout, the novelty factor raised turnout, with people turning out to vote in lower numbers in subsequent EP elections.[43] Given these factors, it is more likely that turnout in the future Euro-elections will be closer to the dismal 31.4 per cent in 1999 than to the respectable 60 per cent achieved in 1996.[44]

According to the law on EP elections, registered parties and voters' associations can nominate candidates. Parties can form electoral alliances with one another, and voters' associations can set up joint lists. The maximum number of candidates per party or per electoral alliance is 20 (16 in 1996). The whole country forms one single constituency. In the 1996 elections, the parties and voters' associations had the right to field both nationwide and regional candidates in the four constituencies, but all lists fielded only nationwide candidates. Voters choose between individual candidates from non-ordered party lists. In 1999, 11 parties nominated altogether 140 candidates. This was fewer than in the first Euro-elections of October 1996, when 14 parties and one voters' association fielded a total of 207 candidates. In candidate selection, parties tried to ensure two goals: that their pool of candidates would be socially, geographically, and ideologically representative of their voters, and that the candidates would also have nationwide appeal.

Smaller or new parties have not really benefited from the second-order logic of Euro-elections.[45] Gains and losses experienced by parties owe at least as much to the individual candidates as to the parties. The only note-worthy exception is the electoral triumph of the Green League in the 1999 EP elections, but that was probably explained largely by the personal popularity of their leading candidate, the MEP Heidi Hautala. Party-switching was thus most evident in the case of Green League supporters. The breakdown by party of the share of voters who cast their vote for the same party in the March 1999 Eduskunta elections and subsequent Euro-elections was 85 per cent for the SDP, 85 per cent for the KESK, 75 per cent for the KOK, 73 per cent for the VAS, and 53 per cent for the VIHR.[46] The two anti-EU membership movements established prior to the 1994 referendum, the League for a Free Finland (*Vapaan Suomen Liitto*) and Alternative to the EU (*Vaihtoehto EU:lle*), won between them 2.7 per cent of the votes in the 1996 Euro-elections, but neither participated in the 1999 EP elections nor have they fielded any candidates in Eduskunta elections.[47] The third anti-EU movement, calling for Finland to leave the EU, is the minor Communist Party of Finland (SKP), which has no representation in Eduskunta.

The parties clearly put more effort into the 1996 elections, both programmatically and particularly in terms of campaigning. In 1999, the busy electoral calendar, with the Eduskunta elections held less than three months earlier in March and presidential elections forthcoming in January 2000, strained the parties' resources and diverted attention from the EP elections. Absence is the best word to describe the behaviour of the party leaders during the campaign. They did not take part in a single televised debate, with only the leading individual candidates representing their parties. This stands in stark contrast to national parliamentary elections, where party chairpersons participate in a series of long televised debates. The collective absence of the party leaders gave the citizens the impression that the EP elections do not matter. If the party leaders do not bother, why should the voters? Given the strong open-list electoral system, the input of party leaders is also crucial in terms of facilitating constructive debates. Since the most efficient electoral strategy of the overwhelming majority of individual candidates is to focus on personal qualities, the party leaders could have counterbalanced this through articulating their parties' views to the voters.

As a reflection of the overall ideological moderation necessitated by forming multi-party governments, and the personalized campaigns resulting from the candidate-centred electoral system, differences between parties were rather difficult to identify in both elections. One issue that separated the parties in 1999 was employment policy.[48] The parties of the left saw the EU as a potential bulwark against the dominance of uncontrolled market forces. The SDP emphasized in its election manifesto the need to fight unemployment through European-level action and closer coordination of national economic policies. The parties of the right argued instead against European-level employment policies. For example, the National Coalition (KOK) stressed that the elections constituted a clear choice between a bourgeois and a socialist Europe. The government parties (the SDP, the KOK, the VAS, the VIHR, and the RKP) argued in favour of increasing qualified majority voting, thus defending the objectives listed in the government's programme, while the opposition parties resisted such moves towards more supranational decision-making. In a candidate survey carried out by the newspaper *Helsingin Sanomat*, 65 per cent of the respondents agreed with the statement that EU membership had been beneficial for Finland, including all SDP, KOK, and RKP candidates. Nearly two-thirds supported EMU membership, including all SDP, KOK, and RKP candidates. Seventy-one per cent of the respondents answered negatively when asked whether the EU should become a defence alliance, with only the KOK and the RKP having a majority of candidates in favour of a defence alliance. Two-thirds of the respondents wanted to increase the powers of the EP.[49]

The strongly candidate-centred electoral system, together with the collective absence of party leaders from the campaigns, clearly affected the citizens' voting behaviour. The personal qualities of candidates weigh heavily in people's minds when making their voting decisions. The electoral system leads to more competition within than between parties. Individual candidates from the same party list pursue personal campaigns, with party programmes being almost completely in the background. In two surveys carried out before the 1996 elections, 57 per cent and 63 per cent of respondents, respectively, agreed with the statement that the individual candidate is more important than the party when making the voting decision.[50] In 1999, 56 per cent of the voters chose first their preferred party while 44 per cent chose their candidates irrespective of their party affiliation.[51] Voters did not consider more specifically EU-level policy objectives, such as the federalization or the enlargement of the EU, important in terms of choosing their party or candidate. In general, voters were far more concerned about the ability of the candidates to defend Finland's national interests in the EU than about wider questions related to European integration.[52]

Considering the potentially divisive impact of European integration on party unity, party leaders have good cause to support the existing rules of the electoral game. Protest or dissenting opinions get channelled through individual candidates, whereas in member states with closed lists organized factions often appear to contest the official party line. The introduction of four regional constituencies together with a system of allocating seats according to the national vote share deserves serious consideration. Prime Minister Lipponen and the KESK both supported the idea of dividing Finland into four constituencies after the disastrous turnout of 1999.[53] Smaller parties (the VAS, the RKP, and the VIHR) have resisted attempts to divide the country into four constituencies, as their prospects of gaining seats are bound to diminish without the use of additional adjustment seats which will distribute seats according to the share of votes gained throughout the country. Moreover, the establishment of four constituencies would mean once again changing the electoral system. In October 1998, the Eduskunta approved the existing law on Euro-elections, according to which the whole country operates as one single constituency. Splitting the country into four constituencies has been argued to ensure the representation of the regions in the EP and to stimulate debate on locally important issues such as the CAP and regional policy. Geographical representativeness is indeed a fundamental problem, and the division of the country into several constituencies would most likely facilitate more intensive campaigns and improve turnout. Of the 16 MEPs elected in 1999, ten live in the capital area, even though only around 20 per cent of the population live there. The reform would also most probably lead to more equal competition among candidates, as the cost of the campaigns would be reduced.

SUMMARY

The recent literature on parties has largely been dominated by studies examining the direction and extent of party change. The thesis about party decline or transformation is primarily based on the eroding linkage between parties and citizens. Finland is no different in this respect: turnout in national parliamentary elections has gradually fallen and is below the EU average, party identification and membership are similarly in decline, and the severe recession of the 1990s further reduced citizens' trust in politicians. European integration arguably consolidates these trends, particularly as the ideological convergence among party elites dilutes rather than intensifies competition between parties.

When we look at the shape of the party system, the new specifically anti-EU movements have remained marginal, and opposition to the EU manifests itself primarily through individual MPs and MEPs, notably in the KESK and the Left Alliance. However, in the end, this should not come as a surprise. The weak mobilization potential characteristic of the Finnish political system weakens the chance that social movements coming from outside the traditional parties will attract the support of the wider public.[54] Furthermore, lack of resources is another effective obstacle to the rise of new parties. Political parties, in terms of both their extra-parliamentary organizations and parliamentary groups, receive public funding based on the share of seats won in the most recent Eduskunta election. Parties not represented in the Eduskunta are not entitled to public funding.[55]

Nevertheless, European integration has added a new significant cleavage to the Finnish political system. Public opinion surveys show that Finns are more sceptical of integration than the average EU citizen (see Chapter 2). However, despite the widespread unease, the political and business elites, led by the Lipponen rainbow governments, have without hesitation taken Finland into the inner core of the EU. The integration cleavage cuts across the traditional left–right spectrum, and parties have tried to cope with the new challenge by indicating that their ranks are open to politicians and people with both pro- and anti-integration views. The Finnish situation seems to be in line with that in other European countries, where, according to Taggart, 'there is very little relationship between levels of Euroscepticism and electoral support for Eurosceptical parties'.[56] The EU dimension is therefore potentially significant in terms of restructuring party competition and vote choice, especially as the ideological convergence has narrowed the differences between parties.[57]

The Finnish system of formulating national integration policy is a key factor in producing ideological convergence and defusing competition between parties. The bargaining involved in building multi-party coalition governments and the corporatist nature of the political system reduce the likelihood of ideological conflicts, but the independent effect of the national EU coordination system is also significant, especially as the agendas of the EU and its member states are increasingly interdependent. The goal of 'speaking with one voice' in Brussels is specifically designed to manufacture national consensus over integration, with the opposition accorded a strong role in the process. As will be argued in the next chapter, this strategy may well ensure consistency in national integration policy, but at the same time it limits party competition over integration.

NOTES

1. See P. Taggart, 'A Touchstone of Dissent: Euroscepticism in Contemporary Western European Party Systems', *European Journal of Political Research* 33:3 (1998), pp. 363–88; S. Hix and C. Lord, *Political Parties in the European Union* (Basingstoke: Macmillan, 1997); J. Gaffney (ed.) *Political Parties and the European Union* (London: Routledge, 1996); and L. Ray, 'Measuring Party Orientations Towards European Integration: Results from an Expert Survey', *European Journal of Political Research* 36:2 (1999), pp. 283–306.
2. See, for example, the contributions in Gaffney, *Political Parties and the European Union*, and K. Heidar and L. Svåsand (eds) *Partier uten grenser?* (Otta: Tano Aschehoug, 1997).
3. The interviews were conducted by the author in connection with a project on the impact of EU membership on Finland. The parties were as follows: SDP, KESK, KOK, VAS, VIHR, and RKP. See T. Raunio, 'Puolueet : Ideologista lähentymistä yhtenäisyyden kustannuksella', in T. Raunio and M. Wiberg (eds) *EU ja Suomi: Unionijäsenyyden vaikutukset suomalaiseen yhteiskuntaan* (Helsinki: Edita, 2000), pp. 43–65.
4. For information on the Finnish party system, see D. Arter, *Scandinavian Politics Today* (Manchester: Manchester University Press, 1999), Parts Two and Three; J. Sundberg, *Partier och partisystem i Finland* (Esbo: Schildts, 1996); and S. Borg and R. Sänkiaho (eds) *The Finnish Voter* (Tampere: The Finnish Political Science Association, 1995).
5. See A. Lijphart, *Patterns of Democracy: Government Forms and Performance in Thirty-Six Countries* (New Haven, CT: Yale University Press, 1999), pp. 74–7.
6. The only exception is from 1916 when the Social Democrats won an absolute majority of Eduskunta seats. See M. Wiberg and T. Raunio, 'Where's the Power: Controlling Voting Outcomes in the Nordic Parliaments 1945–

1995', in G.-E. Isaksson (ed.) *Inblickar i Nordisk Parlamentarism* (Åbo: Meddelanden från Ekonomisk-Statsvetenskapliga Fakulteten vid Åbo Akademi, Ser. A:470, 1997), pp. 245–59.

7. See J. Sundberg, 'The Enduring Scandinavian Party System', *Scandinavian Political Studies* 22:2 (1999), p. 228.

8. In a comparative survey of party positions carried out in 1993, in which country experts were asked to place the parties on the left–right spectrum, the positions of the Finnish parties were (on a scale of 1 to 10, with 1 being the left end and 10 the right end of the dimension) as follows: VAS 3.50, VIHR 4.00, SDP 4.38, RKP 6.57, KESK 7.00, SMP (PS) 7.00, KOK 7.38, KD 9.00. See J. Huber and R. Inglehart, 'Expert Interpretations of Party Space and Party Locations in 42 Societies', *Party Politics* 1:1 (1995), pp. 73–111.

9. See J. Nousiainen, 'Finland: The Consolidation of Parliamentary Governance', in W.C. Müller and K. Strøm (eds) *Coalition Governments in Western Europe* (Oxford: Oxford University Press, 2000), pp. 265–68.

10. Ibid., p. 270.

11. Arter, *Scandinavian Politics Today*, p. 63.

12. On the policy profiles of the Green League and the Left Alliance, see K.O.K. Zilliacus, '"New Politics" in Finland: The Greens and the Left Wing in the 1990s', *West European Politics* 24:1 (2001), pp. 27–54.

13. See P. Mair, 'The Limited Impact of Europe on National Party Systems', *West European Politics* 23:4 (2000), p. 30.

14. This section draws on previous work by the author. See T. Raunio, 'Miten käy puolueiden yhtenäisyyden? Euroopan unioni haaste suomalaisille puolueille?', in S. Borg (ed.) *Puolueet 1990-luvulla: Näkökulmia suomalaiseen puoluetoimintaan* (Turku: Turun yliopisto, Valtio-opillisia tutkimuksia n:o 53, 1997), pp. 186–214; and T. Raunio, 'Facing the European Challenge: Finnish Parties Adjust to the Integration Process', *West European Politics* 22:1 (1999), pp. 138–59.

15. For analyses of party positions in the referendum, see H. Paloheimo, 'Kansalaismielipiteiden kehitys Suomessa', in P. Pesonen (ed.) *Suomen EU-kansanäänestys 1994: Raportti äänestäjien kannanotoista* (Helsinki: Ulkoasiainministeriö, Eurooppatiedotus, ja Painatuskeskus, 1994), pp. 41–52; H. Paloheimo, 'Pohjoismaiden EU-kansanäänestykset: puolueiden peruslinjat ja kansalaisten mielipiteet Suomessa, Ruotsissa ja Norjassa', *Politiikka* 37:2 (1995), pp. 113–27; R. Sänkiaho, 'Puoluesidonnaisuutta vai sitoutumattomuutta', in Pesonen (ed.) *Suomen EU-kansanäänestys 1994*, pp. 164–73; and O. Listhaug, S. Holmberg, and R. Sänkiaho, 'Partisanship and EU Choice', in A.T. Jenssen, P. Pesonen and M. Gilljam (eds) *To Join or Not to Join: Three Nordic Referendums on Membership in the European Union* (Oslo: Scandinavian University Press, 1998), pp. 215–34.

16. Sänkiaho, 'Puoluesidonnaisuutta vai sitoutumattomuutta', pp. 167–8. Translation by the author.

17. Ibid., p. 167.

18. The party congress had twice, in 1997 and 1999, rejected attempts at changing the name to 'Christian Democrats'. In the party congress held in Jyväskylä in May 2001, congress delegates took the floor over 70 times during a debate that lasted over three hours. In the final vote, 223 delegates voted for the new name, with 101 in favour of retaining the old name. The decision rule was a two-thirds majority.

19. In the first round of the presidential elections held in January 2000, the True Finns candidate, Ilkka Hakalehto, won only one per cent of the votes. Hakalehto was the only anti-EU candidate.
20. The European programmes of the parties analysed in this section are available at their websites: SDP (*www.sdp.fi*), Centre Party (*www.keskusta.fi*), National Coalition (*www.kokoomus.fi*), Left Alliance (*www.vasemmistoliitto.fi*), Green League (*www.vihrealiitto.fi*), Swedish People's Party (*www.rkp.fi*), Christian Democrats (*www.kristillisdemokraatit.fi*), and True Finns (*www.perussuomalaiset.fi*). Most programmes are available also in English.
21. See P. Lipponen, speech at the College of Bruges, Belgium, 10 November 2000; and P. Lipponen, speech at the European University Institute, Florence, 9 April 2001.
22. See Huber and Inglehart, 'Expert Interpretations of Party Space and Party Locations in 42 Societies'; O. Knutsen, 'Expert Judgements of the Left–Right Location of Political Parties: A Comparative Longitudinal Study', *West European Politics* 21:2 (1998), pp. 63–94; M.L. Caul and M.M. Gray, 'From Platform Declarations to Policy Outcomes: Changing Party Profiles and Partisan Influence over Policy', in R.J. Dalton and M.P. Wattenberg (eds) *Parties without Partisans: Political Change in Advanced Industrial Democracies* (Oxford: Oxford University Press, 2000), pp. 208–37; and S. Hix, 'Dimensions and Alignments in European Union Politics: Cognitive Constraints and Partisan Responses', *European Journal of Political Research* 35:1 (1999), pp. 69–106.
23. P. Mair, *Party System Change: Approaches and Interpretations* (Oxford: Oxford University Press, 1997), p. 132. For a contrary interpretation, see H. Kitschelt, 'Citizens, Politicians, and Party Cartellization: Political Representation and State Failure in Post-Industrial Democracies', *European Journal of Political Research* 37:2 (2000), pp. 149–79.
24. See K.M. Johansson and T. Raunio, 'Partisan Responses to Europe: Comparing Finnish and Swedish Political Parties', *European Journal of Political Research* 39:2 (2001), pp. 225–49.
25. Ray, 'Measuring Party Orientations Towards European Integration', p. 293.
26. Taggart, 'A Touchstone of Dissent: Euroscepticism in Contemporary Western European Party Systems', p. 369.
27. D. Hine, 'Factionalism in West European Parties: A Framework for Analysis', *West European Politics* 5:1 (1982), pp. 38–9.
28. See M. Franklin, M. Marsh, and L. McLaren, 'Uncorking the Bottle: Popular Opposition to European Unification in the Wake of Maastricht', *Journal of Common Market Studies* 32:4 (1994), p. 465.
29. See N. Aylott, *Swedish Social Democracy and European Integration: The People's Home on the Market* (Aldershot: Ashgate, 1999), pp. 133–56.
30. See Aylott, *Swedish Social Democracy and European Integration*, pp. 133–56; and Johansson and Raunio, 'Partisan Responses to Europe: Comparing Finnish and Swedish Political Parties'.
31. P. Väisänen, 'EU:ta vastustaneet poliitikot eivät innostu ei-puolueesta', *Helsingin Sanomat*, 17 November 1994.
32. See Hix, 'Dimensions and Alignments in European Union Politics'; G. Marks and C.J. Wilson, 'The Past in the Present: A Cleavage Theory of Party Response to European Integration', *British Journal of Political Science* 30:3 (2000), pp. 433–59; and D. Jahn, 'Der Einfluss von Cleavage-Strukturen auf

die Standpunkte der skandinavischen Parteien über den Beitritt zur Europäischen Union', *Politische Vierteljahresschrift* 40:4 (1999), pp. 565–90.

33. Ray, 'Measuring Party Orientations Towards European Integration', p. 293.

34. See particularly R.S. Katz and P. Mair (eds) *How Parties Organize: Change and Adaptation in Party Organizations in Western Democracies* (London: Sage, 1994); K. Heidar and R. Koole (eds) *Parliamentary Party Groups in European Democracies: Political Parties Behind Closed Doors* (London: Routledge, 2000); L. Helms, 'Parliamentary Party Groups and Their Parties: A Comparative Assessment', *Journal of Legislative Studies* 6:1 (2000), pp. 104–20; S.E. Scarrow, P. Webb, and D.M. Farrell, 'From Social Integration to Electoral Contestation', in R.J. Dalton and M.P. Wattenberg (eds) *Parties Without Partisans: Political Change in Advanced Industrial Democracies* (Oxford: Oxford University Press, 2000), pp. 129–53; and W.C. Müller, 'Political Parties in Parliamentary Democracies: Making Delegation and Accountability Work', *European Journal of Political Research* 37:3 (2000), pp. 309–33.

35. See Sundberg, *Partier och partisystem i Finland*; J. Sundberg, 'Compulsory Party Democracy: Finland as a Deviant Case in Scandinavia', *Party Politics* 3:1 (1997), pp. 97–117; J. Sundberg and C. Gylling, 'Finland', in R.S. Katz and P. Mair (eds) *Party Organizations: A Data Handbook on Party Organizations in Western Democracies, 1960–90* (London: Sage, 1992), pp. 273–316; and J. Sundberg, 'Finland: Nationalized Parties/Professionalized Organizations', in R.S. Katz and P. Mair (eds) *How Parties Organize: Change and Adaptation in Party Organizations in Western Democracies* (London: Sage, 1994), pp. 159–84.

36. See Raunio, 'Puolueet : Ideologista lähentymistä yhtenäisyyden kustannuksella', pp. 50–1.

37. Ibid., p. 51.

38. On Europarties, see Hix and Lord, *Political Parties in the European Union*; R. Ladrech, *Social Democracy and the Challenge of European Union* (Boulder, CO: Lynne Rienner, 2000); K.M. Johansson, 'Tracing the Employment Title in the Amsterdam Treaty: Uncovering Transnational Coalitions', *Journal of European Public Policy* 6:1 (1999), pp. 85–101; and D.S. Bell and C. Lord (eds) *Transnational Parties in the European Union* (Aldershot: Ashgate, 1998).

39. See C. Sandström, 'Europeiskt partisamarbete och partiernas idémässiga utveckling', paper presented at the meeting of the Nordic Political Science Association, Uppsala, 19–21 August 1999.

40. See J. Rauramo, 'Euroopan parlamentin puolueryhmien koheesio ja koalitionmuodostus 1994–1998', in T. Martikainen and K. Pekonen (eds) *Eurovaalit Suomessa 1996: Vaalihumusta päätöksenteon arkeen* (Helsinki: Helsingin yliopisto, Yleisen valtio-opin laitos, Acta Politica 10, 1999), pp. 281–97.

41. See M. Linnapuomi, 'Täällä Strasbourg, kuuleeko Helsinki? Suomalaiset europarlamentaarikot eurooppalaisen ja kansallisen tason yhteensovittajina', in Martikainen and Pekonen (eds) *Eurovaalit Suomessa 1996*, pp. 228–80; and T. Raunio, 'Kulisseista puoluejohdon valvontaan? Euroedustajien ja kansallisten puolueiden yhteydet', *Politiikka* 41:1 (1999), pp. 23–39.

42. For information on the 1996 elections, see Martikainen and Pekonen (eds) *Eurovaalit Suomessa 1996*; and D. Anckar, 'The Finnish European Election

of 1996', *Electoral Studies* 16:2 (1997), pp. 262–6. The 1999 elections are analysed in P. Pesonen (ed.) *Suomen europarlamenttivaalit* (Tampere: Tampere University Press, 2000); and in T. Raunio, 'Finland', in J. Lodge (ed.) *The 1999 Elections to the European Parliament* (Basingstoke: Palgrave, 2001), pp. 100–16.
43. See M. Franklin, 'European Elections and the European Voter', in J. Richardson (ed.) *European Union: Power and Policy-Making* (London: Routledge, 2001), pp. 201–16.
44. S. Borg, J. Pehkonen, and T. Raunio, 'Äänestämässä käynti ja äänestämättömyys', in P. Pesonen (ed.) *Suomen europarlamenttivaalit* (Tampere: Tampere University Press, 2000), p. 121.
45. On the consequences of second-order elections, see C. van der Eijk and M.N. Franklin (eds) *Choosing Europe: The European Electorate and National Politics in the Face of Union* (Ann Arbor, MI: University of Michigan Press, 1996); and M. Marsh, 'Testing the Second-Order Election Model after Four European Elections', *British Journal of Political Science* 28:4 (1998), pp. 591–607.
46. See S. Borg, 'Puolueet, ehdokkaat ja äänestäjien valinnat', in Pesonen (ed.) *Suomen europarlamenttivaalit*, p. 130.
47. For more information, see the websites of Alternative to the EU (*www.kaapeli.fi/~veu/*) and League for Free Finland (*www.vapaansuomenliitto.fi*).
48. For a detailed analysis of the electoral programmes of the parties and the preferences of the candidates, see H. Paloheimo, 'Vaaliohjelmat ja ehdokkaiden mielipiteet', in Pesonen (ed.) *Suomen europarlamenttivaalit*, pp. 50–81.
49. Of 140 candidates, 116 answered the survey. See Paloheimo, 'Vaaliohjelmat ja ehdokkaiden mielipiteet', pp. 70–1.
50. See P. Majonen, 'Kauniita ja rohkeita vai aatteellisia ammattipoliitikkoja? Suomen eurovaalien vaaliteemat ja vaalikampanjointi 1996', in Martikainen and Pekonen (eds) *Eurovaalit Suomessa 1996*, p. 76.
51. Borg, 'Puolueet, ehdokkaat ja äänestäjien valinnat', p. 136.
52. T. Raunio, 'Valitsijoiden EU-tavoitteet', in Pesonen (ed.) *Suomen europarlamenttivaalit*, pp. 102–4.
53. See P. Rautio, 'Puolueissa ei sopua eurovaalien asettelusta', *Helsingin Sanomat*, 17 June 1997; 'Virrankoski: Vaalipiirijako EU-vaaleissa uusiksi', *Helsingin Sanomat*, 11 June 1999; 'Aho: Suomi jaettava neljään vaalipiiriin eurovaaleissa', *Helsingin Sanomat*, 20 June 1999; P. Uotila, 'Paavo Lipponen: Alueelliset EU-vaalit lääkkeeksi vaaliapatiaan', *Helsingin Sanomat*, 18 July 1999; and 'Keskustelu eurovaaleista meni ylikierroksille', *Helsingin Sanomat*, 20 July 1999.
54. See S. Borg, 'Kansalaisten suhde politiikkaan murroksessa', in P. Suhonen (ed.) *Yleinen mielipide 1997* (Helsinki: Tammi, 1997), pp. 99–118; and S. Borg (ed.) *Puolueet 1990-luvulla: Näkökulmia suomalaiseen puoluetoimintaan* (Turku: Turun yliopisto, Valtio-opillisia tutkimuksia n:o 53, 1997).
55. See M. Wiberg (ed.) *The Public Purse and Political Parties: Public Financing of Political Parties in Nordic Countries* (Jyväskylä: The Finnish Political Science Association, 1991).
56. Taggart, 'A Touchstone of Dissent: Euroscepticism in Contemporary Western European Party Systems', p. 373.
57. See M. Gabel, 'European Integration, Voters and National Politics', *West European Politics* 23:4 (2000), pp. 52–72.

71

4

Parliament

National parliaments are normally described as the political institutions losing most in the process of European integration. Constitutionally, a wide range of policy competencies has been shifted – by the national parliaments – to the European level. The treaty revisions are usually presented as 'take-it-or-leave-it' packages to national parliaments in which the only realistic option is to accept the revisions without amendments.[1] Politically, the increased application of QMV in the Council effectively removes the ability of national parliaments to force governments to make *ex ante* commitments before taking decisions at the European level. Nevertheless, the legislatures of member states remain, at least potentially, important forums for formulation, scrutiny, and implementation of EU legislation. Perhaps more significantly, they legitimize European integration by providing a channel for incorporating public opinion into the governance of the EU, a function highlighted recently in the debates on democratic deficit in the EU.

The systemic features of the EU policy process disadvantage national parliaments. No matter how tightly MPs control their governments in EU matters, their input is always indirect, involving a delegation of authority to governments that represent member states in the EU political system. Therefore, the main problem facing legislatures is how to reduce informational asymmetry in order to ensure effective parliamentary accountability so that the government behaves according to the preferences of the parliamentary majority. National legislatures have four basic functions in EU decision-making: contributing to national policy formulation on European legislation, monitoring government behaviour in the Council of Ministers and in the European Council, treaty amendment, and implementation of EC directives. The first two aspects are not regulated by European legislation, and it is up to each national parliament – constitutional and political limitations notwithstanding – to decide to what extent it seeks to influence EU governance.[2]

There is broad consensus, among both scholars and MPs themselves that the procedures are not working. According to an MP/MEP survey carried out in 1996–97, the overwhelming majority of parliamentarians throughout the EU thought that national parliamentary scrutiny of EU decision-making is too weak and should be strengthened.[3] Summing up the role of national parliaments in the coordination of national EU policies, Kassim observes that parliaments have 'very little ability to scrutinize Union proposals, still less to influence their content, and are able only in very exceptional cases to direct the actions of their respective governments'.[4] Indeed, the Austrian case illustrates well how difficult it is in practice for the parliament to influence national EU policy, no matter how extensive its formal powers are. The Nationalrat has a constitutional right to issue binding mandates to Austrian ministers, but it seldom uses this right. The sheer volume and technical nature of most EU legislation make it very difficult for MPs to acquire much needed expertise on European matters. More importantly, rigid positions are seen as counter-productive in pursuing national goals, as the government representatives must be able to negotiate compromises with their counterparts in the Council and its working groups.[5]

Comparative research has indicated that the variation between member states is primarily explained by two factors: the role of the parliament in the domestic political system and public and party opinion on European integration. The key variable has been argued to be the executive–legislature relationship, with the parliament controlling the government to the same extent in European matters as it does in the context of domestic legislation. Similarly, the contentiousness of the European dimension is important, with divisions over integration leading to tighter scrutiny mechanisms.[6] The two previous chapters showed that Finnish parties and especially voters are divided over integration. Further-more, recent constitutional changes have significantly altered the Finnish political system, bringing Finland closer to standard parliamentary democracy and strengthening the powers of the Eduskunta. Therefore, both preconditions for tight control of government are in place.

This chapter analyses the role of the Eduskunta in controlling the government in EU matters and in influencing national integration policy. The next section examines the changing nature of executive–legislature relations in Finland. Then we present a section exploring the constitu-tional powers of the Eduskunta and its ability to shape the direction of national EU policy and of government behaviour in the Council. The concluding discussion highlights the main benefits and problems of the Finnish system. The main argument is that the decentralized model established to monitor the government in EU matters works rather well, and that, constitutionally, the Eduskunta has considerable powers to control the government. Nevertheless, the oversized coalition governments, together with the problems involved in adjusting to the pace and timetable of EU decision-making, reduce the influence of MPs over national integration choices.

EXECUTIVE–LEGISLATURE RELATIONS

Finland used to be characterized by short-lived and unstable governments living under the shadow of the president.[7] Of the western European countries, only Italy had more cabinets between 1945 and 2000 than Finland.[8] The president influenced heavily the process of forming governments until the 1990s. The fragmented party system, with no clearly dominant party emerging after the elections, strengthened the president's hand in steering government negotiations. The president appointed a prime ministerial candidate, or *formateur*, whose task was to form the government, and he also intervened in the choice of coalition partners. The last case of direct presidential intervention was in 1987, when President Mauno Koivisto 'exerted decisive influence' in the formation of the cabinet headed by Harri Holkeri.[9]

The new constitution that came into force in March 2000 has fundamentally changed the situation, reducing the president's powers and parliamentarizing the government formation. With the president now in the background, the largest party has the leading role in government formation. Led by the prime ministerial candidate, parties negotiate the partisan composition of the coalition, along with the government programme and portfolio allocation. The nomination of individual ministers is largely an internal party matter, with little interference from coalition partners. The Eduskunta elects the prime minister with a simple majority of the votes cast. The president then formally appoints the prime minister as well as the other ministers in accordance with a proposal made by the prime minister. The government then submits its programme to the Eduskunta in the form of a statement.

Of the 45 cabinets formed since 1945, 28 have been majority coalitions; six, minority coalitions; four, single-party minority governments; and seven, caretaker cabinets. Reflecting the fragmented shape of the party system, the mean number of cabinet parties in 1945–99 was 3.49, the highest figure in western Europe.[10] Until the 1970s, ideological differences between the left and the right were sharp and highly salient in government formation, but the moderation of ideological tensions has led to a situation where basically all coalitions are possible. The Centre Party (KESK) has traditionally occupied the median position on the left–right spectrum, and this ideological centrism primarily explains its strong position in government formation. The dominant coalition from the Second World War until 1987 was the red–green alliance between the SDP and the KESK, while the National Coalition (KOK) was kept out of the government until 1987 due to foreign policy imperatives.

Since the early 1980s, Finnish governments have stayed in office for the whole electoral period of four years. As a rule, governments are formed around two of the three main parties: the KESK, the KOK and the SDP. However, no Eduskunta party is non-coalitionable. Table 6 shows the size and partisan composition of Finnish governments since 1987, that is, the period when European integration has figured on the domestic political agenda. None of the four cabinets formed since 1987 have been minimum winning coalitions, and each government has included at least four parties. After the 1995 and 1999 elections, the Lipponen governments controlled around 70 per cent of parliamentary seats. Despite their ideological heterogeneity, the governments have been surprisingly stable without any major internal conflicts. While two small parties have left the governments, the Rural Party in 1990 over budgetary disagreements and the Christian Democrats in 1994 due to the government's pro-EU stance, these situations have not threatened the overall stability of the cabinet, as the main coalition partners were committed to keeping the coalition together. Disagreements between coalition partners are solved in ministerial committees, informal sessions of the whole cabinet or, plenary meeting of the government. The chairpersons of the governing parties' parliamentary groups are closely involved in governmental decision-making, thus reducing the likelihood of conflicts between the government and the parliament.[11]

The governments formed since the early 1980s, enjoying broad parliamentary majorities and bringing together parties across the left–right spectrum, have been able to rule without much effective dissent by the Eduskunta. Criticism of government policies is normally channelled through political parties, with parliamentary groups and occasionally also other party organs putting pressure on their ministers. While coalition discipline and solidarity are normally maintained without serious problems inside the cabinet, the more radical MPs from the governing parties occasionally voice dissent either by voting against the government or by publicly criticizing the government's policies. During the two rainbow governments led by Lipponen, dissent has mainly focused on the economic austerity measures imposed by the government, with more left-wing Left Alliance, SDP, and the Green League MPs voting occasionally with the opposition. European matters have not produced any notable dissent since 1995.

Table 6
The Partisan Composition and Size of Finnish Governments Since 1987

Government	Duration	Parties	Prime minister	Government strength (percentage of MPs)
Holkeri I/II[1]	1987–91	KOK, SDP, RKP, SMP	Holkeri (KOK)	65.5
Aho I/II[2]	1991–95	KESK, KOK, RKP, KD	Aho (KESK)	57.5
Lipponen I	1995–99	SDP, KOK, VAS, VIHR, RKP	Lipponen (SDP)	72.5
Lipponen II	1999–	SDP, KOK, VAS, VIHR, RKP	Lipponen (SDP)	69.5

1 The Rural Party left the cabinet in August 1990 due to conflicts over the state budget.
2 The Christian Democrats left the government in June 1994 because it disagreed with the government's pro-EU line.

The Eduskunta can be categorized as a working parliament. We follow here the approach of Arter, who distinguishes a working parliament from a debating parliament according to three operational criteria: a) a committee system that reflects the structure of central government departments; b) parliamentary standing orders that elevate committee work above plenary sessions; and c) members who focus in their work on detailed legislative scrutiny instead of grand debates on the floor.[12] The nature of parliamentary work and the fragmented shape of the party system have facilitated a consensual style of politics, with relations between the government and the opposition based primarily on compromise and interparty negotiations. Oppositional influence may have weakened in domestic politics since the early 1990s, but in EU and foreign policy matters, the goal of building broad majorities ensures that the views of the opposition parties are not completely neglected.

The 200 members of the Eduskunta are elected for a four-year term from one single-member (Åland) and 14 multi-member electoral districts. Each electoral district is a separate subunit in the electoral process; thus, the total nationwide vote share does not affect the distribution of seats within districts. The d'Hondt method is used in allocating seats to parties. The method works so that the party with most votes in the electoral district will get the first seat. That party's total vote is divided by two and compared with the vote totals of the other parties. Whoever has the highest number of votes at that point gets the second seat. The process is then repeated until all the seats in the district have been distributed.

Parties, electoral alliances (that is, technical coalitions of parties), and other groups are allowed to put forward candidates. Voters choose between individual candidates from non-ordered lists. Candidate selection is decentralized and based on primaries in district organizations.[13] This has consequences for party discipline in the Eduskunta, as the party leadership is usually not able to prevent reselection, especially as district organizations have traditionally resisted stubbornly any interference from national party organs.[14] The cohesion of party groups in the Eduskunta has indeed been lower than in the other Nordic legislatures.[15]

Parliamentary decision-making is based on continuous interaction between party groups and committees.[16] Most of the legislative work is carried out in committees, with emphasis on detailed scrutiny of government initiatives. Committee deliberation is mandatory and precedes the plenary stage. According to Section 40 of the Constitution, 'Government proposals, motions by Representatives, reports submitted to the Parliament and other matters, as provided for in this Constitution or in the Parliament's Rules of Procedure, shall be prepared in Committees before their final consideration in a plenary session of the Parliament.'[17] Following the 1999 elections, the Eduskunta has 14 committees and the Grand Committee (*Suuri valiokunta*), which is the equivalent of a European Affairs Committee. The Grand Committee (25 members), the Constitutional Law Committee (17), the Foreign Affairs Committee (17), and the Finance Committee (17) are recognized in the Constitution, with MPs free to decide on the number and jurisdiction of other permanent committees (at least 11 MPs per committee) and possible ad hoc committees. The final committee report on a legislative proposal contains a recommendation to the Eduskunta and a statement explaining the majority position. Committee members opposed to the majority resolution may add their dissenting opinions to the report. The decision rule in committees is a simple majority. Committees meet behind closed doors, but may declare their proceedings open to the public if this is seen as necessary for collecting relevant information. The quorum is two-thirds of committee members, unless a higher quorum has been specifically required for a given matter.

Legislative initiatives are considered in plenary session in two readings. Other matters require only one reading. The decision rule is a simple majority of the votes cast, unless otherwise provided in the constitution. In the event of a tie, the decision is made by drawing lots, except where a qualified majority is required for the adoption of a motion. Until 1992, one-third of MPs (67/200) could postpone the final adoption of an ordinary law over the elections, with the proposal being adopted if a majority in the new parliament supported it. This qualified majority rule explained partially the propensity to form oversized coalitions and contributed to the practice of inclusive, consensual decision-making that reduced the gap between the government and opposition.[18] Constitutional amendments are left in abeyance by a simple majority in the second reading until the first parliamentary session following parliamentary elections. The proposal then needs to be adopted by the new parliament without material alterations in one reading in a plenary session by a decision supported by at least two-thirds of the votes cast. However, the proposal may be declared urgent by a decision that has been supported by at least five-sixths of the votes cast. In such cases, the proposal is not left in abeyance and can be adopted by a decision supported by at least two-thirds of the votes cast.

The MPs have a variety of ways to control the executive, the most important of which are votes of no confidence and parliamentary questions. There are three types of votes of no confidence: those following interpellations, government-initiated votes, and votes held without prior warning during plenary debates. The most important are votes following interpellations.[19] Members have the right to table written and oral questions as well as questions to the government. Other scrutiny mechanisms include parliamentary motions and debates following government reports.[20] Between 1991 and 1998, less than ten per cent of parliamentary questions and 12 per cent of interpellations concerned EU issues, with a large share of them dealing with agriculture and regional policy.[21] A key factor in controlling the government is access to information. The informational rights of the Eduskunta are extensive and are regulated in Section 47 of the Constitution:

> The Parliament has the right to receive from the Government the information it needs in the consideration of matters. The appropriate Minister shall ensure that Committees and other parliamentary organs receive without delay the necessary documents and other information in the possession of the authorities.
>
> A Committee has the right to receive information from the Government or the appropriate Ministry on a matter within its competence. The Committee may issue a statement to the Government or the Ministry on the basis of the information.
>
> A Representative has the right to information which is in the possession of authorities and which is necessary for the performance of the duties of the Representative, in so far as the information is not secret or it does not pertain to a State budget proposal under preparation. In addition, the right of the Parliament to information on international affairs is governed by the provisions included elsewhere in this Constitution.[22]

The last sentence of the constitutional passage refers mainly to the right of the Foreign Affairs Committee, regulated in Section 97 of the Constitution, to receive 'from the Government, upon request and when otherwise necessary, reports of matters pertaining to foreign and security policy',[23] and to the right of the Eduskunta to receive information on EU matters.

Recent constitutional reforms have parliamentarized Finnish politics, with the government and the prime minister emerging from the shadow of the president as the leaders of the political process (see Chapter 5). Freed from the imperative of the Cold War and encouraged by President Koivisto, parties and MPs were eager to use the opportunity to strengthen parliamentarism. Until the early 1980s, Finnish governments tended to be relatively unstable and short-lived, but, since then, the governments have stayed in office for the whole electoral period of four years. While the executive branch still dominates national politics, at least now the executive is accountable to the Eduskunta. Therefore, membership in the EU presented a challenge to the parliament, which was concerned not to see its position weakened as a result of the political dynamics of the EU policy process.

THE EDUSKUNTA AND NATIONAL EU POLICY [24]

Adaptation to European integration within the Eduskunta started already in 1990, when the Foreign Affairs Committee demanded that the parliament and particularly its standing committees have access to information and be able to influence national policy in EEA decision-making. The constitutional reforms that reduced presidential powers and increased parliamentary involvement in foreign-policy decision-making, especially in integration matters, were implemented by broad consensus. The goal was to guarantee the Eduskunta as powerful a position in EU decision-making as is possible for any national legislature. However, the constitutional amendments aimed at respecting the separation between the executive and the legislative branches: the parliament was given the right to participate in national policy formulation in EU matters, while the government was given the right to decide on such matters and to represent Finland at the European level.[25]

The Grand Committee and the Foreign Affairs Committee are the main committees responsible for European questions, the former being equivalent to the European Affairs Committee found in all national parliaments of EU member states. The former handles first (EC) and third-pillar (JHA) issues, and the latter second-pillar (CFSP) matters. The Foreign Affairs Committee prepares decisions relating to treaty amendments. The Grand Committee has 25 members and 13 substitutes. In addition, the MP representing the Åland Islands is always entitled to participate in Grand Committee meetings. The committee usually convenes on Wednesdays and Fridays, with an average meeting time of from two to two and a half hours. The committee had 40 meetings in 1995, 56 in 1996, 45 in 1997, 55 in 1998, and 38 in 1999.[26] The Grand Committee tends to attract prominent Eduskunta members. Following both the 1995 and 1999 elections, the committee membership included five chairpersons of standing committees and representatives from the leadership of the three main party groups.

Finnish MEPs are not allowed to attend the meetings of the Grand Committee, and, so far, the committee has not invited MEPs to give testimony. The EU Secretariat of the Eduskunta forwards all agendas and press releases, and, upon request, the minutes of the meetings of the Grand Committee to the Finnish MEPs. The Eduskunta's representative in the EU acts also as a link between the MEPs and the MPs. The Grand Committee and the Finnish MEPs hold a joint seminar twice a year, once in Strasbourg/Brussels and once in Helsinki. The autumn seminar focuses on the EU budget while the spring meeting focuses on topical issues. Lasting only a couple of hours, the seminar is more a social occasion than a forum for exchanging detailed policy information. Only a minority of Grand Committee MPs and MEPs has so far attended the seminars. Moreover, the standing committees have made little use of the MEPs' policy expertise. The Foreign Affairs Committee heard one MEP from each party during the 1996–97 IGC, but, otherwise in 1994–98, only three committees invited MEPs to provide information on European matters. It appears that there is little genuine interest in the Eduskunta in developing contacts with MEPs, the main reason being that the MPs do not see MEPs as useful sources of information or as an effective channel for influencing EU decision-making.[27]

While the Grand Committee meets behind closed doors, the documents considered by it, together with the minutes of the meeting, usually become public when the minutes are signed as a correct record. Additionally, a press release is published after each meeting and is also available at the Eduskunta's website. At the request of the government, however, the committee may decide that its members will maintain the confidentiality of certain questions. This usually occurs when the government cannot reveal its margin of manoeuvre in the negotiations. It is also customary not to publish the negotiating positions of other member states. When the committee decides to maintain the confidentiality of the question, the relevant documents and the views of the committee are not appended to public documents.

The involvement of the Grand Committee in EU matters is threefold. It participates in national policy formulation on issues decided at the European level, gives instructions to cabinet ministers attending the meetings of the Council of Ministers, and scrutinizes the behaviour of Finnish representatives in the European Council.[28] The role of the Eduskunta in European matters is defined in Section 96 of the Constitution:

> The Parliament considers those proposals for acts, agreements and other measures which are to be decided in the European Union and which otherwise, according to the Constitution, would fall within the competence of the Parliament.
>
> The Government shall, for the determination of the position of the Parliament, communicate a proposal referred to in paragraph (1) to the Parliament by a communication of the Government, without delay, after receiving notice of the proposal. The proposal is considered in the Grand Committee and ordinarily in one or more of the other Committees that issue statements to the Grand Committee. However, the Foreign Affairs Committee considers a proposal pertaining to foreign and security policy. Where necessary, the Grand Committee or the Foreign Affairs Committee may issue to the Government a statement on the proposal. In addition, the Speaker's Council may decide that the matter be taken up for debate in plenary session, during which, however, no decision is made by the Parliament.
>
> The Government shall provide the appropriate Committees with information on the consideration of the matter in the European Union. The Grand Committee or the Foreign Affairs Committee shall also be informed of the position of the Government on the matter.[29]

Figure 3 depicts the main stages of processing EU matters in the Eduskunta. The government must inform the parliament without delay of any proposal for a Council decision. These 'U-matters' are usually the European Commission's legislative proposals that fall within the competence of the parliament. Table 7 shows the number and categorization of U-matters processed by the parliament in 1995–2000. The government must also send the Grand Committee information on the preparation of any issue relating to the EU that might belong to the competence of the parliament. Moreover, according to Section 97 of the Constitution, 'the Grand Committee of the Parliament shall receive reports on the preparation of other matters in the European Union'.[30] These 'E-matters' are not legislative proposals nor do they require a

Figure 3
Parliamentary Scrutiny of EU Legislation at the National Level

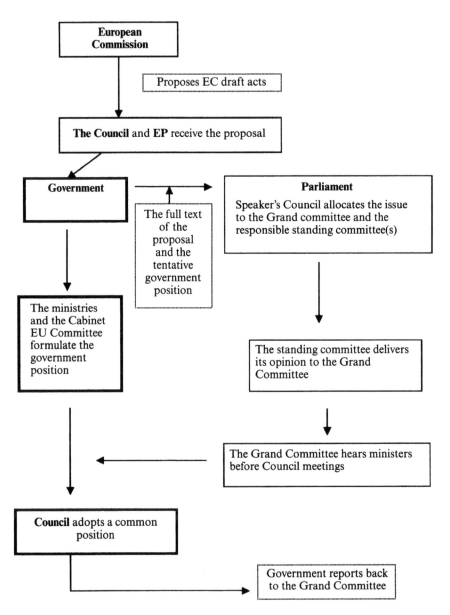

Table 7
Categorization and Number of U-Matters Processed by the Eduskunta (1995–2000)

Year	Directives	Regulations	Community agreements with third parties	Third-pillar conventions	Other	Total
1995	32	20	6	5	2	65
1996	28	25	11	10	6	80
1997	27	21	7	7	4	66
1998	31	47	6	5	7	96
1999	9	25	4	–	11	49
2000	31	34	3	2	12	82

Source: The Eduskunta.

decision by the Eduskunta. Typical E-matters are the Commission's legislative initiatives that fall outside the jurisdiction of the Eduskunta and non-legislative documents published by the Commission (that is, Green and White Papers and the Commission's opinions). Other E-matters include reports on Finland's integration policy or on cases concerning Finland before the European Court of Justice.[31]

The handling of EU matters in the Eduskunta begins with the government sending a formal letter to the speaker. The letter includes a summary and normally the full text of the proposal, its relevance and consequences for Finland, and the (tentative) position of the government. The government also has the constitutional obligation to provide, on its own initiative, the Grand Committee and the competent standing committees with all relevant documents relating to the decisions taken by the parliament. Occasionally, the Eduskunta has complained that the information provided by the government is too extensive, making it difficult for MPs to identify the key points of the proposals.[32] The speaker forwards the matter to the Grand Committee and requests the competent specialized committee or committees to give their opinion to the Grand Committee.

The majority of U-matters are processed by more than one standing committee. Committee involvement in European matters depends on their policy jurisdiction. In 1995–2000, the standing committees issued, on average, 147 written opinions on EU matters (Table 8). The Finance Committee has been most burdened with EU legislation, followed by the Agriculture and Forestry Committee and the Economic Affairs Committee. The Defence Committee has processed least EU issues. The number of domestic legislative initiatives was approximately 250 per year during the same period. Table 9 shows the sources of the U-matters transmitted

Table 8

Written Opinions on EU Matters Issued by Standing Committees on
U- and E-Matters (1995–2000)

Committee	1995	1996	1997	1998	1999	2000
Committee for Constitutional Law	1	10	3	8	1	10
Legal Affairs Committee	4	16	4	7	13	8
Foreign Affairs Committee	4	24	5	14	11	5
Finance Committee	10	31	27	60	29	26
Administration Committee	5	6	16	25	7	14
Transport and Communications Committee	9	14	12	31	7	18
Committee for Agriculture and Forestry	13	22	14	25	19	15
Defence Committee	–	–	–	–	–	–
Committee for Education and Culture	2	2	3	7	2	5
Social Affairs and Health Committee	4	12	8	8	6	9
Economic Affairs Committee	13	19	20	30	11	12
Committee for the Future	–	–	–	–	–	11
Committee of Labour and Equality	2	11	8	8	6	7
Environment Committee	7	2	18	16	6	1
Total	74	169	138	239	118	141

Source: The Eduskunta.

Table 9

The Source of U-Matters Transmitted to the Eduskunta (1995–2000)

Ministry	N	Share (%)
Ministry of Finance	114	26
Ministry of Agriculture and Forestry	60	14
Ministry of Transport and Communications	51	12
Ministry of Justice	40	9
Ministry of Foreign Affairs	39	9
Ministry of Trade and Industry	35	8
Ministry of Social Affairs and Health	31	7
Ministry of the Interior	28	6
Ministry of the Environment	17	4
Ministry of Labour	13	2
Ministry of Education	11	3
Ministry of Defence	0	0
Total	439	100

Source: The Eduskunta.

by the government to the Eduskunta in 1995–2000. The Ministry of Finance produced most U-matters for parliamentary consideration.

The specialized committees prepare their opinions in light of information about the government's tentative position and after having heard expert testimony. It has been estimated that in approximately 90 per cent of the cases the Grand Committee agrees with the opinion of the specialized committee.[33] When more than one specialized committee delivers an opinion, the Grand Committee summarizes and mediates. After debating the issue, the Grand Committee formulates a position (which is a parliamentary recommendation, not a formal decision), in the form of a summary from the chairperson. The government representatives are notified of the decision. In order to enhance the ability of the Eduskunta to monitor and guide government behaviour in the Council, an effort is made to formulate the view of the Grand Committee before the consideration of the matter begins in the preparatory organs of the Council. This enables the parliament to monitor the preferences of the other member states, the European Commission, and the EP, and to frame its own position accordingly.

Hearings with civil servants also enable the Eduskunta to identify key points and to learn about issues under preparation at the European level and in national ministries. For example, the Environment Committee has regular meetings with civil servants from the Environment Ministry. Such direct contacts with civil servants are important, for, according to a report based on extensive interview data, middle-level civil servants have a central role in the preparation and processing of European legislation in Finland. Ministers or even high-level bureaucrats seldom have a significant impact on the substance of the issues.[34] Civil servants appreciate these meetings, particularly in politically controversial matters, for the committee hearings enable the civil servants to hear the MPs' views and to acquire the backing of the relevant Eduskunta committee for their preparatory work. Meetings also serve as occasions for conflict management, where possible differences between the ministries and the parliament are ironed out, and thereby reduce conflicts between the cabinet and the parliament. The government has occasionally failed to inform the Eduskunta of legislative amendments enacted by the Council and the EP, forcing the committees to take steps to acquire the relevant information.

The Grand Committee convenes, usually on Fridays, to hear the views of ministers about Council meetings scheduled for the following week. Committee members receive the agendas of the meetings, as approved by the Committee of Permanent Representatives (Coreper), in advance. They also receive, for each agenda item, a standardized memo with appropriate document references, a historical background summary, and a summary of outstanding questions and the government's proposed course of action. The ministers must give the committee the chance to express its opinion on all matters before final decisions are taken in the Council. The Grand Committee has insisted on this, and the government representatives have used this parliamentary scrutiny reserve in negotiations at the European level, particularly during the 1996–97 IGC. After Council meetings, the Grand Committee always receives a report on the Council meeting. Ministers must be prepared to appear before the committee to explain in detail any deviations from the given policy guidelines.

Advance scrutiny of the Council's agenda items means, in most cases, discussing the relevant issues and their implications, usually from the Finnish perspective. Actual voting instructions are given only at the final stage of the process and constitute a minor share, albeit an important one, of all instructions. These voting instructions by the Grand Committee are not constitutionally binding. Politically, however, they are important because the government must enjoy the support of the legislature. The Grand Committee usually does not impose strict mandates, thus giving ministers a certain amount of freedom of manoeuvre. This is reflected in the behaviour of the Finnish government in the Council, which is mainly characterized by flexibility and the desire to compromise. Moreover, the Grand Committee focuses its scrutiny on selected issues, often those of special interest to the MPs. The overwhelming majority of European matters do not cause controversy. Excluding two cases, there have been no major differences of opinion between the Eduskunta and the cabinet, although standing committees do occasionally insist that the government adopt a more stringent and detailed negotiating mandate.[35]

Basically the same model applies to the summits of the European Council. According to Section 97 of the Constitution, 'The Prime Minister shall provide the Parliament or a Committee with information on matters to be dealt with in a European Council beforehand and without delay after a meeting of the Council. The same applies when amendments are being prepared to the treaties establishing the European Union.'[36] The prime minister must therefore inform the Grand Committee in advance of questions to be addressed by the European Council. After European Council meetings, the prime minister must provide the plenary session or the Grand Committee with information on what took place. The prime minister informs the Foreign Affairs Committee about CFSP matters discussed in the European Council.

The functional capacity of the Grand Committee has been enhanced by its secretariat. In 2000, the Grand Committee employed three counsels and three secretaries, who, together with the secretariat of the Foreign Affairs Committee, the Eduskunta's representative in the EU, and the information officer of the Grand Committee, form the EU Secretariat of the parliament. When additional staff are required, the Grand Committee primarily relies on the staff of the specialized committees. Committee counsels with personal experience of EU matters have been especially important, suggesting that it would facilitate parliamentary scrutiny if each committee had one functionary specializing in European issues. The Eduskunta has its own EU information service. All members and staff of the Eduskunta have unrestricted on-line access to the sources of the government, including its central and non-public database of EU documents, and to the public services of the EU institutions.

The plenary (the full session of the parliament) can become involved both before and after decisions are taken at the European level. The plenary session may, after a proposal by the Speaker's Council, request the Grand Committee to submit European Commission proposals to the whole parliament, along with all information provided to the committee by the government. The plenary session may debate the proposals, but does not make formal decisions in such cases. A formal Act of Parliament, that is, a decision made after plenary debate, is necessary when the implementation of directives requires legislation. Treaty amendments also require the consent of national parliaments. While routine EU legislation is rarely debated on the floor, far-reaching political decisions such as EMU, and notably the development of CFSP, have inspired long plenary debates. As in the case of scrutinizing European legislation in the committees, the debates have been conducted primarily from a national perspective, with broader, EU-wide implications of the matters receiving less attention. Some MPs who do not sit in the Grand Committee have expressed their concern about the difficulty of following European matters, arguing that more EU issues should be debated on the floor.

EVALUATING THE FINNISH MODEL

The government, the Eduskunta, and all Finnish political parties have consistently emphasized that national parliaments are the primary channel for providing democratic legitimacy to EU decision-making, with the EP complementing the role of national legislatures. For example, in 1995, the Grand Committee asserted that 'national parliaments are now and for the foreseeable future the primary representatives of the political sovereignty of the peoples of the member states and of the democratic legitimacy of their political systems. Differences in the languages, cultures, historical experience and political traditions of the populations of the member states inhibit political organization at the European level and the formation of truly European parties and political movements.'[37] Finnish politicians have also repeatedly argued in favour of increasing the openness and transparency of EU decision-making, partially in order to enhance national parliamentary scrutiny of European matters. The importance attached to national legislatures reflects the parliamentari- zation of the Finnish political system, with the Eduskunta trying to ensure that its strengthened position will not evaporate as a result of European integration.

While the Eduskunta cannot be categorized as a strong policy- influencing legislature in domestic legislation, it has subjected the govern- ment to relatively tight scrutiny in EU matters. The close scrutiny of government in European matters has arguably had a positive spill-over effect, with the MPs exercising tighter control also in domestic issues. This phenomenon is at least partially explained by the overlap between national and EU agendas, and the interaction between the two levels of decision-making. Moreover, the active scrutiny of European legislation has improved the dialogue between the government and the Eduskunta. The regular appearance of ministers before the Grand Committee has had an impact on the internal work of the government, leading to improved policy coordination within the cabinet and between the ministries, and forcing the ministers to study the issues more thoroughly than might otherwise be the case.

There is no doubt that the institutional rules established for parlia- mentary scrutiny of European matters work well. Both the MPs and politicians in Finland, as well as civil servants from other EU member state legislatures, have considered the Finnish model a success, at least in comparative terms. The scrutiny model of the Eduskunta has four main strengths: the position of the parliament is regulated in the constitution, the Eduskunta gets involved relatively early in the processing of EU legislation, the parliament enjoys unlimited access to information from the government, and the responsibility of preparing and monitoring European matters is delegated downwards to specialized committees.[38] Particularly the decentralization of scrutiny and policy formulation to standing committees increases the ability of the whole parliament to influence the position of the government. The delegation of authority to standing committees benefits both the government and opposition MPs, as a strong committee system facilitates efficient control over govern- ment.[39] More centralized arrangements which give specialized committees a much smaller role, such as those found in the majority of member states, fail to benefit from the cumulative expertise of the standing committees. However, a decentralized system enables all representatives to engage in EU matters.[40]

The constitutionally regulated, practically unlimited access to information from the government is crucial, particularly as MPs across Europe often find it difficult to separate the important documents from the huge amount of EU material dispatched to the national legislatures. The constitutional rules encourage the government to provide the Eduskunta with information of its own accord without any specific requests by the MPs. The 'Protocol on the Role of National Parliaments in the European Union', included in the Amsterdam Treaty (1997), set a minimum time limit of six weeks for the enactment of EU legislation and detailed which documents should be forwarded to national legis- latures. The Eduskunta is usually informed of the European Commission's legislative initiatives months before the six-week time limit of the Amsterdam Treaty begins. Thus, the Eduskunta normally becomes involved in the processing of the initiative long before the Commission officially publishes it. The access to information is particularly impor- tant for written reports from the government to the Grand Committee ('E-matters') and hearings with ministers in the Grand Committee prior to Council meetings, as the main difference between E-matters and U-matters is that the former do not belong to the remit of the parliament.

Participation in EU governance has internationalized legislatures and brought issues previously decided by national governments under increased parliamentary control. Through parliamentary scrutiny of EU affairs, national parliaments are now routinely involved in foreign-policy decision-making, a domain traditionally dominated by the executive branch and foreign ministry in particular.[41] This applies particularly to Finland. In decision-making related to the foreign and security policy of the EU, the Foreign Affairs Committee enjoys the same right to receive information and to express the view of parliament as the Grand Com- mittee enjoys in relation to other EU matters. As foreign policy leadership is now shared between the government and the president, and as the government primarily decides on CFSP matters, the Eduskunta has a genuine opportunity to influence national foreign policy.[42]

Parliamentary scrutiny of government in EU matters has so far operated smoothly. Particularly noteworthy has been the lack of conflict, or even of tension, between the government and the Eduskunta, on the one hand, and between the government and the opposition, on the other hand. Overall, the parliament has been more critical of integration than the two rainbow governments led by Lipponen, notably on EMU and the development of the CFSP. This applies not only to the opposition, but also to the parliamentary groups of the governing parties. All parties are, to a varying degree and depending on the policy area, divided over European matters (see Chapter 3), and the government is usually criticized by individual MPs from both opposition and government parties rather than by a united opposition or even by unitary party groups. However, while the Eduskunta has been more critical of the EU than the government, and has subjected the cabinet to tight scrutiny in European matters, neither the KESK-led Aho government (1991–95) nor the Lipponen governments (1995–) have faced any major internal crisis or parliamentary rebellions over integration matters.[43]

What explains this low level of institutional and partisan conflict in the Eduskunta? Institutionally, the emphasis is on pragmatic examination of the EU's legislative initiatives in the committees, with hardly any partisan ideological debates about national integration policy or the overall development of integration. Indeed, in line with the image of a working parliament, the debating function of the parliament has so far remained marginalized in European matters. Plenary involvement has been weak, with lack of constructive debates on national European policy or on the future of integration. Apart from the centrality of committees in processing legislation, the brevity of integration debate is explained by partisan considerations. Despite the overall consensus in the Grand Committee, European matters continue to produce disagreement within and between parties, and public debates on the floor might damage the parties by highlighting these internal cleavages.

Politically, committee scrutiny of European matters differs in one important respect from domestic legislation: the government–opposition division does not play the only significant role either in the Grand Committee or in specialized committees. While stable majority coalitions may exclude opposition power, the traditional government–opposition cleavage is often blurred on European questions, as the anti/pro-integration cleavage cuts across the familiar left–right spectrum. The Grand Committee has refused to act as the government's rubber stamp and insists that all relevant information be made available to both the government and opposition representatives on equal terms. The main goal is to achieve parliamentary, and thus national, unanimity or at least broad consensus, which can be translated into additional influence in the Council.[44] While an active role for the parliament may create problems for national EU coordination, through slowing the process down, divergent preferences, or institutional rivalry,[45] the Finnish case illustrates that the inclusion of parliamentary views is important in terms of building elite consensus and of policy consistency. Granting the opposition a larger role in European matters, especially on more important issues such as treaty amendments, increases the legitimacy of the decisions, as parties share the responsibility for the outcome.[46] The multi-party coalition governments, together with the role accorded to the opposition in the Grand Committee, facilitate broad backing for governmental action at the European level.

NOTES

1. National parliaments have only twice rejected treaties or treaty amendments. In 1954, the French National Assembly failed to ratify the plan for a European Defence Community, and, in January 1986, the Danish Folketinget rejected the Single European Act (SEA), only for the will of the parliamentary majority to be overturned by a referendum held in February that year.
2. On the role of national parliaments in EU governance, see T. Bergman, 'National Parliaments and EU Affairs Committees: Notes on Empirical Variation and Competing Explanations', *Journal of European Public Policy* 4:3 (1997), pp. 373–87; T. Bergman and E. Damgaard (eds) *Delegation and Accountability in European Integration: The Nordic Parliamentary Democracies and the European Union* (London: Frank Cass, 2000), published also as a Special Issue of *Journal of Legislative Studies* 6:1 (2000); T. Bergman, 'The European Union as the Next Step of Delegation and Accountability', *European Journal of Political Research* 37:3 (2000), pp. 415– 29; D. Judge, 'The Failure of National Parliaments', *West European Politics* 18:3 (1995), pp. 79–100; F. Laursen and S.A. Pappas (eds) *The Changing Role of Parliaments in the European Union* (Maastricht: EIPA, 1995); P. Norton (ed.) *National Parliaments and the European Union* (London: Frank Cass, 1996); T. Raunio, 'Always One Step Behind? National Legislatures and the European Union', *Government and Opposition* 34:2 (1999), pp. 180–202; T. Raunio and M. Wiberg, 'Does Support Lead to Ignorance? National Parliaments and the Legitimacy of EU Governance', *Acta Politica* 35:2 (2000), pp. 146–68; and T. Raunio and S. Hix, 'Backbenchers Learn to Fight Back: European Integration and Parliamentary Government', *West European Politics* 23:4 (2000), pp. 142–68.
3. The MPs and MEPs were asked, using a scale from 1 (too much) to 7 (too little), to give their views on whether their national parliament 'is exercising too much or too little supervision over the positions of the [country] government in the Council of Ministers of the European Union?' The averages were 5.35 for MEPs and 5.22 for MPs. The same survey also asked the MPs and MEPs about the roles of national parliaments and the European Parliament: 'Some people regard the European Parliament as the democratic heart of the Union, because democratic legitimacy of the Union can only be based on a supranational parliament. Others say that this is a wrong ambition because the legitimacy of the Union is already based on the national parliaments.' The respondents were again asked to rate their opinions on a scale from 1 (EP) to 7 (national parliaments). The averages were 3.04 for MEPs and 3.57 for MPs. An additional question showed that, on average,

MPs think that the EP should have more influence on EU decision-making than national legislatures, with only the Swedish MPs ranking the institutions in the opposite order. MPs from Austria, Denmark, Finland, France, and the UK were not included in the survey. The responses indicate that while MPs are dissatisfied with domestic parliamentary supervision, the majority of them also feel that controlling EU decision-making is primarily the job of the EP. See R.S. Katz, 'Representation, the Locus of Democratic Legitimation and the Role of the National Parliaments in the European Union' in R.S. Katz and B. Wessels (eds) *The European Parliament, the National Parliaments, and European Integration* (Oxford: Oxford University Press, 1999), pp. 21–44.

4. H. Kassim, 'Conclusion: The National Co-ordination of EU Policy: Confronting the Challenge', in H. Kassim, B.G. Peters and V. Wright (eds) *The National Coordination of EU Policy: The Domestic Level* (Oxford: Oxford University Press, 2000), p. 258.
5. See G. Falkner, 'How Pervasive Are Euro-Politics? Effects of EU Membership on a New Member State', *Journal of Common Market Studies* 38:2 (2000), pp. 223–50; and W.C. Müller, 'Austria', in H. Kassim, B.G. Peters and V. Wright (eds) *The National Coordination of EU Policy: The Domestic Level* (Oxford: Oxford University Press, 2000), pp. 210–13.
6. See Bergman, 'National Parliaments and EU Affairs Committees'; R. Pahre, 'Endogenous Domestic Institutions in Two-Level Games and Parliamentary Oversight of the European Union', *Journal of Conflict Resolution* 41:1 (1997), pp. 147–74; and Raunio and Wiberg, 'Does Support Lead to Ignorance?'
7. For detailed information on Finnish governments in 1945–2000, see J. Nousiainen, 'Finland: The Consolidation of Parliamentary Governance', in W.C. Müller and K. Strøm (eds) *Coalition Governments in Western Europe* (Oxford: Oxford University Press, 2000), pp. 264–99.
8. See W.C. Müller and K. Strøm, 'Conclusion: Coalition Governance in Western Europe', in Müller and Strøm (eds) *Coalition Governments in Western Europe*, p. 561.
9. Nousiainen, 'Finland: The Consolidation of Parliamentary Governance', p. 268.
10. Müller and Strøm, 'Conclusion: Coalition Governance in Western Europe', p. 561. The figure excludes caretaker cabinets.
11. For an excellent analysis of recent developments in executive–legislature relations, see J. Nousiainen, 'Suomalaisen parlamentarismin kolmas kehitysvaihe: konsensuaalinen enemmistöhallinta, vireytyvä eduskunta', *Politiikka* 42:2 (2000), pp. 83–96.
12. See D. Arter, *Scandinavian Politics Today* (Manchester: Manchester University Press, 1999), p. 213.
13. The electoral law adopted in 1969 changed the rules for candidate selection. Prior to 1969, the party leadership was able to control the nomination process in the districts. Under the present law, parties must use membership voting as a means of selecting candidates in constituencies where the number of candidates exceeds the constituency's number of parliamentary seats.
14. See J. Sundberg, 'Organizational Structure of Parties, Candidate Selection and Campaigning', in S. Borg and R. Sänkiaho (eds) *The Finnish Voter* (Tampere: The Finnish Political Science Association, 1995), pp. 45–65.

15. See T.K. Jensen, 'Party Cohesion', in P. Esaiasson and K. Heidar (eds) *Beyond Westminster and Congress: The Nordic Experience* (Columbus, OH: Ohio State University Press, 2000), pp. 210–36.
16. On Finnish party groups, see M. Wiberg, 'The Partyness of the Finnish Eduskunta', in K. Heidar and R. Koole (eds) *Parliamentary Party Groups in European Democracies: Political Parties Behind Closed Doors* (London: Routledge, 2000), pp. 161–76; and the chapters in Esaiasson and Heidar, *Beyond Westminster and Congress*.
17. The Constitution of Finland, 11 June 1999 (731/1999), Section 40.
18. On the consequences of the abolition of the deferment rule, see M. Mattila, 'From Qualified Majority to Simple Majority: The Effects of the 1992 Change in the Finnish Constitution', *Scandinavian Political Studies* 20:4 (1997), pp. 331–45.
19. According to Section 43 of the Constitution, 'A group of at least twenty Representatives may address an interpellation to the Government or to an individual Minister on a matter within the competence of the Government or the Minister. The interpellation shall be replied to in a plenary session of the Parliament within fifteen days of the date when the interpellation was brought to the attention of the Government. At the conclusion of the consideration of the interpellation, a vote of confidence shall be taken by the Parliament, provided that a motion of no confidence in the Government or the Minister has been put forward during the debate.' The Constitution of Finland, 11 June 1999 (731/1999), Section 43.
20. See M. Wiberg (ed.) *Parliamentary Control in the Nordic Countries: Forms of Questioning and Behavioural Trends* (Jyväskylä: The Finnish Political Science Association, 1994).
21. T. Raunio and M. Wiberg, 'Building Elite Consensus: Parliamentary Accountability in Finland', *Journal of Legislative Studies* 6:1 (2000), pp. 71–2.
22. The Constitution of Finland, 11 June 1999 (731/1999), Section 47.
23. Ibid., Section 97.
24. This section draws on previous work by the author. See Raunio and Wiberg, 'Building Elite Consensus: Parliamentary Accountability in Finland'; T. Raunio and M. Wiberg, 'Efficiency Through Decentralisation: The Finnish Eduskunta and the European Union', in M. Wiberg (ed.) *Trying to Make Democracy Work: The Nordic Parliaments and the European Union* (Stockholm: Gidlunds, 1997), pp. 48–69; and M. Wiberg and T. Raunio, 'Strong Parliament of a Small EU Member State: The Finnish Parliament's Adaptation to the EU', *Journal of Legislative Studies* 2:4 (1996), pp. 302–21. See also N. Jääskinen and T. Kivisaari, 'Parliamentary Scrutiny of European Union Affairs in Finland', in M. Wiberg (ed.) *Trying to Make Democracy Work: The Nordic Parliaments and the European Union* (Stockholm: Gidlunds, 1997), pp. 29–47; M. Boedeker and P. Uusikylä, 'Interaction between the Government and Parliament in Scrutiny of EU Decision-Making; Finnish Experiences and General Problems', in *National Parliaments and the EU – Stock-Taking for the Post-Amsterdam Era* (Helsinki: Eduskunnan kanslian julkaisu 1/2000), pp. 27–42; and especially N. Jääskinen, 'Eduskunta: Aktiivinen sopeutuja', in T. Raunio and M. Wiberg (eds) *EU ja Suomi: Unionijäsenyyden vaikutukset suomalaiseen yhteiskuntaan* (Helsinki: Edita, 2000), pp. 114–34.

25. Jääskinen, 'Eduskunta: Aktiivinen sopeutuja', pp. 114–17.
26. Information provided by the Eduskunta. Parliamentary elections were held in 1995 and 1999.
27. M. Linnapuomi, 'Täällä Strasbourg, kuuleeko Helsinki? Suomalaiset europarlamentaarikot eurooppalaisen ja kansallisen tason yhteensovittajina', in T. Martikainen and K. Pekonen (eds) *Eurovaalit Suomessa 1996: Vaalihumusta päätöksenteon arkeen* (Helsinki: Helsingin yliopisto, Yleisen valtio-opin laitos, Acta Politica 10, 1999), pp. 246–50.
28. The technical details of the procedures are explained in Suuren valiokunnan lausunto 3/1995 vp, Euroopan unionin asioiden käsittelystä suuressa valiokunnassa ja sille lausunnon antavissa erikoisvaliokunnissa, 22.11.1995 (SuVL 3/1995 vp). Information on the processing of EU matters, together with statistics, is also found in English and in French at the Eduskunta's website (*www.eduskunta.fi*).
29. The Constitution of Finland, 11 June 1999 (731/1999), Section 96.
30. Ibid., Section 97.
31. It is not possible to determine the exact number of EU documents processed by the Eduskunta. The data reported in Table 2 shows the number of dossiers opened each year. The number of documents included in the dossiers is much higher. Dossiers remain open until the item is no longer on the agenda of the EU institutions.
32. According to Boedeker and Uusikylä, 'given the vast amount of information flowing into the Eduskunta and the tight schedules of the affairs under preparation, its real opportunities to influence the Finnish EU-positions seem to be rather limited. The Eduskunta also seems to have difficulties in monitoring and following up the decision-making process after it has given its opinion on a particular matter.' See Boedeker and Uusikylä, 'Interaction Between the Government and Parliament in Scrutiny of EU Decision-Making', p. 41.
33. See R. Lampinen and I. Räsänen, 'Eduskunnan asema EU-asioiden valmistelussa', in R. Lampinen, O. Rehn, P. Uusikylä et al., *EU-asioiden valmistelu Suomessa* (Helsinki: Eduskunnan kanslian julkaisu 7/1998), pp. 121–32.
34. R. Lampinen, O. Rehn, P. Uusikylä et al., *EU-asioiden valmistelu Suomessa* (Helsinki: Eduskunnan kanslian julkaisu 7/1998).
35. Both conflicts emerged in 1995, at early stages of adaptation to membership, when the parliamentary routines for government scrutiny in EU matters were yet to be effectively established. More importantly, on a few occasions, the Grand Committee has received information after a considerable delay, or it has not received all the relevant information, notably in third-pillar matters. In these cases, the Chancellor of Justice has ruled that the delays have been accidental, resulting from misunderstandings, and the government has accepted the criticism voiced by the parliament. See Jääskinen, 'Eduskunta: Aktiivinen sopeutuja'.
36. The Constitution of Finland, 11 June 1999 (731/1999), Section 97.
37. Grand Committee, Opinion No 2/1995 Session, Preparing for the Inter-Governmental Conference of the European Union, Opinion of the Grand Committee to the Council of Ministers, 22.11.1995 (SuVL 2/1995 vp), p. 10.
38. See Jääskinen, 'Eduskunta: Aktiivinen sopeutuja'.

39. See, for example, I. Mattson and K. Strøm, 'Parliamentary Committees', in H. Döring (ed.) *Parliaments and Majority Rule in Western Europe* (New York: St. Martin's Press, 1995), pp. 249–307; P. Norton (ed.) *Parliaments and Governments in Western Europe* (London: Frank Cass, 1998); and L.D. Longley and R.H. Davidson (eds) *The New Roles of Parliamentary Committees* (London: Frank Cass, 1998).
40. See Raunio, 'Always One Step Behind? National Legislatures and the European Union'; and Raunio and Wiberg, 'Does Support Lead to Ignorance? National Parliaments and the Legitimacy of EU Governance'.
41. See K. von Beyme, 'Niedergang der Parlamente: Internationale Politik und nationale Entscheidungshoheit', *Internationale Politik* 53:4 (1998), pp. 21–30.
42. See T. Raunio and M. Wiberg, 'Parliamentarizing Foreign Policy Decision-Making: Finland in the European Union', *Cooperation and Conflict* 36:1 (2001), pp. 61–86; D. Arter, 'Finland', in R. Elgie (ed.) *Semi-Presidentialism in Europe* (Oxford: Oxford University Press, 1999), p. 64; and Arter, *Scandinavian Politics Today*, p. 239.
43. Despite the more cautious attitude shown by the Eduskunta, MPs and the political elite in general are still far more supportive of integration than their voters. According to a survey carried out in 1995, Finnish MPs were considerably more pro-integrationist than the citizens. See T. Raunio and M. Wiberg, 'Parliaments' Adaptation to the European Union', in P. Esaiasson and K. Heidar (eds) *Beyond Westminster and Congress: The Nordic Experience* (Columbus, OH: Ohio State University Press, 2000), pp. 344–64.
44. See E. Tuomioja, 'Konsensus tärkeää pienelle maalle', *Hallinto* 4 (1998), pp. 3–7.
45. See H. Kassim, B.G. Peters and V. Wright, 'Introduction', in H. Kassim, B.G. Peters and V. Wright (eds) *The National Coordination of EU Policy: The Domestic Level* (Oxford: Oxford University Press, 2000), pp. 16–17.
46. See M. Maor, 'The Relationship between Government and Opposition in the Bundestag and House of Commons in the Run-Up to the Maastricht Treaty', *West European Politics* 21:3 (1998), pp. 187–207.

5

The Dual Executive:
The Government and the President

The Finnish political system is normally categorized as semi-presidential. A semi-presidential system of government is a combination of presidentialism and parliamentary democracy, with the executive functions divided between an elected president and a government that is accountable to the parliament. This division of powers is also clearly stated in Section 3 of the new constitution that came into force in March 2000: 'The legislative powers are exercised by the Parliament, which shall also decide on State finances. The governmental powers are exercised by the President of the Republic and the Government, the members of which shall have the confidence of the Parliament.'[1]

Under the old Constitution, the president was recognized as the supreme executive power: 'Sovereign power in Finland shall belong to the people, represented by Parliament convened in session. Legislative power shall be exercised by Parliament in conjunction with the President of the Republic. Supreme executive power shall be vested in the President of the Republic. In addition, for the general government of the State there shall be a Council of State comprising the Prime Minister and the requisite number of ministers.'[2] According to the old constitution, the president had the right to influence the legislative process; he appointed governments and routinely dictated the partisan composition of governments, and was empowered to dissolve the government and the parliament, and to call early elections. The president had exclusive control over foreign policy, headed the armed forces, granted pardons, and enjoyed wide-ranging appointment powers that included judges, senior civil servants, and even university professors.[3]

Apart from constitutional regulations, the widely acknowledged priority of maintaining amicable relations with the Soviet Union concentrated power in the hands of the president. The constitution itself left room for interpretation, which the presidents, particularly Urho

Kekkonen, used to their advantage. Without a system of checks and balances such as those enshrined in the constitution of the United States, Kekkonen was able to influence and even dictate domestic politics far beyond his constitutional powers. The balance between government and the president was therefore both constitutionally and politically strongly in favour of the latter until the constitutional reforms enacted in the 1990s.

The constitutional reforms of the 1990s were indeed a response to the excesses of the Kekkonen era. A period of parliamentarization started in 1982 when Mauno Koivisto took the office after a quarter of century of politics dominated by Kekkonen. President Koivisto and the political elite in general favoured the strengthening of parliamentarism and curtailing the powers of the president. A further impetus to change came from the end of the Cold War. At the highest level, relations with the Soviet Union were primarily based on negotiations between the Finnish president and the leaders in the Kremlin, and the dissolution of the Soviet empire reduced the importance of such personalized foreign policy leadership. The gradual consolidation of parliamentary democracy was also facilitated by government stability. Since 1983, the governments have stayed in office for the whole electoral term of four years, and have done so without serious internal problems or even without real effective opposition (see Chapter 4). Partisan cooperation inside the cabinet and in the parliament is in turn made easier by an ideological convergence that has downplayed the importance of bloc politics and of the left–right division (see Chapter 3).[4]

The constitutional and political changes have therefore drastically changed the nature of the Finnish polity, with the government and particularly the prime minister emerging as the dominant players. Now the government is the supreme executive authority, not the president, and the powers of the latter are more clearly restricted. EU membership has contributed to this development in two ways. According to the constitution, the government formulates and decides national EU policy, with the president's powers limited to second-pillar matters. Secondly, the process of European integration effectively blurs the distinction between foreign and domestic policy, with trade and increasingly also traditional foreign policies being decided collectively by member states or together with the EU institutions at the European level. Therefore, the share of matters falling under the jurisdiction of the Finnish president is gradually declining. Nevertheless, the president is not (at least, not yet) a mere ceremonial figurehead.

As a result, the new Finnish political system sits rather uneasily in the semi-presidential category. According to Lijphart, classifying the

Finnish system is difficult. While Lijphart categorizes Finland as a semi-presidential system, he concludes that the Finnish political system is 'certainly much closer to a parliamentary than a presidential system'.[5] Paloheimo meanwhile defines Finland as 'an almost parliamentary democracy',[6] while Arter concludes that 'it is clear that Finland is en route to becoming an orthodox parliamentary democracy'.[7]

The chapter is structured as follows. In the next section, we analyse the division of competences between the president and the government. Apart from the president being almost completely excluded from national EU policy coordination, we show that the increasing interdependence between the member states and the EU and the gradual development of the EU's common foreign policy set further limits to presidential powers. In the third section, the coordinating system established to formulate national EU policies is explored. While the Finnish system is fairly decentralized in routine legislation, the goal in important issues is to speak with one voice in the various EU bodies. The concluding section summarizes our main findings and discusses the balance of power between the government and the president in integrating Europe.

DIVISION OF POWERS BETWEEN THE PRESIDENT AND THE GOVERNMENT

The starting point for the historical division of powers between the president and the government was given in the first Finnish constitution, which came into force in 1919, two years after Finland had achieved independence.[8] The division of powers between the two state agencies could be characterized as highly dualistic. In domestic politics, the government was to be the key player, the role of the president being above all to guarantee the functionality of the parliamentary system. In this role of a *pouvoir neutre* in domestic politics, the president was not given powers in any policy field directly.[9] He was, however, provided with strong instruments with which to control the parliamentary machinery. These included the right to influence the legislative process by postponing legislative proposals to the new parliament. The president was also entitled to appoint governments, as well as to dissolve the government and the parliament and to call early elections.

In contrast to his position in domestic politics, the president was given a position in foreign policy corresponding to that of an autocrat. It is traditionally pointed out that this was not necessarily the intention of the drafters of the constitution. The formulation of Section 33 of the old Constitution Act, according to which 'Finland's relations with foreign powers shall be determined by the President' has been considered very vague. This was a result of the fact that in the constitutional deliberations preceding the work of the 1917–19 constitutional committee, Finland's status as a Russian Grand Duchy had formed the starting point, and foreign policy was still considered within the competence of the Russian tsar. When Finnish independence had been confirmed, the powers of the tsar in foreign policy were simply transferred to those of the Finnish president.[10] The Swedish Gustavian model of ruler-centred foreign policy direction functioned as the precedent.[11]

The dualistic division of powers combined with the indefinite formulation of the president's position in foreign policy put the emphasis on the conceptions and interpretations of those individuals holding the presidency. Before the new constitution entered into force in 2000, Finland, consequently, had ten very different presidencies. According to Jaakko Nousiainen, the constitution and the political culture – that is, the prevailing attitudes towards authority – constituted a stable setting within which the incumbents operated as individuals, the variable factors being parliamentary party arrangements and historical situations.[12] The Second World War, including Finland's two wars with the Soviet Union, constituted an important divide as far as the exercise of presidential powers is concerned. After the war, foreign policy, wherein a normal system of ministerial decision-making had become typical, was made the prerogative of the president. The main reason for this could be found in Finland's relations with the Soviet Union, where good personal relations between the political leaderships were, from the Finnish perspective, seen as a guarantee of the country's security. This development culminated during the long incumbency of President Urho Kekkonen (1956–81), who even utilized his powers in foreign policy to strengthen his authority in domestic politics and extend it to areas of the government's competence.[13]

During the term of office of Kekkonen's successor, Mauno Koivisto (1982–94), the measures taken to reduce presidential powers were reinforced. Together with a new electoral system – direct election of the president – a number of limitations in presidential power came into force in 1991.[14] These amendments were, with the exception of the limitation of re-election to one term, all related to the powers exerted in domestic politics. The president could no longer dismiss the government without a vote of no confidence by the parliament or the initiative of the government. Similarly, the president could no longer dissolve the parliament without the initiative of the prime minister. However, Section 33 of the Constitution Act had remained intact, and still in the beginning of the 1990s, the willingness to touch upon this 'foreign policy reserve' was not very firm.

In this sense, Finland was faced with a new situation when its political system had to adapt itself to European integration, first in the form of EEA membership and then through membership in the EU. Already Finland's participation in the EEA system would have implied, in accordance with a strict interpretation of the Finnish constitution, the inclusion of the entire EEA policy in the competence of the president. The constitution had, consequently, to be amended in order to redress this and to enable the participation of both the parliament and the government in EEA matters. The result was first an addition to Section 33 of the Form of Government Act, and, finally, the whole section was modified in the new constitution. It can thus be concluded that even if integration was not the only force behind the reduction of presidential powers in Finland, it was *the* force that introduced the reduction of power into the president's competence in foreign policy.

In connection with EEA membership, a specific Section 33a was added to the main section. It purported to balance the division of powers between the president and the government in EEA matters, and to prevent the powers that, by definition, belonged to the sphere of domestic policy from being transferred to the president.[15] According to Subsection 33a, 'The Parliament shall participate in the approval of those decisions taken by international organs which according to the Constitution require the consent of the Parliament in the manner stipulated by the Parliament Act. The Council of State shall decide on the approval and implementation of the decisions covered by the subsection 1 if the decision does not require the Parliament's approval and does not because of its substance necessitate that an order is issued.' Section 33a was historical in the sense that, for the first time in Finland's history, the government had been brought into the sphere of foreign policy.

Furthermore, the importance of the amendment increased when Finland joined the EU. Section 33 of the Government Act was applied to Finland's EU membership in the sense that, as a part of his general foreign policy leadership, the CFSP, as well as amendments to the EU treaties, was seen to belong to the president's competence while other parts of EU policies belonged to the government. In the preparation of Finland's EU membership, an unusual disagreement appeared between the parliament and the president as far as a detail in this division of powers was concerned. The Committee for Constitutional Law of the Eduskunta, exerting its power of the preliminary examination of laws, adopted a position according to which the government – instead of the president – was the key player representing Finland in the European Council.[16] The national preparation for the European Council meetings was to take place under the auspices of the government, and the prime minister was to brief the parliament and its committees on these meetings (see Chapter 4). The Committee for Constitutional Law, therefore, came to the conclusion that the decision on Finland's participation in the summits of the European Council belonged to the government on the basis of Section 33a of the Form of Government Act. When President Martti Ahtisaari confirmed the laws enforcing the amendments caused by Finland's EU membership, he adopted an interpretation deviating from the position of the committee. According to President Ahtisaari, in order not to undermine the division of powers in foreign policy, the president should have the right to decide whether to participate in the European Council meetings. This was confirmed between Prime Minister Lipponen and President Ahtisaari, and it forms the current praxis, at least as long as Lipponen holds his seat.

Separately from these EU amendments, a comprehensive revision of the Finnish constitution was going on in the 1990s, purporting, for the first time, to consolidate the four separate constitutional acts into one constitution, whose text would be modernized. Another purpose was the further parliamentarization of the political system. The result of this revision, a new Finnish constitution, entered into force in March 2000. Those drafting the new constitution were faced with the difficult task of coordinating the pressures to change the presidential powers, thus bringing about a more modern outcome even in this sense. In the new constitution, the government, which for the first time is placed on a par with the president as far as powers in foreign policy are concerned, becomes the key player in EU policy. The text of the new Section 93, in its entirety, is as follows:

> The foreign policy of Finland is directed by the President of the Republic in co-operation with the Government. However, the Parliament accepts Finland's international obligations and their denouncement and decides on the bringing into force of Finland's international obligations in so far as provided in this Constitution. The President decides on matters of war and peace, with the consent of the Parliament.
>
> The Government is responsible for the national preparation of the decisions to be made in the European Union, and decides on the concomitant Finnish measures, unless the decision requires the approval of the Parliament. The Parliament participates in the national preparation of decisions to be made in the European Union, as provided in this Constitution.
>
> The communication of important foreign policy positions to foreign States and international organizations is the responsibility of the Minister with competence in foreign affairs.

In foreign policy decision-making, the new constitution practically confirmed the decision-making practices that had come into being in the mid-1990s. The president had kept his position as the general director of Finnish foreign policy. This position had, however, been substantially reduced because the leadership of Finland's EU policy had, to a very large extent, become the prerogative of the government and particularly of the prime minister. In the government's proposal for the new constitution, the relationship between the president and the government was further-more clarified by counting even the national preparation for the CFSP as a competence of the government. In fact, it can be argued that the new cooperative foreign policy leadership essentially circumscribes presiden-tial powers. First, as EU membership in present conditions forms the very starting point for Finland's foreign and security policy (see Chapter 7), the president's 'general leadership' of foreign policy becomes very limited as far as both its material extension and policy principles are concerned. In the future, the president's position is dependent on the development of the CFSP. The more the CFSP is developed, and extended to new policy areas such as defence, the more the roles of the prime minister and the government are emphasized at the expense of the powers of the president.

The new constitution also decreased the presidential powers in domestic politics, mainly by taking further the reforms launched already in the early 1990s. The president's powers in government formation were also restricted by strengthening the role of the parliament in the election of the prime minister. The parliament, consequently, elects the prime minister, who is then appointed to the office by the president. The president appoints all other ministers in accordance with a proposal made by the prime minister. The purpose of the amendment was to bind the composition of the government directly to the result of the general elections without the interference of the president. In the legislative process, the presidential powers were reduced by transferring the power to issue decrees to the government and by abolishing the suspensive veto of the president. If the president does not ratify a law within three months, the parliament can, according to the new constitution, adopt it without material alterations.

It is too early to draw any definitive conclusions on how the division of powers between the president and the government in Finland's EU policy will function. One reason for this is the continuous revision of the constitution that has been going on since the beginning of Finland's EU membership. The other reason is that, as the president and the prime minister have so far come from the same party (SDP), the system of dual leadership has not yet been put to a real political test. The key principle in the application of the new constitution has been that the president takes all the most important decisions on foreign and security policy in cooperation with the government and on the basis of the government's reports. The main forum for discussion and decisions is the weekly meeting of the ministerial committee on foreign and security policy, the Cabinet Foreign and Security Policy Committee, which can be chaired by the president, and the decisions of which are based on papers presented by the minister of foreign affairs. As a rule, the decision is based on consensus, conforming to the position of the government, rather than a unilateral statement by the president. Matters requiring a formal decision proceed to the plenary session of the government, there to be decided by the president.

NATIONAL EU POLICY COORDINATION

As in the case of the Eduskunta (see Chapter 4), the basic features of the national coordination system for EU policies were established already in connection with EEA membership, which took effect from the start of 1994. The Finnish model was influenced by the Danish system, which was 'designed to ensure parliamentary control, overall national policy coordination and utilization of civil service expertise. It was also designed to enable the interests of organized groups to be articulated and, not least, to achieve a national consensus.'[17] While EU membership has necessitated the establishment of new administrative structures, the overall organization of the state bureaucracy has remained intact. This is not surprising, for institutional change is typically incremental, and organizations usually respond to new challenges by adapting their existing structures instead of establishing new units.

Figure 4 shows the institutions involved in formulating national EU policies, and Table 10 depicts the processing of EU matters at the European level and in the Finnish state administration. At the bottom of the coordination system are the sections that formally operate under the Committee for EU Matters. In 2000, this committee had 39 sections, and their function is to coordinate European matters within the respective ministries. Sections are chaired by an official from the responsible ministry, and they include representatives from relevant interest groups, those from other ministries, and one from the EU Secretariat. Officials present matters to the sections for discussion and inform them of issues under preparation. When agreement is reached, the section procedure provides a sufficient basis for determining Finland's final position. Otherwise, the matter is presented to the Committee for EU Matters and the Cabinet EU Committee.

Figure 4
The Institutions Participating in the Formulation and Coordination of Finnish
National EU Policy

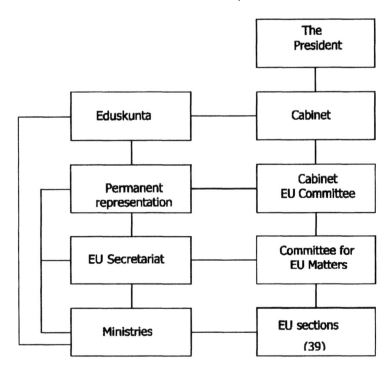

Source: M. Mattila, 'Valtioneuvosto: Suomen EU-politiikan määrittelijä', in T. Raunio
and M. Wiberg (eds) *EU ja Suomi: Unionijäsenyyden vaikutukset suomalaiseen
yhteiskuntaan* (Helsinki: Edita, 2000), p. 140.

The main interministerial coordinating body is the Committee for
EU Matters located in the Foreign Office. It has 17 members: high-level
officials (*kansliapäälliköt*) from ministries, and representatives of the
Prime Minister's Office, the Office of the President, the Bank of Finland,
the Office of the Attorney General, and the autonomous Åland region.
The committee is chaired by the representative of the EU Secretariat, and
it convenes on a weekly basis. As most matters are decided by the civil
servants in the sections or by ministers in the Cabinet EU Committee, the
committee has played a relatively minor role in the coordination system.

The Foreign Ministry was initially given the overall responsibility for
European matters. It was in charge of coordinating ministerial policies
and provided the home for the EU Secretariat. However, the EU
Secretariat was transferred to the Prime Minister's Office in the summer

Table 10
The Processing of EU Matters in the EU Institutions and in the Finnish State
Administration

EU level	Finland
1) The European Commission starts to draft a legislative proposal	1) The responsible ministry begins to process the matter
2) The European Commission enters into negotiations with interest groups and national ministries	2) The ministry negotiates with the European Commission and formulates the initial national position
3) The European Commission publishes the initiative	3) The ministry decides the initial Finnish position. The Eduskunta is informed of the matter
4) The European Commission sends the initiative to the Council	4) Interministerial negotiations determine possible changes to Finland's position
5) The EP starts to process the matter	5) The permanent representation presents the Finnish position to Finnish MEPs
6) Council working groups debate the initiative	6) The responsible civil servant takes part in the Council working group and reports back to superiors. The Grand Committee is informed of the matter and presents its views on the proposal
7) Coreper processes the matter	7) The permanent representative, the minister and civil servants fine-tune the national position
8) The proposal is put on the agenda of the Council	8) The Cabinet EU Committee decides on the negotiating mandate of the minister. The minister appears before the Grand Committee prior to the Council meeting

Sources: Adapted from O. Rehn, 'EU-asioiden kansallinen koordinaatio ja poliittinen ohjaus', in R. Lampinen, O. Rehn, P. Uusikylä et al., *EU-asioiden valmistelu Suomessa* (Helsinki: Eduskunnan kanslian julkaisu 7/1998), p. 16; and M. Mattila, 'Valtioneuvosto: Suomen EU-politiikan määrittelijä', in T. Raunio and M. Wiberg (eds) *EU ja Suomi: Unionijäsenyyden vaikutukset suomalaiseen yhteiskuntaan* (Helsinki: Edita, 2000), p. 139.

of 2000. It was argued that moving the responsibility for European issues from the Foreign Ministry to the Prime Minister's Office would enhance the capacity of the whole state bureaucracy and the parliament to process EU issues, particularly as most European matters are relevant to traditional domestic policies, and as the government and the prime minister are in charge of directing national integration policy.[18] Other ministries also raised concerns about the objectivity of the EU Secretariat, as they felt that the foreign ministry was safeguarding its own interests.[19] The main function of the EU Secretariat is to ensure the smooth functioning of the national coordination system and to provide relevant information and documentation to those involved in preparing national positions.

The Cabinet EU Committee, in full, Cabinet Committee on European Union Affairs, is the main forum for deciding national positions in important matters and for building compromises between coalition partners on integration issues.[20] Government work is coordinated through its four statutory ministerial committees, the other three being the Cabinet Foreign and Security Policy Committee, the Cabinet Finance Committee, and the Cabinet Economic Policy Committee. The prime minister chairs all ministerial committees, and they prepare decisions that are given the final seal of approval by the plenary session of the whole cabinet. Established in 1995, the Cabinet EU Committee handles all politically sensitive EU matters. With all government parties represented, and headed by the prime minister, the ministerial committee ensures that all key decisions are coordinated at the highest political level. Before the decisive Council meeting, the Cabinet EU Committee determines the final Finnish position and gives guidelines to the ministers attending the meeting.[21]

The government's voice in the EU is Finland's permanent representation, which employs over 100 civil servants. The president appoints the permanent representative. The permanent representation has performed a crucial role during the first years of membership, both as a source of information to Finnish civil servants, ministers, and MEPs, and as a key player in preparing and formulating national positions prior to Council meetings.[22] The Finnish experience is thus in line with the research by Thorhallsson on small member states. Comparing the administrative procedures of 12 large and small member states in 1986–94 in regional policy and CAP issues, Thorhallsson underlined the importance and relative autonomy of permanent representations. The permanent representations of larger countries get regular instructions from national capitals whereas those of smaller countries often need to find their own solutions. This makes permanent representations key players in the game and strengthens their role in relation to domestic ministries.[23]

While the overall aim 'is to speak with one voice on all levels of decision-shaping in Brussels',[24] the importance attached to achieving such consistency varies between policy areas and individual legislative initiatives. When a proposal is perceived as having significant national repercussions, the matter is debated at the highest political level in the Cabinet EU Committee. In these cases, the permanent representative in Brussels also often informs (all) Finnish MEPs of the national position.

Examples of such high-profile issues are IGCs and the Agenda 2000 negotiations. In less important matters, the process is decentralized, with the competent ministries and the responsible civil servants enjoying much autonomy in formulating the national stance.[25] The Finnish situation corresponds again with the results of Thorhallsson. Ministers in smaller EU member states often grant civil servants considerable autonomy in policy-making. When the issue is not very important, national officials have much freedom of manoeuvre. However, in certain prioritized matters, the officials of small member states are instructed to keep a close eye on their countries' special interests.[26]

If we keep in mind this variation among issues, the Finnish co-ordination system can be categorized as fairly centralized.[27] The prime minister is in charge of the overall direction of national EU policy, and the EU Secretariat is located in the Prime Minister's Office. Routine matters are delegated downwards to individual ministries, but sensitive matters are dealt with at the highest political level in the Cabinet EU Committee. Moreover, the Finnish coordination system, together with the implementation of EU legislation, is broadly inclusive and is based on wide consultation among both public and private actors. The basic idea is to manufacture broad (elite-level) societal backing for national positions, including the parliament, relevant interest groups, and government representatives.

An often-mentioned feature of the EU policy process is bureaucra-tization, the involuntary or unintended shift of power from directly elected office-holders to civil servants. The EU political system is arguably highly sectorized, with emphasis on networks, problem-solving, and technical expertise within policy communities. The internal organization of the EU institutions – the European Commission, the sectoral councils, the committees of the EP – is very sectionalized, and thus each policy domain (agriculture, environment, transport, social affairs, etc.) has gradually built its own policy networks with relatively little interaction with other policy sectors. Likewise in Finland (see Table 10), civil servants perform a central role at all stages of the game, from the initial formula-tion of the national position in the ministries in Helsinki to the top-level negotiations among the permanent representatives in Brussels. Directly elected office-holders (MPs and ministers) rarely possess similar expertise; thus, the ability of politicians to control or monitor the processing of EU initiatives is rather limited.[28] However, the autonomy of civil servants is at least partially counteracted by the active scrutiny of the Eduskunta in EU matters that encourages the ministers to familiarize themselves with the European issues handled in their ministries (see Chapter 4).

The most important development in the executive branch is the emergence of the prime minister as the unrivalled leader in both domestic and European policy. The strengthened position of the prime minister results from several factors: constitutional reforms that have parliamentarized decision-making, the personalization of modern democracy as a result of media coverage and electoral campaigns, and increased government stability since the 1980s. In no small measure, EU membership has reinforced these domestic changes, as will be argued in the concluding section.

TOWARDS NORMAL PARLIAMENTARY DEMOCRACY

Membership in the EU has acted as an important external factor in parliamentarizing decision-making in Finland. This applies particularly to foreign policy. During the post-1945 period, foreign policy decision-making had been firmly in the hands of the president and a narrow circle of the political elite. Constitutional amendments enacted since the early 1990s have strengthened the role of the government and the Eduskunta in foreign policy decision-making. Most notably, EU matters belong almost exclusively to the jurisdiction of the cabinet. The government largely dictates national integration policy, with the president intervening mainly when questions of the utmost importance from the point of view of Finland's foreign policy are on the agenda.

The prime minister has emerged as the undisputed leader in both domestic and integration policy. The constitutional and political powers of the president have been reduced to such an extent that Finland can arguably no longer be classified as a semi-presidential system.[29] The president directs foreign policy, but does so together with the government and through the government's ministerial committee.[30] The president now focuses on promoting foreign trade and on what is left (and that is not much) of so-called traditional foreign policy matters, that is, Finland's relations with countries outside the EU that are not handled via the Union. In recent debates, the role of the president as a moral leader – instead of a political one – has been asserted.[31] In this role, the president would bring moral perspectives to political debates whose horizons tend to be limited. Nevertheless, the tradition of presidential powers has a firm position in Finnish political culture. The incumbents have – with the support of their own parties – taken advantage of this by being very committed to the maintenance of presidential powers. As the public also seems to favour strong leadership, the system of dual executive may result in tensions between the government and the president.[32]

If the powers of the Finnish president are compared with those of the other strong presidents in Europe, such as the French, both similarities and differences can be found. Since 1962, the extent and nature of the president's role in France has depended both on the personality of the incumbent and on the balance of forces in the parliament. The president is in charge of foreign policy, but his influence in other policy areas depends on the ability to command support in the French National Assembly. In Finland, the president lacks an active connection with the parliament. In both countries, the president has mainly influenced policy-making through contacts with the prime minister and other cabinet members.

During De Gaulle's presidency, integration matters were the domain of the president, but his successors have assumed a more limited role. French presidents usually get involved primarily when constitutional or institutional questions and second-pillar matters are on the EU agenda, such as IGCs, the single currency, enlargements of the Union, a foreign crisis, or the balance of power between the EU institutions. When coordination problems between the French president and the government have emerged, they have usually resulted from the president's intervention in policy-making in matters normally handled by the government, that is, first-pillar questions. During cohabitation, with the president and the prime minister representing different parties, the personalities and ideological differences have occasionally led to disputes over the direction of French integration policy. However, on the whole, the relationship between the two heads of the executive branch over integration has been smooth.[33]

In Finland, the situation is much the same, with the government and the prime minister exercising firm leadership on EU affairs and the president adopting a more limited role. Treaty amendments, however, belong formally to the president's competence. The prime minister is the primary representative of Finland in the EU, a role which is, among other things, indicated by the fact that it is the prime minister, and not the president, who is the key player in formulating national policy, and who also reports to the parliament on EU issues. The president has, however, participated in the European Council meetings, with the exception of a few extraordinary meetings. An institutional amendment that gives further proof of the prime minister's position in EU affairs is the transfer of the coordinative unit, the EU Secretariat, from the Ministry of Foreign Affairs to the Prime Minister's Office. In Finland's case, it is too early to assess how the relationship between the two heads of the executive over integration functions in the long run. Ambiguity in the constitutional definition of this relationship is, in this respect, another feature in common with the French system.

NOTES

1. The Constitution of Finland, 11 June 1999 (731/1999), Section 3.
2. The Constitution Act of Finland, 17 July 1919/94, Section 2. The 'Council of State' is the term used when the legal-institutional framework of the government is referred to. In certain contexts, the term includes also the president.
3. See D. Arter, 'Finland', in R. Elgie (ed.) *Semi-Presidentialism in Europe* (Oxford: Oxford University Press, 1999), pp. 48–66; and H. Paloheimo, 'Divided Executive in Finland: From Semi-Presidential to Parliamentary Democracy', paper presented at the ECPR Joint Sessions of Workshops, Copenhagen, 14–19 April 2000.
4. See Paloheimo, 'Divided Executive in Finland', pp. 19, 27; and Arter, 'Finland'.
5. A. Lijphart, *Patterns of Democracy: Government Forms and Performance in Thirty-Six Countries* (New Haven, CT: Yale University Press, 1999), p. 123.
6. See Paloheimo, 'Divided Executive in Finland', p. 26; and H. Paloheimo, 'Divided Government in Finland: From a Semi-Presidential to a Parliamentary Democracy', in R. Elgie (ed.) *Divided Government in Comparative Perspective* (Oxford: Oxford University Press, 2001) pp. 86–105.
7. See Arter, 'Finland', p. 49.
8. The constitution was drafted in a constitutional committee nominated in 1917 and led by the man who in 1919 was elected the first Finnish president, K.J. Ståhlberg. The drafting of the constitution was based upon a republican form of government until the monarchical aspirations were reinforced, with the result that a German prince (the Prince of Hessen, Friedrich Karl) was elected Finland's king in 1918. After Germany had lost the First World War, the decision was annulled and a republican form of government adopted for Finland. See O. Jussila, S. Hentilä and J. Nevakivi, *From Grand Duchy to Modern State: A Political History of Finland Since 1908* (London: Hurst, 1999).
9. *Pouvoir neutre* is a concept originally used by the French constitutional theorist Benjamin Constant (1767–1830). It referred to the role of the monarch as a moderating force in a situation where political conflicts were blocking the functionality of the political machinery. See A. Jyränki, *Presidentti* (Helsinki: WSOY, 1981), p. 26.
10. See O. Meres-Wuori, *Suomen ulko- ja turvallisuuspoliittinen päätöksentekojärjestelmä* (Helsinki: Lakimiesliiton Kustannus, 1998), p. 56.
11. See Arter, 'Finland', p. 54.
12. See J. Nousiainen, 'From Semi-Presidentialism to Parliamentary Government: The Political and Constitutional Development of Finland', in L. Karvonen and K. Ståhlberg (eds) *Festchrift for Dag Anckar on his 60th Birthday on February 12, 2000* (Åbo: Åbo Akademi University Press, 2000), p. 340.
13. Nousiainen sums up Kekkonen's position in the following way: 'He used his presidential regulative powers in a very personal way: he selected prime ministers, pushed parties into coalitions, forced governments to resign, appointed non-partisan presidential cabinets and dissolved parliaments. On the policy-making side, certain behavioural rules were established: the president had the right to be informed about important matters, the right to

take initiatives, and the right to exercise his veto. These powers also applied to matters belonging to the cabinet's formal jurisdiction.' See Nousiainen, 'From Semi-Presidentialism to Parliamentary Government', p. 343.

14. In presidential elections, three different electoral systems have been used. First, the president was elected by an electoral college consisting of 301 electors elected by the people. In the 1988 presidential elections, a combination of the old system and a direct election was used. In this model, the people voted both for a presidential candidate and for an electoral candidate. If no presidential candidate achieved a majority (which was the case), the electors were supposed to elect the president. The current electoral system, direct elections, was used for the first time in the 1994 presidential elections. In this system, the people vote directly for the presidential candidates nominated by parties and other civic groupings. If none of the candidates get a majority in the first ballot, another ballot is arranged between the two most successful candidates.

15. Meres-Wuori, *Suomen ulko- ja turvallisuuspoliittinen päätöksentekojärjestelmä*, p. 256.

16. Ibid., pp. 294–8.

17. E. Damgaard, 'Conclusion: The Impact of European Integration on Nordic Parliamentary Democracies', in T. Bergman and E. Damgaard (eds) *Delegation and Accountability in European Integration: The Nordic Parliamentary Democracies and the European Union* (London: Frank Cass, 2000), p. 164. Indeed, the Danish model resembles closely the Finnish system. In Denmark, the structure is pyramidal, with over 30 special committees at the base of the structure. These committees consist of civil servants from the ministries and of relevant interest group representatives and are chaired by the ministry whose jurisdiction the matter belongs to, and which prepares the initial paper for discussion. Within the cabinet, there are two ministerial committees, the Foreign Policy Committee and the EC Committee, to decide the final positions and resolve interparty conflicts. See T. Pedersen, 'Denmark', in H. Kassim, B.G. Peters and V. Wright (eds) *The National Coordination of EU Policy: The Domestic Level* (Oxford: Oxford University Press, 2000), pp. 219–34.

18. See, for example, O. Rehn, *Pieni valtio Euroopan unionissa* (Helsinki: Kirjayhtymä, 1996), pp. 113–16.

19. R. Lampinen, O. Rehn and P. Uusikylä, 'Loppupäätelmät', in R. Lampinen, O. Rehn, P. Uusikylä et al., *EU-asioiden valmistelu Suomessa* (Helsinki: Eduskunnan kanslian julkaisu 7/1998), p. 136.

20. A new portfolio of a Minister of European Affairs was created following the March 1995 parliamentary elections. The minister was responsible for coordinating government's EU policy, but the experiment did not work as planned, as individual ministries dominated decision-making. There is therefore no Minister of European Affairs in the second Lipponen government, which took office after the elections held in March 1999.

21. The cabinet can also appoint internal ad hoc committees and working groups for the preparation of particular matters and routinely holds informal sessions, in advance of the plenary session of the whole cabinet, which take place on Thursdays. Further information on the working procedures of the cabinet is available at *www.government.fi*.

22. See T. Raunio and M. Wiberg, 'Building Elite Consensus: Parliamentary

Accountability in Finland', *Journal of Legislative Studies* 6:1 (2000), pp. 59–80.
23. See B. Thorhallsson, *The Role of Small States in the European Union* (Aldershot: Ashgate, 2000); and B. Thorhallsson, 'The Administrative Working Procedures of Smaller States in the Decision-Making Process of the EU', paper presented at the ECPR Joint Sessions of Workshops, Copenhagen, 14–19 April 2000.
24. See A. Stubb, H. Kaila and T. Ranta, 'Finland: An Integrationist Member State', in E.E. Zeff and E.B. Pirro (eds) *The European Union and the Member States: Cooperation, Coordination, and Compromise* (Boulder, CO: Lynne Rienner, 2001), p. 306.
25. See Lampinen et al., 'Loppupäätelmät', p. 134.
26. See Thorhallsson, *The Role of Small States in the European Union.*
27. See also Mouritzen, according to whom the Finnish EU decision structure is cohesive and centralized. See H. Mouritzen, *External Danger and Democracy: Old Nordic Lessons and New European Challenges* (Aldershot: Dartmouth, 1997), pp. 73–8, 131–2.
28. A potential solution would be to introduce junior ministers into the ministries who would specialize in European affairs. See Lampinen et al., 'Loppupäätelmät', p. 136; and M. Mattila, 'Valtioneuvosto: Suomen EU-politiikan määrittelijä', in T. Raunio and M. Wiberg (eds) *EU ja Suomi: Unionijäsenyyden vaikutukset suomalaiseen yhteiskuntaan* (Helsinki: Edita, 2000), p. 145.
29. Nousiainen, 'From Semi-Presidentialism to Parliamentary Government', pp. 337–52.
30. D. Arter, *Scandinavian Politics Today* (Manchester: Manchester University Press, 1999), p. 239.
31. A. Jyränki, 'Jutun nimi', *Helsingin Sanomat*, 9 May 1999.
32. See Paloheimo, 'Divided Executive in Finland', pp. 27–8; and T. Raunio and M. Wiberg, 'Parliamentarizing Foreign Policy Decision-Making: Finland in the European Union', *Cooperation and Conflict* 36:1 (2001), pp. 70–1.
33. See A. Cole and H. Drake, 'The Europeanization of the French Polity: Continuity, Change and Adaptation', *Journal of European Public Policy* 7:1 (2000); pp. 26–43; and A. Guyomarch, H. Machin and E. Ritchie, *France in the European Union* (Basingstoke: Macmillan, 1998), pp. 45–53.

6

Finland's First Presidency of the European Union

The presidency of the EU is not an easy task for a member state to undertake. In part, this has to do with the particular type of leadership required in the EU. The presidency concerns directly only one of the major bodies in the Union – the Council of Ministers. The division of powers with the other bodies is not always clear-cut. The other reason relates to the character of the organ headed by the presidency. To lead a Council which comprises 15 nation states gradually transferring their sovereignties to a supranational union, is a real challenge for any country.

In Finland, the presidency of the EU, falling on the last term of the second millennium, was regarded as the greatest international challenge since Finland's independence. Finland had to cope with the task only four and a half years after it had joined the EU, which increased the presidency's role as the first real showcase for national EU policy. The Finnish state administration took the task very seriously – preparations for the presidency were started already years before the term of office. While the domestic preconditions for a successful presidency seemed excellent, the external conditions were extremely challenging. This chapter provides an analysis of the first Finnish presidency of the EU. First, the conditions of the task are discussed from the point of view of the EU. Then, the Finnish success in fulfilling these is discussed. Finally, attention is paid to the impact of the presidency on Finnish EU membership.

THE LEADERSHIP OF THE UNION

The EU can be viewed as a hybrid in many respects. The reason for this characterization is the vacillating legitimacy of federalism in Europe since the establishment of the original three communities. The original communities were based upon a federalist plan taking expression, for instance,

113

in the institutional structures they created. In the course of history, the federalist tendencies have been increasingly challenged by growing intergovernmentalism, which reached its peak when Great Britain and Denmark entered the EC in the 1970s. The result has been a steady concurrence between federalist goals, on the one hand, and intergovernmental ones, on the other hand, which has left its imprint on almost every single element of European integration.[1]

In many ways, the hybrid, or compromise, character of the EU takes expression in its present institutional structures. Originally, as mentioned, these structures were based upon a federalist plan with the European Commission as an evolving European government, politically responsible to a directly elected EP. The role of the Council of Ministers was planned to have been gradually toned down and, even if this was not explicitly stated in the original treaties, it was considered not a remote possibility that the Council might end up as a second chamber of the EP.[2] This federalist structure was completed by a system of law, a large part of which was directly binding and the interpretation of which belonged in the final analysis to another independent 'European' organ, the European Court of Justice. The completion of this federalist structure has, however, been hampered, and the intergovernmental elements have maintained – and arguably even strengthened – their position.[3] Instead of forming a second chamber of the EP, the Council of Ministers still functions as a kind of second government, sharing, in part, the role of the European Commission as well as that of the EP. The European Council, which was established as a political directorate of the evolving political cooperation in the 1970s, has been transformed into the directorate of the entire EU – a factor which puts still more weight upon the intergovernmental angle.[4]

Thus, an analysis of the EU presidency must begin from the peculiar structure of multi-leadership which is typical of the Union and which has become still more accentuated due to the pillar structure with which it is connected. If political leadership is perceived as traditional executive and representative powers, the EU clearly has a dual leadership in first-pillar issues, where leadership is divided between the European Commission, on the one hand, and the Council of Ministers and the European Council, on the other hand. The ultimate form and effectiveness of the EU's leadership then depend on the leadership capacities of each of these two organs as well as on the nature of the cooperation between them. In second-pillar issues, the leadership belongs more clearly to the two Councils.

The Council of Ministers presidency participates in the dual leadership of the EU by managing the intergovernmental part of the EU machinery and representing the Union in the framework of the CFSP. The recent evolution in which the Council presidency has been transformed into a

more and more political institution – as opposed to its original administrative role – has made the presidency an important candidate for EU
leadership. Emil Kirchner has divided the functions of the presidency into
the administrative function, initiative function, coordination function,
and representational function.[5] The last three are clearly linked with the
political role that the presidency has adopted in the EU leadership.

THE PRECONDITIONS FOR THE FINNISH PRESIDENCY

All presidencies are, of course, different in their agendas and the general
political environment in which they take place. Anyhow, there are certain
elementary qualifications that a good presidency should possess which
can more or less be deduced from the particular form of leadership
represented by the EU. These qualifications can first be divided into those
that get emphasized in the presidency's role as an operator of the intergovernmental machinery – as mediator and builder of compromises – and
those related to the general leadership of the EU.[6] Another division can
be made between the internal and external preconditions of a good
presidency.

Finland's small size (see Chapter 1) and short membership history
could have made the starting point for its EU leadership quite vague.
However, Finland had achieved international recognition as a mediator
in other diplomatic contexts during both the Cold War and the post-Cold
War era.[7] It had been hosting the meetings of superpower leaders, and its
credibility had been recently confirmed by the nomination of the former
president, Martti Ahtisaari, as mediator in the Kosovo crisis just on the
eve of the Finnish presidency. For a country in the role of a mediator,
small size connected with a history of neutrality could be assumed to
develop into an advantage, too.

Small size and new membership were also compensated for through
an effective national system for preparation and decision-making in EU
issues (see Chapter 5). On the basis of this machinery, national preparations for the EU presidency had been started as early as 1996.[8] A particular
unit (Unit for EU Affairs) had been established in the Prime Minister's
Office for the national direction and coordination of the EU presidency.
A corresponding ad hoc unit had been established in the Ministry of
Foreign Affairs for the direction and coordination of the practical
arrangements – such as meetings and interpreter services – related to the
presidency. An extensive training programme of civil servants had taken
place to reinforce the language proficiencies and administrative skills of
those functioning in key positions during the presidency.[9]

As for the general leadership function connected with the EU presidency, the internal preconditions for a successful presidency appeared almost perfect in the case of Finland. Commitment to integration had been firm in the form of governmental policy throughout Finnish membership history by that time. In the general elections just a few months before the presidency, the government had renewed its mandate, which made its political position solid behind the presidency. Even at the EU level, the Lipponen government had achieved recognition for its flexible and pro-European policy.

However, the external preconditions were not so favourable for Finland. As Finland assumed the last presidency of the millennium, the Finnish agenda appeared to be overloaded. In general, it seemed as if almost all key projects related to integration – everything from enlargement and the defence dimension to the constitutional development and the new IGC in institutional issues – should arrive at an important stage during the Finnish presidency.[10] At the same time, the political machinery of the EU appeared to have serious malfunctions. Due to the resignation of the European Commission headed by Jacques Santer in March 1999, the new Commission would enter office in the middle of the Finnish presidency. Another element of instability was caused by the EP elections just a few weeks before the start of the Finnish presidency and the change of political alignments they would bring to the EU government. In addition to all this, the stabilization of the situation in Kosovo after the crisis there became a special issue that virtually dominated the EU agenda.

THE FINNISH PRIORITIES

The presidency can be analysed as Finland's effort to assess her identity in the unification project. The conception of Finland as a small and northern member state seemed to constitute the basis for Finnish action. There appeared to be a slight discrepancy between the way this identity was expressed in external and internal policies. This discrepancy even made itself evident in the title of the programme for the Finnish presidency, 'A Strong and Open Europe into the New Millennium'.[11]

One of the main tasks of the Finnish presidency was to contribute to the creation of a globally active and influential EU. Even if this part of the agenda was to a large extent determined by forces other than Finland herself, it well suited Finnish priorities. The Finnish government had frequently emphasized the value of a strong EU to a small member state.[12] The EU's international position was first promoted by developing the common crisis-management capacity at the rapid rate agreed upon by the European Council in Cologne. The crisis-management project was, even in the new form it had taken since Saint Malo, a pleasant task for Finland, which regards herself as one of the inventors of the whole project.[13] Another task that Finland adopted concerning the institutional setting of the CFSP was the promotion of coherence in the EU's external operations. The efficiency and coherence of decision-making were among those Nordic principles of administration that formed the basis for the Finnish claims concerning general institutional reform in the EU.

'Northernness' was clearly the geographical dimension of the EU's external relations that Finland tried to promote, even if it was self-evident that it was not the only dimension that would need the presidency's attention during the Finnish term. The implementation of the newly adapted Common Strategy on Russia suited the Finnish agenda. The EU's relations with Russia were further emphasized through the Northern Dimension Initiative (NDI), whereby a ministerial conference of the EU member states and partners in the northern dimension – Iceland, Norway, Latvia, Lithuania, Poland, Russia and Estonia – was planned to speed up the project.[14] In the enlargement process, the Helsinki meeting of the European Council was supposed to examine, on the basis of the European Commission's progress reports, the scope for opening EU accession talks with new applicant countries. Finland emphasized the principle according to which all applicant countries participate in the process on an equal footing and can join the EU on the basis of the same criteria.

As far as the internal policies of the EU were concerned, Finland's identity as a northern small state was reflected in the emphasis put on the reform of the EU political machinery in accordance with the administrative principles of the northern member countries. Finland stressed the openness and transparency of EU decision-making, the necessity of enhancing the efficiency and coherence of the Council of Ministers, and the need to improve action to combat fraud in the European Commission. The preparations for an IGC on institutional reform, a task assigned to Finland by the Cologne meeting of the European Council, was a more problematic project from the Finnish point of view. Basically, it corresponded to the Finnish demand for the efficiency of the EU. The whole agenda, however, seemed to be based on the interests of the big member states, a supposition which had led to the original Finnish aim of keeping the agenda as limited as possible. A society based on information and knowledge, and social and ecological responsibility were other large-scale goals in the programme for the Finnish presidency that expressed northern values. Even the topic of the Tampere meeting of the European Council, the creation of an area of freedom, security, and justice, assigned to the Finnish presidency by the Vienna summit, fitted well the Finnish aspirations concerning integration.

THE INTERNAL FUNCTIONS OF THE EU PRESIDENCY

The success of the Finnish presidency can be estimated on the basis of various criteria. One basis for this is formed by the set of functions that the presidency is associated with. To start with the administrative function, Finland seemed to carry out well – even if not without the traditional scandals – the technical burdens of the Council presidency. Around 200 meetings were arranged in Finland in the context of EU presidency, the most visible of them being the European Council meetings in Tampere (October 1999) and Helsinki (December 1999).[15] The problems in this respect appeared unexpectedly, when Germany and Austria decided to boycott the informal ministerial meetings due to the Finnish decision to exclude German from its official languages. No solution to this linguistic problem was found during the Finnish presidency.

Another originally administrative task of the presidency, which nowadays carries a remarkable political weight, is the management of the Council agenda. Finland seemed to be able to cope well with the huge agenda accruing to it. The Helsinki meeting of the European Council was able to take the decisions on almost all of the big issues that were assigned to it. In some of these issues, the decision was still more far-reaching than the original goal.[16] In some questions, however, the objectives could not be achieved. The most visible of these failures concerned the tax package, for which an agreement should have been reached before the Helsinki meeting of the European Council. When agreement could not be found in one of the three proposals for EU directives – the one concerning the taxation of savings – a political working group was set up to solve the problems.

Problems appeared also when it came to the preparations for the IGC. It was Finland's task to confirm the agenda of the Conference and to review and assess the various options concerning each issue on it.[17] The member states' opinions concerning the agenda were apparently ambiguous, making it very difficult for the presidency to define the issue. The presidency, consequently, had to change its position as late as during the Helsinki European Council meeting.[18] The result was that the final agenda for the IGC was left open and was not fixed before the launch of the Conference.[19]

Another issue, one affecting Finland's key interests, in which the objectives could not be reached, concerned the implementation of the TEU (Treaty on European Union) Article 255 on transparency.[20] According to this article, the Council was to approve, jointly with the EP, general principles and restrictions for such transparency which took account of public and individual interests, following a proposal from the European Commission. Finland aimed to create the political preconditions and efficient procedures for preparation of the transparency legislation and to reach agreement on its main elements. This aim could not, however, be fulfilled due to the postponement of the European Commission's proposal.

Finally, the Finnish presidency can be analysed through the co-ordinative function that is linked with the Council presidency. This function refers both to relations between the member states and to relations between the Council of Ministers and other EU institutions. It is a common conception that the coordinative function between differing interests can best be managed by an agent whose own position and interests in the issue are not inflexible. Therefore, small member states are arguably often better arbitrators in EU politics than big ones.[21] The smooth management of the EU agenda has already indicated that Finland did well in the coordinative function. Her own interests with the presidency were moderate – aspirations for general success rather than for the realization of her national interest. Relations with the European Commission and the EP were handled smoothly, although both of these bodies started with new memberships, and although new decision-making rules entered into force along with the Amsterdam Treaty.

With respect to the coordinative function of the Council presidency, two decisions may be considered the supreme achievements of the Finnish presidency because of their historic significance. The first was the decision to approve Turkey's candidature for membership of the EU.[22] In the preparation of this historic decision, Finland took advantage of the momentum created for rapprochement during the German presidency. In fact, Germany had tried to solve the problem of Turkey's status at the Cologne summit, but the project had been unsuccessful due to Greek and Swedish opposition.[23] It was the task of the Finnish presidency to retain this momentum and to overcome the remaining opposition in the issue. The Finnish strategy, which finally proved successful, was to keep a low profile on the Turkish issue and to prevent it from becoming politicized. The neutrality of the Finnish presidency was emphasized in the sense that Finland was not perceived as having any strong interest of her own in the issue, which was not even included in the programme for the presidency. Confirmation of Turkey's status as a candidate for membership in the EU was the result of many different factors.[24] However, it fell to the Finnish presidency to coordinate these factors so that the very concrete end result was achieved.

The creation of the crisis-management capacity can be treated as the other important achievement, and one which emphasized the coordinative function of the Council presidency. In this issue, it was the flexibility of the Finnish EU policy, as well as Finland's credibility as a compromise builder, that brought success. It was the purpose of the Finnish presidency to start developing the EU's capacity and instruments to act independently in conflict prevention and crisis management in accordance with the guidelines adopted by the Cologne meeting of the European Council.[25] Since defence has been one of the most controversial dimensions of integration, there is still much difference of opinion among the member states concerning the details and formulations of the defence dimension. The results must, consequently, please both those states, like France, who have more ambitious expectations concerning the EU's defence policy, and those states, like Sweden and Ireland, who are highly sceptical of the entire military dimension.

During the Finnish presidency, the big member states reached an agreement on the main forms of the crisis-management system, and it fell to the presidency to obtain the support of the rest of the EU for this policy. Flexibility was needed from Finland herself, as was shown by the fact that the first drafts produced by the Finnish presidency were more moderate than what was to become the decision of the Helsinki meeting of the European Council.[26] Thanks to the firm position of the government, the new guidelines of the crisis-management system were accepted in the Eduskunta without difficulty. The compromise created by the presidency was a rapid promotion of the defence dimension packaged as crisis-management capacity. Binding the military resources firmly to crisis-management activities was a precondition for the defence dimension being incorporated into the EU from the point of view of the sceptical member states. With her own position of non-alignment, Finland functioned as a credible leader in this respect. However, the achievements pleased even the opposite camp, which saw the results of the Finnish presidency – the creation of military resources and institutions in the EU – as an important step in the process of establishing a European defence.[27]

THE EXTERNAL FUNCTIONS OF THE EU PRESIDENCY

During the Finnish presidency, the focus of the EU's external relations was on the western Balkans and Russia. There were also several multilateral projects that came to a critical stage during the Finnish presidency. Participation in the negotiations of the World Trade Organization (WTO) and the renewal of the Lomé Treaty were the most challenging of these.

Promotion of the stability and reconstruction of Kosovo by different means became one of the key tasks of the Finnish presidency. The presidency's role with respect to the entire western Balkans was in many ways difficult and demanding. First, the implementation of the stability pact for south-eastern Europe was launched under Finnish leadership. The Cologne meeting of the European Council had obligated the Council and the European Commission to maintain the leading role of the EU in the promotion of stability in the region. The implementation of the stability pact was launched by establishing the so-called working tables around three themes with the countries in the regions.[28] The special representative of the EU, and the coordinator of the stability pact, Bodo Hombard, took office during the Finnish term. External pressures were directed at the presidency, as the members of the stability pact were expecting faster movement by the EU in the stabilizing actions.[29]

Another challenge was related to the relations between the EU institutions in connection with the stability pact. Cooperation between the European Council and the European Commission in safeguarding the external unity of the EU was not of the very best, and Finland tried to solve this problem by asking the two bodies to make a common report on the issue to the Helsinki meeting of the European Council (Report to the European Council on the Stability Pact and South-Eastern Europe). The report summed up the guidelines for the EU's action in the implementation of the pact and the roles of both bodies in this connection.

The internal conflicts of the EU – those between member states as well as between EU bodies – came to the fore in connection with many other projects in the Balkan. Two important decisions concerning the reconstruction of Kosovo can be taken as examples. On the eve of the Finnish presidency, the European Commission had taken the initiative to establish a new reconstruction agency for the Balkans. The new agency was to be responsible for channelling reconstruction aid to Kosovo after the damage caused by the air strikes of the North Atlantic Treaty Organization (NATO) and Serbian military action. The European Commission suggested that the new agency would be placed in Priština, or, if that was not possible, in Skopje in Macedonia. The EP suggested Priština. Greece opposed the European Commission's proposal and threatened to veto the whole project if parts of the agency were not – in addition to Priština – based in Tirana (Albania) and Montenegro. The Finnish presidency led the conciliation of this dispute on the basis of a compromise carried out behind the official process.[30] On the basis of this compromise, the administrative headquarters of the agency was located in the Greek city of Salonika and its operational headquarters in the Kosovan capital, Priština.[31]

Another dispute concerning Kosovo arose between the EU bodies on the position of the EU's aid to Kosovo in the Union budget. The EP refused to accept the European Commission's proposal to take the aid funds of 500 million euro from other budget categories, and proposed, instead, that new funds be allocated for Kosovo. The EP's proposal would have necessitated amendments to the financial agreements made by the European Council in Berlin, so the Council did not consent to them. It was the task of the Finnish presidency to mediate between the three bodies in this case, where the prestige of the bodies formed the core of the issue.[32] Finally, a compromise was reached in which, by lowering the sum to 360 million euro, the cost of rebuilding could be funded without undermining the other items in the expenditure for external relations.[33]

During her presidency, Finland was prepared to reinforce the EU's ties with Russia in various ways. The implementation of the Common Strategy on Russia was the general framework inside which Finland had planned to draft a work programme in order to strengthen the basis for democracy and a market economy in Russia. Another aim was to advance the implementation of the Partnership and Cooperation Agreement between the parties. Relations with Russia were supposed to be promoted even through the Northern Dimension programme. The advancement of all projects was, however, seriously delayed by the new course that relations between the EU and Russia took because of the Russian military action in Chechnya. The General Affairs Council of the EU expressed several times during the Finnish presidency its concern over Russia's military campaign in Chechnya, and the EU–Russian summit arranged in Finland in October already reflected the deadlock in relations. Pressures for stronger EU action grew towards the end of the Finnish presidency, until the summit in Helsinki finally decided on concrete sanctions.[34] It also enacted the 'reviewing' of the Common Strategy and the transfer of some funds from Tacis (a programme launched by the EC in 1991 to help the transition process in 13 Eastern European and Central Asian countries by providing grant-financed technical assistance) to humanitarian assistance.[35]

The deterioration of relations with Russia was reflected even in the NDI – based upon Finland's own initiative – which the Finnish presidency was supposed to advance. The NDI is a broad policy programme purporting to emphasize Russia and the Baltic region in the EU's external relations. The Finnish presidency intended to give an important stimulus to the programme, in the form of a ministerial conference between the EU member states and partners in the NDI. The conference was to support the European Commission's design to make the NDI concept more concrete. The programme did not, however, get the political backing that was planned during the Finnish presidency because of the interference of the already mentioned factors. The conflict in Chechnya affected the EU's relations with Russia, resulting in, among other things, the ministerial conference on the NDI being watered down.[36] The entire programme did not, however, get stranded, as the Helsinki meeting of the European Council invited the European Commission to prepare an action plan on the policy area. The European Council even welcomed the Swedish intention to organize a follow-up conference on the NDI. However, the fact, remains that, instead of a celebration of the EU's relations with Russia, it was the lot of the Finnish presidency to have to cope with another crisis in these relations.

Another process in the EU's external relations that, for reasons that had nothing to do with the presidency itself, was unsuccessful was the preparations for the negotiations in the WTO. The European Commission and the member states had reached an agreement on the EU's position concerning the WTO agenda already before the Finnish presidency. The presidency's task was to defend this position in international contexts and to complete it in detail.[37] Due to a systematic approach based on good preparation, Finland coped well with the arbitration between the member states.[38] The EU's position was completed in October 1999. The relationship between the presidency and the European Commission was, however, not entirely trouble-free in this field that embraces both the first and the second pillars, as the division of labour was not always clear-cut.[39] The WTO meeting in Seattle, however, failed to set the agenda for the new round of negotiations, consequently hindering Finland from completing her task in this regard.

SUMMARY

In general, the Finnish presidency of the EU seemed to correspond to the expectations based upon the role of Finland as a small, new, and northern member state. Some general characterizations can be given of the Finnish presidency; however, we must take into account that exceptions to the general rule are evident. To keep the EU machinery functioning seems to have formed the guiding principle of the Finnish leadership. Finland, consequently, tried to get the EU to take the decisions that were assigned to her term of office. The fulfilment of this goal presupposed the effective preparation of issues and a systematic planning.[40] It even presupposed a distancing from immediate national interests in the issues concerned. In the study conducted upon the Finnish presidency,[41] a number of issues could be pointed out where Finland – either before the conciliation process started or during the process – distanced herself from her national objectives. At the level of the very large-scale political projects, the Lome Treaty and the enlargement process can be mentioned as examples of the first case, and the creation of the crisis-management capacity and the agenda of the IGC as examples of the second.[42]

There was, however, one specific field where systematic efforts were taken in order to leave the presidency's own imprint on EU structures. Finland tried, in various forms, to influence the structures and practices of decision-making in the EU, and, in particular, in the Council. This was generally done in the spirit of the Nordic principles of administration: openness, efficacy, and rationality. The Finnish presidency was the first to publish agendas for meetings on the Web, on its home page. Finland even started to apply some points of the Trumpf-Piris report on Council reform before it was adopted by the Helsinki summit.[43] A clear tendency to simplify the EU's practices could be perceived even in the framework of the CFSP and Euro-11 (now Euro-12, the meetings of the finance ministers of the countries in the single currency area).

As for the presidency's working methods, Finland was praised for the professional way in which things falling to her term of office were prepared. The Finnish capacity for conciliation was also considered successful. The role as a small member state with moderate national interests and no hidden agendas evidently increased Finland's credibility as compromise-builder. Success, however, has its reverse, and, in the case of the Finnish presidency, what was pragmatic and well-planned appeared to many to be lack of imagination and political vision. The Finnish effectiveness in planning turned into inflexibility in some cases and an unnecessary insistence on the planned agenda. In general, Finland was not accused of a lack of credibility in representing the CFSP. Some difficulties could still be perceived in Finland's capacity to adopt the harsh rhetoric of the great powers, which even many large members of the EU expected of the one speaking on behalf of the EU.

The Finnish expectations of her first EU presidency could be considered realistic. The closer the presidency approached, the more the aspirations centred on just an efficient management of the overwhelming agenda. In the end, however, the Finns seemed to have left their imprint on the process of unification. The results could be treated as a cautious introduction of the 'northern' values into European integration. Principles such as openness, efficiency, and coherence reinforced their grip on the EU administration. The EU's attention was drawn to the territories and problems around its northern borders, and factors independent of the Finnish presidency helped to show that this area is not free of problems. The successful leadership of the common European project presumably helped Finland to get rid of her old feeling of inferiority stemming from her Cold War identity (as viewed within Finland) as an outsider – a peripheral small state all on her own. At the same time, it forced the country to identify her place – her own goals and values – in the common European community.

NOTES

1. Pinder conceptualizes this as a rivalry between the federal idea and that of national sovereignty. See J. Pinder, *The Building of the European Union* (Oxford: Oxford University Press, 1998), pp. 3–26. Joseph Weiler perceives the EU as an interaction between federalist legal structures and an intergovernmental political system. See J.H.H. Weiler, *The Constitution of Europe* (Cambridge: Cambridge University Press, 1999), pp. 10–96.
2. The two-chamber system of representation was included in the plan for a political community (1952–54), which was finally stranded in the French Parliament. See R. Cardozo, 'The Project for a Political Community', in R. Pryce (ed.) *The Dynamics of European Union* (London: Routledge, 1989), p. 52.
3. For a view of the historical balancing between federalism and inter-governmentalism, see T. Tiilikainen, *Europe and Finland: Defining the Political Identity of Finland in Western Europe* (Aldershot: Ashgate, 1998).
4. See P. Sherrington, *The Council of Ministers* (London: Pinter, 2000), p. 13.
5. See E. Kirchner, *Decision-Making in the European Communities* (Manchester: Manchester University Press, 1992), pp. 80–1. Kirchner's categorization matches that of Helen Wallace, who divides the presidency's roles into the management of the Council, the promotion of political initiatives, the brokering of packages, liaison with other Community bodies, and spokesman. See H. Wallace, 'The Presidency: Tasks and Evolution', in C.O. Nuallain (ed.) *The Presidency of the European Council of Ministers* (London: Croom Helm, 1985), pp. 10–20.
6. Schout specifies the elements of success as mediation skills, technical expertise, networks, luck, careful preparation, good people, and neutrality. See A. Schout, 'The Presidency as a Juggler: Managing Conflicting Expectations', *Eipascope* 2 (1998), pp. 2–10. Verbeke and van de Voorde define the key skills as neutrality, credibility, skill and tact, in-depth knowledge of the dossiers, good collaboration with other institutions, and attentiveness to the full participation of all member countries in decision-making and internal cohesion. See J. Verbeke and W. van de Voorde, 'The Presidency of the European Union; Some Reflections on Current Practice and Recent Evolutions', *Studia Diplomatica* 47:3 (1994), pp. 29–40.
7. Finland was in a key position in the Security and Co-operation in Europe - process (currently Organization for Security and Cooperation in Europe [OSCE]), whose first conference it hosted in Helsinki in 1975. In the 1980s, Finland hosted several meetings of the US and Soviet leaders.
8. Concerning national preparations, see A. Simula, 'Suomen EU-puheenjohtajuus hallinnollisten järjestelyjen näkökulmasta', in T. Martikainen and T. Tiilikainen (eds) *Suomi EU:n johdossa: Tutkimus Suomen puheenjohtajuudesta 1999* (Helsinki: Helsingin yliopisto, Yleisen

valtio-opin laitos, Acta Politica 13, 2000), pp. 21–50. Stubb refers to the fact that decisions on the calendar for informal and formal Council meetings were taken as early as 1997, when preparations for the presidency programme began. See A. Stubb, 'The Finnish Presidency', *Journal of Common Market Studies*, Annual Review of the EU 1999/2000, p. 50.

9. All in all, 1,500 people participated in these training programmes, the costs (1996–99) of which rose to 88 million Finnish marks (15 million euro).
10. In its meeting in Cologne, the European Council paid attention to the fact that the European Commission was supposed to give its progress reports on the applicant countries in autumn 1999 and that these reports formed the basis for any decisions to be taken by the Helsinki meeting of the European Council. The Cologne summit even invited the Finnish presidency to draw up, in relation to the Intergovernmental Conference on institutional questions, a comprehensive report explaining and taking stock of options for resolving the issues to be settled. In the framework of the Common European Security and Defence Policy, the Cologne meeting of the European Council invited the Finnish presidency to continue the work of creating a crisis-management system in accordance with the outlines approved by it (Presidency Conclusions, Cologne European Council, 3 and 4 June 1999).
11. See Programme for the Finnish Presidency of the European Union, SN 2940/2/99 REV 2.
12. See, for instance, 'Finland's points of departure and objectives at the 1996 Intergovernmental Conference', Report to the Parliament by the Council of State, 27 February 1996.
13. The crisis-management capacity of the EU that was agreed upon in the IGC held in 1996–97 was largely based upon a Finnish-Swedish initiative. According to an official Finnish interpretation, the creation of a military crisis-management system in the EU will not compromise the Finnish policy of non-alignment.
14. An extensive analysis of the NDI can be found in D. Arter, 'Small State Influence Within the EU: The Case of Finland's "Northern Dimension Initiative"', *Journal of Common Market Studies* 38:5 (2000), pp. 677–97.
15. In addition to the two summits, 14 ministerial meetings were arranged and 64 meetings for civil servants. The rest were other meetings related to the presidency. See Simula, 'Suomen EU-puheenjohtajuus', p. 34.
16. The agreement on Turkey's status as an official membership candidate was not a part of the original Finnish programme for the presidency. The progress report presented on the common crisis-management capacity is much more far-reaching than what is referred to in the programme for the Finnish presidency or in the Cologne declaration. See Presidency Conclusions, Annex III: European Council Declaration on Strengthening the Common European Policy on Security and Defence.
17. Finland's role with the IGC was given in the following way in the Cologne declaration: 'The European Council invites the incoming Presidency to draw up, on its own responsibility, for the European Council meeting in Helsinki, a comprehensive report explaining and taking stock of options for resolving the issues to be settled.'
18. *European Report* (2459), 15 December 1999.
19. The formulation in the Presidency conclusions was as follows: 'The Conference will examine the size and composition of the Commission, the

weighting of votes in the Council and the possible extension of qualified majority voting in the Council, as well as other necessary amendments to the Treaties arising as regards the European institutions in connection with the above issues and in implementing the Treaty of Amsterdam' (Presidency Conclusions, Helsinki European Council, 10 and 11 December 1999).

20. According to Article 255, 'Any citizen of the Union, and any natural or legal person residing or having its registered office in a Member State, shall have right of access to European Parliament, Council and Commission documents, subject to the principles and the conditions to be defined in accordance with paragraphs 2 and 3.'

21. See Kirchner, *Decision-Making in the European Communities*, p. 83.

22. The analysis concerning Finland's role is based upon P. Peltonen, 'Päätöksenteko Euroopan unionissa – kahdeksan esimerkkitapausta puheenjohtajan näkökulmasta', in Martikainen and Tiilikainen (eds) *Suomi EU:n johdossa*, pp. 107–62. For her study, Peltonen conducted extensive interviews both during the Finnish presidency and afterwards.

23. Peltonen, 'Päätöksenteko Euroopan unionissa', p. 112.

24. One of these factors was the European Commission's positive stance on the issue taken during the Finnish presidency. Another was the US contribution through its contacts with Greece and Turkey. See Peltonen, 'Päätöksenteko Euroopan unionissa', p. 116.

25. The exact formulation in the Cologne summit was as follows: 'In pursuit of our Common Foreign and Security Policy objectives and the progressive framing of a common defence policy, we are convinced that the Council should have the ability to take decisions on the full range of conflict prevention and crisis management tasks defined in the Treaty of European Union, the "Petersberg tasks". To this end the Union must have the capacity for autonomous action, backed up by credible military forces, the means to decide to use them, and a readiness to do so without prejudice to actions by NATO.' See Presidency Conclusions, Annex III.

26. The Finnish drafts departed from the idea that the size and forms of EU military units (the headline goals) will not be confirmed in Helsinki. The Finnish drafts did rely more upon cooperation between the EU and NATO than the final decision. Even the level of EU military organization became higher than the one presented in the original drafts. See The Finnish Presidency, Non-Paper, 'Elements for the Presidency Progress Report to the Helsinki European Council on Strengthening of the Common European Policy on Security and Defence'.

27. The French newspaper *Le Monde*, for instance, interpreted the results of the Helsinki Summit as an important step in the creation of a European identity due to the strengthening of the defence dimension. The other daily newspaper, *Le Figaro*, announced in its headline, 'A 60,000 man army for Europe'. See Ministry of Foreign Affairs, Media Report, HELD 103–1, 7 January 2000.

28. The working table on economic reconstruction, development and cooperation started its activities first. The working tables on democratization and human rights and defence and security affairs also held their inaugural meetings during the Finnish presidency. See General Affairs Council, 11 October 1999, 11651/99.

29. T. Tiilikainen, 'Suomi johtajana EU:n ulkosuhteissa', in Martikainen and

Tiilikainen (eds) *Suomi EU:n johdossa*, p. 173.
30. Ibid., p. 174.
31. Greece had insisted that the headquarters would be based in Salonika, whereas the Commission, supported by a majority of member states, preferred Priština. See *European Report*, no. 2426, V, p. 10.
32. See Peltonen, 'Päätöksenteko Euroopan unionissa', p. 151.
33. See *European Report*, no. 2460, I, p. 4.
34. Criticism came from the EP, which demanded that the EU freeze Tacis aid to Russia if that country did not stop its military campaign in Chechnya. See *Bulletin EU* 10 (1999).
35. See Presidency Conclusions, Helsinki European Council 10 and 11 December 1999, Annex II.
36. The EU foreign ministers did not attend the ministerial conference as a protest against the Russian policy in Chechnya.
37. The EU favoured an extensive agenda for the WTO negotiations, which implied that areas such as regulation on employment, environmental legislation, and the relationship between trade and investments and trade and concurrence were to be considered together with liberalizing acts. See *Bulletin EU* 6 (1999).
38. A major part of the work took place in the Article 133 committee, whose unofficial meeting in Kittilä was of key importance. Finland's capacity for promoting compromise has been assessed, for example, in 'EU/WTO: Florence Trade Council to Settle Seattle Strategy', *European Report* 2438 (1999); or in 'EU/WTO: EU Still Split over Seattle Agenda', *European Report* 2443 (1999).
39. This came up in those (about 100) interviews done in the context of the research project on the Finnish presidency, the results of which were summed up in the volume edited by Martikainen and Tiilikainen, *Suomi EU:n johdossa*.
40. The preparation of issues has been regarded as one of the great virtues of the Finnish presidency. See Stubb, 'The Finnish Presidency', p. 49.
41. See Martikainen and Tiilikainen, *Suomi EU:n johdossa*.
42. The Finnish government had been critical of the structure of the Lomé system, and in the enlargement process it had been in favour of a more restricted second round. In the creation of the crisis-management system, Finland had originally supported a more cautious approach; concerning the IGC, it had worked for the confirmation of a closed agenda. See Tiilikainen, 'Suomi johtajana EU:n ulkosuhteissa', pp. 171 and 176; and Peltonen, 'Päätöksenteko Euroopan unionissa', p. 110.
43. The guidelines for reform and operational recommendations are based upon the so-called Trumpf-Piris report published in March 1999. The report was drawn up by a working party chaired by the Secretary-General of the Council, Mr Trumpf, with Mr Piris as its deputy chairperson.

7

The Common Foreign and Security Policy

Prior to its accession to the EU, Finland was not regarded as an ideal member of the CFSP. In Maastricht, the 12 member states of the EC had agreed on deepening the former political cooperation into the form of a common foreign and security policy. The entrance of the three non-aligned states to the newly established EU was widely expected to hamper further integration in this policy field where the deepening of integration had proved to be problematic from the start.

The advent of Finnish membership proved these expectations wrong. The Finnish policy has indicated a wholehearted commitment to the project of European integration, implying loyal and constructive participation even in the CFSP. Non-alignment, like other key principles of Finnish Cold War foreign policy, has not placed any constraints on Finnish participation in the common EU policy. In this chapter, Finnish participation in the CFSP is analysed from the point of view of national objectives. First, the starting points for Finland's participation are assessed by analysing the shift from its Cold War foreign policy to the present policy of active and unreserved participation in the CFSP. Then, Finland's position and objectives are analysed, firstly by pinpointing its position in the general institutional structure of the CFSP, and secondly by extending the analysis to the key fields of the CFSP.

THE CONDITIONS OF ENTRANCE

Finnish participation in the CFSP became one of the controversial issues in the political campaign on membership which preceded the membership referendum in 1994. Participation in the CFSP seemed to question all the key principles of Finnish Cold War foreign policy, which had already formed the strongest official arguments against Finnish EC membership up to the beginning of the 1990s (see Chapter 2). These principles – constituting the main tenets of Finnish foreign policy – were neutrality, sovereignty of foreign policy, and good relations with the Soviet Union. When the political situation suddenly changed, and the moment arrived for the achievement of Finnish EC membership, clear difficulties could be perceived in coping with the old principles.

The strategy adopted by the political leadership could be called 'the strategy of continuity'.[1] Elements of change manifested by the new policy were played down and the links – and elements of continuity – between the old and new policies were emphasized. The principles that seemed to be at odds with participation in the CFSP formed the key principles of the old policy; therefore, skilful tactics were needed to dispel the contradictions that existed and to make the old principles seem compatible with the new policy.

The first of these principles was that of neutrality, which was ostensibly in direct contradiction to full-scale participation in the CFSP. The political leadership, however, never declared the old principle of neutrality void. Instead, it was claimed to have been given a new meaning in the new political context.[2] This was expressed by the government in the following way: 'The post-Cold War situation puts the emphasis on the core of Finnish neutrality and its position outside military alliances, purporting to make Finnish neutrality possible in the event of war. The aim is supported by a decent national defence that is credible with respect to the country's security environment.'[3] Gradually, therefore, the concept of neutrality disappeared from the official terminology, being effectively replaced by its 'hard core', that is, military non-alignment.[4] The starting point for Finland's participation in the CFSP has, consequently, been that military non-alignment is compatible with full participation in the CFSP.[5]

The other principle that had furnished a reason for Finland's exclusion from the EC was the sovereignty of foreign policy. Sovereignty was regarded as a necessary condition for the maintenance of the policy of neutrality and of good relations with the Soviet Union.[6] The demand of sovereignty had made Finnish participation in supranational institutions impossible. The conflict between the sovereignty principle and participation in the CFSP was played down by referring to the intergovernmental character of the second pillar, on the one hand, and to the goals of the CFSP that Finland shared, on the other hand.[7] The system of unanimous decision-making was seen to provide Finland with the necessary back door she needed in order to prevent her essential foreign policy interests from being violated. In a speech delivered in August 1995, Foreign Minister Tarja Halonen still asserted that a significant shift to majority decisions in the CFSP could not be anticipated.[8] After only six months, moderate support for use of qualified majority voting in CFSP matters was written into the government's position on the 1996–97 IGC.[9]

The third principle that had to be rendered compatible with participation in the CFSP was the maintenance of good relations with the neighbouring country to the east. As a result of two wars with the Soviet Union in connection with the Second World War, the doctrine which held that the maintenance of good relations with this big neighbour should be a priority for Finnish foreign policy had become unquestionable. Due to the collapse of the Soviet Union in December 1991 – and the consequent lapse of the FCMA treaty with Finland – the doctrine had lost much of its impact. Finland, in any case, shared a common border of more than 1,000 kilometres with the Soviet Union's successor, Russia, which was suffering from immense instability. In the official membership rhetoric, continuity was perceived even between the 'special relationship with the eastern neighbour' and participation in the CFSP.[10] In the new situation, this relationship would be implemented through the EU, whose significance for Russian stability and welfare could be increased by Finnish EU membership.[11]

As a result of the strategy of continuity, Finnish participation in the CFSP was made to appear reasonably compatible with Finland's long-term foreign policy, and the theme was therefore prevented from becoming a major issue in the political campaign preceding the referendum to join the EU.[12] The result was that Finland, in effect, executed a volte-face by turning from a strict policy of neutrality to active and unreserved participation in the CFSP. Consequently, Finland did not seek any reservations as far as her participation in the CFSP was concerned. On the contrary, the country committed herself to develop this policy area, embracing even defence policy openly and constructively.[13]

The reason for this cooperative position can be found in the security policy significance that Finnish EU membership was vested with right from the start. In its 1995 report to parliament, the government stated that 'membership of the European Union strengthens the basis for Finnish security policy and provides Finland with a key channel to promote its interests and bear its responsibility in international relations'.[14] This sentiment was largely shared by the people who, from the first year of EU membership, have perceived that Finnish membership has strengthened Finland's security.[15] In the course of Finnish EU membership, and linked with the deepening of the common security and defence policy (ESDP), the security policy role of EU membership has been defined more and more concretely. In the latest report to parliament, issued by the government in June 2001, the security policy role of EU membership was defined in the following way: 'A strong Union based on solidarity will also benefit Finland's security situation and help to prevent the eruption of crises that may affect Finland, as well as improve Finland's ability to deal with such crises.'[16]

Right from the outset of its EU membership, Finland made it clear that her former policy of neutrality would not put any constraints on her participation in the CFSP. Like the other non-aligned members of the EU, Finland gained observer status in the Western European Union (WEU) at the beginning of 1995. The relationship between this status and the position of non-alignment did not evoke any criticism in the domestic political debate.[17] Thus far, and due also to the intensive cooperation with NATO, it had become clear that in the new political situation the policy of non-alignment could be vested with a flexibility that would not have been possible in the Cold War climate.[18]

In spite of this openness and flexibility, the fact remains that no serious debate took place about the future of Finnish non-alignment in the EU during the initial years of membership. It seemed to be the general assumption that the reference to the possibility of a common defence included in the Maastricht Treaty would remain a dead letter and that Finnish non-alignment would not be challenged by its EU membership.[19] However, a certain division of opinion seemed to prevail in the coalition government as far as the defence dimension of the EU was concerned. Among the Left Alliance and the Green League, the attitude towards the deepening of the defence dimension has been more critical from the very beginning, whereas the National Coalition has been more neutral in this respect (see Chapter 3). A clash could be perceived even between the key players in Finnish foreign and security policy. Prime Minister Paavo Lipponen, who has been in favour of a deepening of the EU in general, showed from the beginning more sympathy for the defence dimension than Foreign Minister Tarja Halonen, who, although also a member of the same SDP, remained true to the radical values of her past.[20]

The IGC of 1996–97 brought the issue of a deepening defence dimension into open political debate and forced the government to formulate a national position on it. In this situation, the government created a policy line that was to gain some continuity as far as the Finnish position on the development of a common defence was concerned. The policy line even formed the basis of the common Finnish–Swedish initiative made to the IGC.[21] Together, these countries stressed the necessity of creating a military crisis-management capacity for the EU as well as the possibility of the non-aligned members' participation in the activities launched within its framework. The message of the initiative was twofold. Firstly, it expressed the willingness of the two non-aligned EU members to extend the project of integration into the military field. But, secondly, it also expressed the aspiration to limit this field of integration to crisis management, leaving territorial defence to NATO.

Even if the Finnish government has been eager to guide the EU's defence dimension in the direction of crisis management, it has not – at least not publicly – opposed more far-reaching forms of integration in this field. The national position in the 1996–97 IGC was formulated in the following way in the government's report to parliament:

> Crisis-management tasks can be separated from actual defence functions which, for the countries that are NATO members, are still under the responsibility of the organisation and which the militarily non-aligned countries take care of themselves. In the TEU, a common defence is mentioned as a possible long-range objective. In the present conditions, development of the defence dimension means strengthening crisis-management and peacekeeping capabilities.[22]

As far as the other issues on the IGC's agenda were concerned, Finland seemed to have taken a flexible position towards the strengthening of the CFSP. In line with the general argument presented at the EU level in favour of the deepening of the second pillar, the Finnish government stressed the need to make the EU more effective in international relations.[23] For this purpose, the government accepted the increase of majority decisions as well as the establishment of the policy-planning and early-warning unit within the Council Secretariat. But Finland was even willing to accept the much more far-reaching amendment – and one of the hot potatoes of the IGC – conferring a legal personality on the EU.[24] Finland, however, was not among those few member states that wished to make CFSP matters subject to similar rules and practices as the first pillar (EC), but supported instead the maintenance of the CFSP as intergovernmental cooperation.[25]

The Amsterdam Treaty, signed in 1997, seemed to bring relief to the non-aligned members of the EU, as it responded to the need to deepen the defence dimension by creating a military crisis-management capacity for the Union, and failed, consequently, to merge the EU and the WEU.[26] Finland and Sweden celebrated the success of their common initiative on crisis management, even though an important change of formulations had been made at the insistence of the large member states.[27] Things, however, started to change as a result of the Saint Malo process launched in the autumn of 1998, with the sudden turnabout in British EU policy, which led to a swift acceleration in the common defence policy.[28] As it soon became evident that Finland had to deal with the new turn of the defence dimension as one of the key challenges of its first EU presidency, demands grew concerning the solidity of its national position (see Chapter 6).

The Finnish government was none too eager to deliberate on the changes that the Saint Malo process and the British change of policy would bring to the EU. It tended to emphasize that the process was fully in line with the Amsterdam Treaty, the fulfilment of which it would only accelerate.[29] The flexibility of the Finnish position was practically tested when the Cologne meeting of the European Council invited the Finnish presidency of the EU to advance the creation of a military crisis-management system. In this situation, the government chose to ignore the national suspicions connected with the deepening military dimension of the EU and exerted effective leadership of the process at the EU level. The results of the Helsinki meeting of the European Council – the decision on the size and details of the crisis-management troops as well as on the new military organization – were more far-reaching than the Finnish national goals.[30] This did not, however, ignite any controversy in the national political debate, even if the newspapers did refer to the key role that the large member states were playing in the crisis-management process.[31] The decision of the Helsinki meeting of the European Council was approved by the Eduskunta in November 1999. Finland has, subsequently, offered to make available to the EU its rapid deployment force set up for the purposes of international crisis management. Its total strength is 2,000 soldiers.

Due to the comprehensive reasons for Finnish EU membership, the Finnish government has treated the deepening of European integration as beneficial from the Finnish point of view. In this context, it has even been able to accept the integration of the new military dimension, as this dimension inevitably plays a major role when it comes to the credibility and effectiveness of the EU in the international arena. But clear limits to this positive attitude do seem to exist – limits that are dictated more by general Finnish security policy interests than by its commitment to the principle of non-alignment.

In parallel with the support given to the EU's defence dimension, the Finnish government has started to stress the value of the transatlantic alliance and the US presence in Europe.[32] The same message has been signalled by a formulation according to which it is not meaningful to create a double system of defence in Europe. At the general European level, Finland sees the US presence as a necessary counterbalance to the position that Russia, armed with its nuclear weapons, takes in Europe. As long as the future of a purely EU-based defence system is highly unclear, it is not rational – from the point of view of Finnish security needs – to question the existing transatlantic system. Still, one cannot disregard the possibility that the protection afforded by this transatlantic system can best be achieved through the EU and the mutual dependence that has been created between it and NATO. This leads to a political readiness to partici-pate in the deepening of the EU's defence dimension. The possible extent of this process is anticipated by the programme of the second Lipponen government, in which the traditional policy of Finnish non-alignment is relaxed and becomes simply an instrument for national security policy. The programme defines credible defence as the basis of Finnish security policy and states that stability in northern Europe can, under the present circumstances, be best promoted by military non-alignment.[33]

The government is, therefore, not actively striving for membership of NATO. At the same time, however, it does not vehemently oppose a development that might be transformed into a heavy argument for Finnish NATO membership, namely, the deepening of the EU's defence dimen-sion. It seems that membership of NATO would be even easier for the Finnish people to accept if it were conceived as a part of the deepening defence dimension of the EU. In general, the Finnish people have demon-strated a more positive attitude towards defence cooperation in the framework of the EU, as is indicated, for instance, by a survey carried out in July 2000, according to which 60 per cent of Finns supported the attachment of security guarantees to EU treaties.[34]

From the perspective of Finnish security policy, the worst alternative – and one that might well increase pressure against Finnish non-alignment – is the establishment of a defence core with explicit security guarantees inside the EU. Even if such a development could be regarded as reinforcing the international position of the EU in accordance with Finnish aspirations, it would make the position of the non-aligned EU members more unclear. The position adopted by the government in the IGC held in 2000 reflected its flexibility even in this delicate matter of core-building. The Finnish government did not oppose 'flexible integration' in defence policy even if a general condition for flexibility was that it should take place inside the existing institutions and in accordance with common rules.[35]

ADAPTATION TO THE GEOGRAPHICAL SCOPE OF THE CFSP

Adaptation to the CFSP has, in Finland's case, implied that a new profile has been given to Finnish foreign policy in terms of both its geographical and ideological scope. Before EU membership, the immediate focus of

Finnish foreign policy was on relations with its neighbours, the Soviet Union – subsequently, Russia – and the Nordic countries, in particular, Sweden, Norway, and Denmark. EU membership has changed the geographical profile of Finland's external relations, firstly by bringing EU members, for natural reasons, into the very core of this policy area. Finland has formed a close relationship with some large member states, particularly Germany – a key supporter of Finland during the membership negotiations.[36] The security policy motivation and the firm commitment to integration it has brought about have pushed Finland towards the group of EU members most supportive of integration.

Attention has been paid to the fact that Finland's exemplary adaptation to EU membership has decreased the importance of her neighbours in her foreign policy.[37] This problem seems to be most acute in the case of the Nordic countries with whom Finland shares a long common history, and common social and political values. The problem has been further emphasized by the fact that three of the five Nordic countries are EU members, a fact which would, apparently, provide a perfect platform for cooperation. When Finland and Sweden joined the EU (Denmark had joined as early as 1973), the Nordic countries signalled that they did not intend to constitute a Nordic bloc in the Union. Indeed, they purportedly wanted their memberships to be treated individually.[38] However, at times, this has led to criticism of the inability of the Nordic EU members to take advantage of their cultural and geopolitical proximity in the EU.[39] In part, the striking lack of Nordic cooperation in the EU has been explained by defective machinery. Coordination of policies between the Nordic countries has been as non-existent in the CFSP as in other fields of EU policies.[40] The main cause has, however, been found in defective political will and, in particular, in Finland's more pro-European attitude, which causes her to seek other allies.

There is, however, some evidence of coordinated activities between Finland and the other Nordic countries in the CFSP. The Finnish–Swedish initiative on crisis management and its implications for the EU have been discussed earlier in this chapter. The Nordic countries have even established a common pool of forces, NORDCAPS (Nordic Coordinated Arrangement for Military Peace Support), to be utilized in, among other things, EU-led crisis-management operations, in which all the Nordic countries participate. In general, however, coordination is weak when we consider the cultural and historical background that exists for cooperation.

As far as the role of Russia in Finnish foreign policy is concerned, EU membership has contributed both to the normalization and multi-lateralization of relations. The precondition for this change took place when, along with the collapse of the Soviet Union in December 1991, the FCMA treaty lapsed and was replaced by a Treaty on Cooperation and Mutual Amity with Russia. This treaty lacks stipulations concerning military cooperation. Finland's EU membership turned this previously overemphasized area into a part of the CFSP. A major part of Finland's relations with Russia is now handled through this multilateral forum, which, furthermore, has forced Finland to adapt herself to the core principles of the common policy. For Finland, this has put an end both to her cautiousness in relations with Russia and to her previous unwillingness to criticize Russian policies.[41] Pursiainen shows how the Russian wars in Chechnya, starting in 1995 and 1999, respectively, have provided a showcase for the new Finnish policy.[42] As early as the first month of her EU membership, Finland – represented by Prime Minister Esko Aho – was called on to deliver the EU's criticism of the Russian action to the Russian leadership. Finland adopted the new role, and the prime minister appears to have been well aware of the importance of the situation for Finland's EU membership. The situation repeated itself when Finland, during its Council presidency in 1999, had to communicate the EU's increasing criticism of the Russian military action in Chechnya. This time, the EU's policy culminated in the extreme form of imposing political and economic sanctions against Russia, an action that, prior to Finnish EU membership, had been presented as a worst-case scenario of events cuased by EU membership. Finland, however, acquitted herself well in a situation which, from the national perspective at least, was a delicate one.

The change that has occurred in the place of Russia in Finland's foreign policy has not, as stated earlier in this chapter, resulted in a total neglect of Russia among the priorities of Finnish policy.[43] According to Pursiainen, Finland has been one of the most active member states in harmonizing the EU's relations with Russia. Finland promoted the adoption of the Common Strategy on Russia, which – when adopted by the 1999 Cologne meeting of the European Council – was the first common strategy in accordance with the instrument established in the Amsterdam Treaty. The Northern Dimension Initiative (NDI) – even if it does not take place in the framework of the CFSP – has been another more comprehensive project purporting to advance the EU's relations with Russia.

In addition to the transformation of Finnish foreign policy, participation in the CFSP has widened Finnish foreign policy by bringing into its scope countries and territories which were largely ignored previously. The EU's Mediterranean policy forces Finland to pay increasing attention to the Mediterranean area, which has historically been of much greater importance to southern than to northern Europe. Finland has never been a colonial power and consequently lacks those cultural and historical ties that bind the majority of EU members to their geographically distant colonies. During its Council presidency, Finland's adaptation to the geographical scope of the CFSP was practically tested, for instance, when the country led the EU's policies towards the conflict in East Timor and the military *coup d'état* in Pakistan. Both are examples of areas that generally have fallen outside the scope of Finnish foreign policy.[44]

Another important geographical area which has demanded increasing attention during Finland's EU membership is the Middle East. Even in this case, the former policy line, which demonstrated strict neutrality vis-à-vis Israel and the Palestinians has been replaced by the policy line of the EU. In this respect, the EU has been more critical of Israeli action in the crisis than has Finland in the past. Much attention was paid to the change in Finnish policy in connection with a vote in the United Nations (UN) in October 2000. In a vote of the General Assembly in which 92 UN members condemned Israel for the use of force against the Palestinians, Finland was the only Nordic country to support this condemnation in a case where even the EU was divided.[45]

ADAPTATION TO THE IDEOLOGICAL SCOPE OF THE CFSP

In the previous sections, Finland's participation in the CFSP was said to be contoured mainly in terms of a flexible adaptation in which not even those areas of foreign policy that were formerly the most sensitive delayed progress. A similar picture can be drawn of the ideological orientation of Finland's foreign policy, namely, the position with respect to the key institutions and principles of the international system. A gradual movement towards the position adopted by the majority of EU members can be perceived even here in many important issues.

The UN – with its system of collective security – has traditionally had an important place in Finland's foreign policy. The leading principles of the UN Charter have formed the very core of Finnish policy in issues of international politics, and Finland's strong contribution to UN peace-keeping forces has been widely recognized.[46] In a study on Finland's UN policy during the 1990s, Unto Vesa concludes that during her EU membership Finland has clearly moved closer to the other EU members than to her previous allies, the Nordic countries.[47] This is a natural result of the coordination of UN policies taking place in the framework of the CFSP. The Kosovo crisis was an extreme example of this new alliance. Finland clearly distanced herself from her old policy of giving primacy to the Charter principles when the Finnish leadership, together with the rest of the EU, considered the NATO air strikes legitimate even though they lacked a UN mandate.[48] The government's policy became the subject of a heated domestic debate, which – as Forsberg shows – demonstrated new divisions instead of the old polarization of opinion between the political right and left, the typical division in these kinds of questions.[49] While the most vociferous criticism of the air strikes came from the radical left, some notable left-wing politicians (actually 1960s radicals, as Forsberg shows) supported the operation on moral grounds.

The national legislation on peacekeeping can be singled out as another area showing the increasing emphasis on the EU which is taking place at the expense of the UN. Up to 1995, Finland's participation in international peacekeeping operations was based on two leading principles. The first was the necessity for a UN or OSCE (Organization for Security and Cooperation in Europe) mandate for such operations. The second was that participation in peace enforcement was prohibited. Peace enforcement meaning the use of armed forces to create a cease-fire. Finnish soldiers were allowed to use force only for self-defence. Both principles were motivated by the fact that in the sensitive area of peacekeeping, solid ground was needed for international action. Peace enforcement was not regarded as a suitable form of operation for a small state. Since Finland joined the EU, a more flexible attitude has been adopted vis-à-vis both of these principles. Since 1995, Finnish peacekeeping legislation has been amended several times, purportedly to allow Finland to participate in new types of crisis-management operations. An amendment in 1995 authorized 'extended peacekeeping', implying the possibility of more extensive use of force.[50] In this regard, however, parliament must be heard in the case. The amendment of 2001 further increased the compatibility of Finnish peacekeeping legislation with the EU treaties which, since 1999, have entitled the EU to carry out all types of crisis-management operations.[51] The prohibition of participation in peace enforcement was abolished in connections other than those taking place in the framework of Articles 42 or 51 of the UN Charter. The Finnish policy on the NATO air strikes in Kosovo indicated that even the other key principle of Finnish peacekeeping policy, the necessity for a UN or OSCE mandate, has become more flexible. Moreover, an amendment made to the peacekeeping legislation in 2001 enables Finland to participate in humanitarian operations – or in the protection of such operations – at the request of UN organizations or agencies.[52]

There is one particular issue in Finnish foreign and security policy, however, which has received much attention, as Finland has been unusually slow and hesitant to adopt the EU's position. Finland is the only member state of the EU that has not signed the international convention banning anti-personnel landmines, adopted in Ottawa in 1997. This is a result of the key role that landmines play in the defence of Finland's long land borders. Due to the pressure put on Finland by the other EU members, as well as by civil organizations, the government has undertaken to replace the landmines with other weapon systems by 2006.

Finally, the last ideological shift discussed here as a manifestation of the transformation of Finnish foreign policy relates to human rights. Since the early days of Finnish EU membership, the promotion of human rights has taken a prominent position as one of the new fields of Finnish foreign policy. In addition to the impact of EU membership on this new tendency, the role of President Tarja Halonen – foreign minister from 1995 until the start of her presidency in 2000 – cannot be ignored. In 1998, the government committed itself to report to parliament on the progress of its human rights policy at regular intervals. In 2002, the third report will be submitted to parliament. The Finnish human rights policy centres on the rights of women, children, minorities, and indigenous peoples. In addition, the rights of the disabled, human trafficking, and torture are of special importance. Finland also works actively to abolish capital punishment and racism in the world. During its EU presidency, Finland even made an effort to raise the profile of human rights in the Union. The EU's annual human rights report, the discussion forum, and a significant increase in contacts with the non-governmental organizations were initiated during the Finnish presidency.

SUMMARY

The expectations of how Finland would participate in the CFSP were based upon the country's Cold War policy, which has been characterized by neutrality and a cautious attitude vis-à-vis European integration. Finland was assumed to be a highly reluctant member – an assumption that gained weight from the political campaign preceding the EU referendum, and from the country's strong aspiration for the maximum national sovereignty. Once her EU membership came into force, Finland proved all these expectations wrong by adopting a unique flexibility towards the CFSP. This was firstly manifested in the way the Finnish political leadership made participation in the CFSP compatible with the tenets of the old foreign policy. This implied, in practice, that the principles of neutrality, sovereignty of foreign policy, and maintenance of good relations with the Soviet Union (Russia) all had to bend in the face of the demands of the new policy. They were, in other words, made compatible with Finland's EU policy.

The new policy emerged from active and unreserved participation in all areas of EU policies. Participation in European integration firmly replaced the old principles of security policy and became, as a result, the basis of Finland's policy in this field. This has reflected itself in a willingness to contribute to the reinforcement of the CFSP in a very open-minded manner. Finland has promoted the deepening of the CFSP institutions as well as demonstrated a constructive attitude vis-à-vis the creation of a military capacity for the EU. All in all, the Finnish policy indicates that a direct connection is believed to exist between the EU's international role and capacity and Finland's security. Even if the political part of Finland's security policy has changed, the military part still relies on the old concepts of non-alignment and independent defence. Even here, Finland has shown flexibility, implying that she has not been willing to block further integration in defence policy.

In addition to the large issues of the CFSP's institutions and instruments, Finland's policy reflects a smooth adaptation as far as the geographical and ideological frameworks of foreign policy are concerned. The geographical emphasis of Finland's foreign policy is now placed on the EU area. This shift of focus has led to accusations of neglecting the historically important relations with Finland's immediate neighbours, the Scandinavian countries and Russia. Vis-à-vis both of these, Finland had traditionally adopted the role of a subordinate, or at least that of a younger brother, and she has now taken advantage of her membership in the EU to redress the balance. In the ideological framework of foreign policy, commitment to the CFSP has reflected itself in the change which has taken place, above all, in principles concerning international military activities. Loyal to the common positions, Finland accepted the military operation in Kosovo without a UN mandate. The necessity for a UN or OSCE mandate still forms the starting point for Finland's participation in international operations, although some flexibility can be perceived in this rule. Finland has not, consequently, made a big issue of the fact that the EU's crisis-management capacity is not tied to a UN mandate.

In domestic political debate, Finland's participation in the CFSP has been an issue firmly in the hands of the government and the president, and one where open political conflicts have been relatively rare. An important reason for this can be found in the broad coalition government that has been in office since the onset of Finnish membership. Another is the limited knowledge which prevails among the broader public concerning the details of the CFSP.

NOTES

1. Concerning continuity as one of the four key pillars of Finnish security policy, see K. Törnudd, 'Ties That Bind to the Recent Past; Debating Security Policy in Finland Within the Context of Membership in the European Union', *Cooperation and Conflict* 31:1 (1996), pp. 43–50.
2. See also H. Ojanen, 'Finnish Non-Alignment: Drills in Flexibility', H. Ojanen together with G. Herolf and R. Lindahl (eds) *Non-Alignment and European Security Policy* (Helsinki: Finnish Institute of International Affairs and Institüt für Europäische Politik, 2000), pp. 95–6.
3. See 'Finland and Membership of the EC', A Report to Parliament Given by the Council of State, 1992, pp. 15–16.
4. Törnudd refers to the fact that in the 1995 government report on security policy, the concept of neutrality is not used to describe Finland's current security policy. Neutrality policy is, according to him, mentioned only as something belonging to the Cold War period. See Törnudd, 'Ties That Bind to the Recent Past', p. 53.
5. The 1995 government report stated this as follows: 'Finland has joined the EU as a militarily non-aligned country, which participates actively and constructively in the creation and fulfilment of the CFSP. An effective Union corresponds to Finland's needs. Finland takes a reserved attitude towards military alignment. Finland's solutions do not include military guarantees or other obligations connected with common defence.' See 'Turvallisuus muuttuvassa maailmassa', Valtioneuvoston selonteko eduskunnalle, 6 June 1995, p. 56.
6. See R. Väyrynen, 'Finland and the European Community: Changing Elite Bargains', *Cooperation and Conflict* 28:1 (1993), p. 36.
7. According to the 1992 government report ('Suomi ja Euroopan yhteisön jäsenyys', Valtioneuvoston selonteko eduskunnalle ja siihen liittyvä taustaselvitys, 1992), 'EC membership would create important obligations for Finland emanating from the CFSP. The starting point is the level reached by EC members in their present foreign policy co-operation (political *acquis*). A new member shall even accept the goals mentioned in the EC treaties concerning the further development of this cooperation. In the changed situation of Europe neither of these obligations would create problems for Finland. There are no noteworthy differences between EPC statements and Finland's policy. The goals of the CFSP accepted in Maastricht are compatible with the goal-setting of the Finnish foreign policy.' See also Ojanen, 'Finnish Non-Alignment: Drills in Flexibility', pp. 95–8.
8. See T. Halonen, 'Katsaus edustustonpäällikkökokouksessa, Helsinki 14.8.1995', *Suomen ulko- ja turvallisuuspolitiikka 1995* (Helsinki: Ministry of Foreign Affairs, 1997), p. 29.
9. See 'Finland's Points of Departure and Objectives in the EU's Intergovernmental Conference 1996', A Report Given to Parliament by the Council of State, 1996, p. 39.
10. See Törnudd, 'Ties That Bind to the Recent Past', p. 45.
11. See *Suomi ja Euroopan yhteisön jäsenyys*, pp. 8 and 16.
12. The anti-EC camp could, however, to some extent utilize this sensible policy field. See Chapter 2 in this book and D. Arter, 'The EU Referendum in Finland on 16 October 1994: A Vote for the West, Not for Maastricht',

Journal of Common Market Studies 33:3 (1995), pp. 379–80.

13. See P. Salolainen's (Minister of Foreign Trade) speech at the opening of accession negotiations on 1 February 1993; *Helsingin Sanomat*, 2 February 1993.

14. See 'Turvallisuus muuttuvassa maailmassa', p. 5.

15. See *Suomalaisten EU-kannanotot 1998* (Helsinki: EVA, 1998), p. 28. According to this annual opinion poll, more than 60 per cent of Finns had, since 1995, believed that the Finnish position was safer as a result of EU membership.

16. See 'Finnish Security and Defence Policy 2001', Report by the Council of State to Parliament, 13 June 2001.

17. Ojanen ('Finnish non-alignment: drills in flexibility', pp. 106–9) refers to the fact that the Foreign Affairs Committee of the Eduskunta had proposed observer status for Finland in its memorandum, and the matter had even been discussed on the basis of a report given by the government.

18. Concerning the shift from neutrality to non-alignment, see T. Tiilikainen, 'The Finnish Neutrality – Its New Forms and Future', in L. Goetschel (ed.) *Small States Inside and Outside the European Union* (Boston: Kluwer, 1998), pp. 169–79.

19. See 'Turvallisuus muuttuvassa maailmassa', p. 58.

20. In his speeches in 1997 and 1998, Prime Minister Lipponen confirmed the positive Finnish attitude towards the further development of the defence dimension even if he did, at the same time, state that a full European territorial defence was not probable. See, for example, P. Lipponen, 'Jatkuvuus ja muutos Suomen ulkopolitiikassa', Speech at the Paasikivi Association, 3 September 1998. In her speeches, Foreign Minister Halonen stressed the role of the EU's crisis-management system as a part of its more comprehensive crisis management apparatus. See T. Halonen, 'At the luncheon of the Helsinki Diplomatic Association', *Suomen ulko- ja turvallisuuspolitiikka 1998* (Helsinki: Ministry of Foreign Affairs, 2000), p. 29.

21. See 'The IGC and the Security and Defence Dimension: Towards an Enhanced EU Role in Crisis Management', Memorandum from Finland and Sweden, 25 April 1996; see also 'Finland's Points of Departure and Objectives in the EU's Intergovernmental Conference 1996', p. 41.

22. See 'Finland's points of departure and objectives in the EU's Intergovernmental Conference 1996', p. 41.

23. Concerning the agenda of the 1996–97 IGC in CFSP, see C. Gourlay and E. Remacle, 'The 1996 IGC: The Actors and Their Interaction', in K. Eliassen (ed.) *Foreign and Security Policy in the European Union* (London: Sage, 1998), pp. 59–93.

24. According to 'Finland's Points of Departure and Objectives in the EU's Intergovernmental Conference 1996' (p. 37), 'the government is prepared to study the matter of giving the Union legal personality'. According to Foreign Minister Halonen (T. Halonen, 'Alustus Suomen EU-maissa toimivien edustustopäällikköjen seminaarissa Helsingissä 22.1.1998', *Suomen ulko- ja turvallisuuspolitiikka 1998*, p. 50), 'We would have been pleased to reinforce the position of the Union as an international actor, to clarify its representation and increase the comprehensibility of its structure by conferring the Union one legal personality.'

25. See 'Finland's Points of Departure and Objectives in the EU's Inter-governmental Conference 1996', p. 38.
26. Concerning this relationship, see P. van Ham, 'The EU and WEU: From Cooperation to Common Defence?', in G. Edwards and A. Pijpers (eds) *The Politics of European Treaty Reform: The 1996 Intergovernmental Conference and Beyond* (London: Pinter, 1997), pp. 306–25.
27. In the Memorandum from Finland and Sweden ('The IGC and the Security and Defence Dimension'), the EU's new crisis-management powers were formulated to cover 'humanitarian tasks and military crisis management and other elements of the common defence policy to be defined in the long term'. The final formulation of the EU's powers corresponded to the original formulation of the Petersberg tasks (Petersberg Declaration, WEU Council of Ministers, 1992), according to which, these powers 'shall include humanitarian and rescue tasks, peace-keeping tasks and tasks of combat forces in crisis-management including peace-making' (TEU, Article 17, 2).
28. The change in the British policy was followed by a series of summits between the large member states, the high point being the Saint Malo Declaration by Great Britain and France, which emphasized the necessity of building an independent defence capability for the EU (Joint Declaration on European Defence, 4 December 1998). Concerning the background and interpretation of the process, see S. Biscop, 'The UK's Change of Course: A New Chance for the ESDI', *European Foreign Affairs Review* 4 (1999), pp. 253–68; and G. Andréani, C. Bertram and C. Grant, *Europe's Military Revolution* (London: CER, 2001).
29. See Paavo Lipponen, 'Suomi tukee EU:n kriisinhallinnan vahvistamista', *Helsingin Sanomat*, 6 December 1998.
30. They were more far-reaching as far as the EU's autonomy, the level of its military system or the general level of details of the decision were concerned. See T. Tiilikainen, 'Suomi johtajana EU:n ulkosuhteissa', in T. Martikainen and T. Tiilikainen (eds) *Suomi EU:n johdossa: Tutkimus Suomen puheenjohtajuudesta 1999* (Helsinki: Helsingin yliopisto, Yleisen valtio-opin laitos, Acta Politica 13, 2000), pp. 171–2.
31. 'Suomi esittää nyt tarkkaa aikataulua', *Helsingin Sanomat*, 26 November 1999.
32. See the speech of President Tarja Halonen in the Paasikivi Society, 31 August 2000 (*www.tpk.fi/netcomm*). See also T. Forsberg, 'Ulkopolitiikka: Puolueettomasta pohjoismaasta tavalliseksi eurooppalaiseksi', in T. Raunio and M. Wiberg (eds) *EU ja Suomi: Unionijäsenyyden vaikutukset suomalaiseen yhteiskuntaan* (Helsinki: Edita, 2000), pp. 268–9.
33. See *http://formin.finland.fi/finnish/*.
34. See the Planning Commission for Information on National Defence, survey of July 2000.
35. See 'HVK 2000- vahvistettu yhteistyö', VNK 2120-173.
36. Forsberg, 'Ulkopolitiikka', p. 270.
37. Mauno Koivisto, the former president of Finland, has been one of the leading figures to show concern about this. See M. Koivisto, *Venäjän aate* (Helsinki: WSOY, 2001), pp. 298–9.
38. Even in its negotiations for membership, Sweden tried to distance itself from Finland and lobbied the EC to start negotiations, in the first instance only with itself and Austria. See A. Kuosmanen, *Finland's Journey to the European*

Union (EIPA: Maastricht, 2001), p. 21. Later, the reluctance of Denmark and Sweden towards the EU has clearly diminished the Finnish willingness to be perceived as a member of a Nordic club in the EU. For a view on the memberships of the Nordic countries in the European Union, see C. Ingebritsen, *The Nordic States and European Unity* (Ithaca, NY and London: Cornell University Press, 1998).

39. For an analysis of the forms of this incapacity for common action, see K. Jorgensen, 'Possibilities of a "Nordic" Influence on the Development of the CFSP', in M. Jopp and H. Ojanen (eds) *European Security Integration, Implications for Non-Alignment and Alliances* (Helsinki: Finnish Institute of International Affairs and Institüt für Europäische Politik, 1999), pp. 103–46.

40. In their meeting in Finland in July 2001, the Nordic prime ministers decided to reinforce the coordination of EU policies by meeting before the summits of the European Council.

41. As an example of the old policy, Pursiainen refers to the Soviet–Afghan war, in response to which the leadership of Finnish foreign policy remained neutral without criticizing the Soviet Union. See C. Pursiainen, 'Finland's Policy Towards Russia: How To Deal with the Security Dilemma?', in B. Huldt, T. Tiilikainen, T. Vaahtoranta and A. Helkama-Rågård (eds) *Finnish and Swedish Security: Comparing National Policies* (Stockholm: Försvarshögskolan and Programme on the Northern Dimension of the CFSP, 2001), pp. 153–4.

42. See Pursiainen, 'Finland's Policy Towards Russia', pp. 153–4; and C. Pursiainen, 'EU-Suomi ja Tshetshenian kaksi sotaa', *Ydin* 1 (2000), pp. 2–5.

43. See also Forsberg, 'Ulkopolitiikka', p. 272.

44. See Tiilikainen, 'Suomi johtajana EU:n ulkosuhteissa', pp. 180–1 and U. Vesa, 'Suomen YK-politiikan pitkät linjat', *Ulkopolitiikka* 37:3 (2000), p. 23.

45. 'Pohjoismailla välillä eripuraa YK:ssa', *Helsingin Sanomat*, 26 October 2000.

46. Since 1956, more than 40,000 Finnish peacekeepers have participated in over 20 operations. The maximum number of Finnish soldiers in international operations is 2,000 per year. With this contribution, Finland has – from time to time – been one of the leading suppliers of troops.

47. See Vesa, 'Suomen YK-politiikan pitkät linjat', p. 20.

48. See Vesa, 'Suomen YK-politiikan pitkät linjat', p. 21. Forsberg notes that Foreign Minister Tarja Halonen supported only the common position (CFSP), while President Ahtisaari more explicitly supported the NATO operation. See Forsberg, 'Ulkopolitiikka', p. 269.

49. See T. Forsberg, 'Finland and the Kosovo Crisis: At the Crossroads of Europeanism and Neutrality', *Northern Dimensions* 2000, p. 45.

50. Laki Suomen osallistumisesta Yhdistyneiden kansakuntien ja Euroopan turvallisuus- ja yhteistyöjärjestön päätökseen perustuvaan rauhanturvaamistoimintaan (1565/95).

51. Rauhanturvaamislaki (750/2000).

52. Ibid.

8

Conclusion

This book has analysed Finland's membership in the EU. We have mainly focused on domestic policy-making in Finland and on the impact of EU membership on the Finnish political system. It is fair to conclude that Finland has adapted herself well to the EU. The system established for the national formulation of EU issues works effectively, with the coordination mechanism facilitating the formulation of coherent national EU policies. The parliament is firmly involved in the formulation of EU policies through its decentralized system of committees, and thanks to the constitutional obligation of the government to deliver information on EU matters. A gradual revision of the division of powers between the government and the president has taken place, and the political dynamic of the EU policy process has contributed to the prime minister emerging as the undisputed leader in both domestic and integration policy. Perhaps most significantly, Finland has adapted to the CFSP without any problems. From the difficult position of the Cold War era – characterized by limited room for international manoeuvre – Finland has within just over a decade become an active EU/EMU member state with a strong commitment to European integration. However, Finnish citizens remain less convinced of the virtues of integration, and they are more sceptical of integration than the average EU citizen.

This concluding chapter focuses on the broader changes that have resulted from EU membership. In the next section, we discuss the ways in which European integration has altered Finland's international identity and the not always easy interaction between a state-centric political culture and commitment to supranational integration. Then we summarize some of the main findings of this book and offer our explanation of why Finland's adaptation to the EU has been so smooth and unproblematic. The final section contains a brief look into the future, arguing that the 'positive' approach to integration shown thus far by Finland is unlikely to be radically altered by future governments.

Conclusion

STATE-CENTRISM AS THE CORE OF POLITICAL IDENTITY

Finland's integration policy cannot be explained without reference to past experiences and the way they are interpreted. By this, we refer to the formation of the national identity. A firm position taken by the state has constituted the core element in Finnish political culture.[1] The state-centric political culture has its roots in the way 'Finland' as a political entity, and later as a nation, came into being. Finland started for the first time to appear as a political entity when parts of the present Finnish territory was a dominion of the Swedish monarchy between the twelfth century and the year 1809.[2] During the Swedish era, the structures of a centralized state became rooted in Finland. These structures, including indigenous Finnish state organs and constitution, became important as the political basis of an independent Finnish state when Finland was transferred from Swedish rule and became an autonomous Grand Duchy in the Russian Empire in 1809. When nationalism and a nationalist conception of Finland arose in the country in the mid-nineteenth century, it had two objectives. The first was the cultivation of the Finnish national culture, primarily at the expense of Swedish cultural and linguistic elements.[3] The second objective – which finally united both the Swedish and Finnish groups in Finland – was the liberation of Finland from Russian political dominance. The struggle for independence was largely based upon the existing political institutions, including the constitution dating from the Swedish era, which served as an expression of Finnish statehood legitimizing independence.[4] The process was successful, as Finland managed to take advantage of the 1917 revolution in Russia to declare independence.

The early history of Finland engendered a state-centric tradition in Finnish political culture. Nationalism and the wars with the Soviet Union in 1939–40 and 1941–44 reinforced this tradition. In Finnish terms state-centrism means that values connected with the state, such as sovereignty and territoriality, have traditionally been strongly emphasized. This has led to a very limited position being given to alternative political communities, such as that of a united Europe or the development of a strong regional identification, in Finnish political thinking. Finnish political culture stems from Lutheran political concepts, a fact which means that a connection to the cultural origins of European unification – that is, to the Catholic political tradition – is very weak. Consequently, Finland has lacked any visible or politically influential federalist political movements or other movements that would have strongly favoured European political unification. In the Cold War era, the state-centric identity was further emphasized by the international situation and by two

147

other attributes of Finnish identity deriving their legitimacy from that situation. These were the small-state tradition and the status of Finland as a borderland. Both of these traditions underlined Finland's position as a land under threat. They have had far-reaching consequences for Finnish policy even after the Cold War era.

The status of Finland as a borderland became very accentuated in the tense international situation of the Cold War, where the borderline between the two political blocs was Finland's border with the Soviet Union. Finland occupied a strange position between the blocs by her commitment to military neutrality, with the FCMA treaty requiring wartime military cooperation with the Soviet Union, while belonging to the west as far as the political and economic basis of Finnish society was concerned. Finland was thus very practically faced with the challenge of walking a tightrope between the two blocs in a difficult international situation, which, in the worst case, could have turned the country into a battlefield. Another tenet that grew out of post-war political thinking in Finland was that pertaining to the status of a small state. As a small player – at least when assessed in terms of the qualities decisive in international politics – Finland was seen to be continually under threat. Finland had to be subordinate in order to guarantee her position, and to submit to the realities of international politics. The international room for manoeuvre that Finland had was characterized by President Urho Kekkonen as follows: 'A small country like Finland cannot have a great impact upon what is happening in the world. Its role in the search for its national interest is to adapt itself to actual conditions of history and economic geography rather than to strive at a change in them.'[5]

By the early 1990s, the Finns had become used to living – for at least five decades – in a world where state sovereignty and security formed the uncontested starting point for political life. When participation in European integration started to be discussed in Finland, it first took place very much in these state-centric terms.[6] The impact that EU membership would have on state sovereignty in several policy fields formed the key perspective of this debate. The lack of a cultural connection to the values and starting points of European integration reflected itself even in the manner in which the Finns arrived at a positive solution to the problem of EU membership. State security was one of the key motives behind the national decision to apply for membership. Still in the mid-1990s, Finnish political identity was very much the identity of a small state situated on the fringes of Europe and seeking protection for its land and people.

The security policy motivations of Finnish EU membership expressed themselves in various ways. In the first place, they formed the basis for the national consensus on the major decisions related to Finland's participation in European integration. Irrespective of the controversies prevailing about the consequences of integration for various sectoral policies, Finnish EU membership, per se, could be shown to lie on solid political ground. Secondly, the security policy motivations of Finnish membership expressed themselves as a firm commitment to integration, extending even to those policy fields where a conflict of values could have been assumed to take place. As was anticipated by several foreign scholars, the state-centric political culture could have brought about a reluctant attitude, in particular to the supranationalization of decision-making. However, such expectations proved very wrong indeed. In the CFSP, the security policy motivations of Finnish EU membership led to an unpreju-diced policy in favour of strengthening the presence of the EU in inter-national politics.

However, the commitment to integration that prevails among the political, administrative, and business elites, and which, to a great extent, can be traced back to economic and security policy motivations, is not shared to the same extent by the Finnish people. The Finns are sceptical of the benefits and desirability of EU membership. In part, this scepticism is an expression of a sense of the EU's deficient legitimacy that is common to the citizens of the EU. But in the Finnish case, it may indicate that an era of dogmatism and respect for authority has ended in Finnish political culture. It is not an exaggeration to state that EU membership has 'normalized' the conception of foreign policy in Finland. Gradually, it has politicized the field that used to be the prerogative of the president and beyond the reach of political controversy. In Finland, scepticism of the EU can, consequently, be treated also as an indication of an increased readiness of people to formulate their own opinions on political issues and question the axioms of the political elite. Thus far, Finland's EU policy has neither formed a dominant topic in any elections nor been significant in the polarization of the political field.

PRAGMATISM AND CONSENSUS POLITICS

Finland has often been characterized as a 'model student' of the EU that is always willing to promote common goals and to respect common rules and obligations.[7] Pragmatism and adaptability are the leading qualities of Finnish integration policy. In part, the roots of this type of behaviour can be traced back to the dominant characteristics of Finnish political culture. The Lutheran mentality of the Finns, combined with the small-state identity, clearly reflects itself in Finland's international action. The status and history as a small state have apparently helped Finland to adapt herself to a political union in the sense that Finland is used to conciliating her interests with those of other states. In this respect, a clear difference has been shown to exist between Finland and Sweden, as Sweden's external identity and behaviour in international politics still reflects the country's history as a big power.[8]

The Finnish political and administrative elite has pragmatically adjusted to life in the EU. EU membership is now 'taken for granted' at the elite level: the choice made in 1994 may be privately lamented, but not publicly questioned. Finland has not made any specific demands or sought any significant opt-outs, either in the membership negotiations or during the first years of EU membership. In the membership negotiations, the government accepted the Maastricht Treaty without reservation, the CFSP included, and, with the exception of the CAP, sought no major exemptions from the *acquis communautaire*.[9] Since the referendum held in 1994, no Finnish party represented in the Eduskunta has demanded that Finland leave the EU, nor has any party significantly criticized the basic objectives or working methods of the EU.

Finland's national European policy can be characterized as flexible and constructive, and it has sought to consolidate Finland's position in the inner core of the EU. The government has constantly underlined the importance of being present where decisions concerning Finland are taken. This argument was used extensively both during the referendum campaign and also in relation to joining the EMU. This logic indicates the basic substance of Finnish EU policy. According to the Lipponen government, national interests can best be pursued through active and constructive participation in decision-making. Underlying this stance is a strong conviction that a strong and efficient EU can best protect the rights and interests of smaller member states, as intergovernmental processes tend to favour the larger member states. The Finnish approach is thus in line with Soetendorp and Hanf, who argue that 'small states in particular can reap advantages from membership of the EU. Here they can exert more influence and achieve more of what they seek than if they were forced to compete on their own in the "international political market" with the larger powers. The formal institutions and procedures of the EU, in this view, provide both opportunities for being heard and protection against being overwhelmed by the larger members.'[10]

Pragmatism and the search for national consensus are also defining features of the system established in Finland for formulating and coordinating national EU policies. The priority of the national EU coordination system is to manufacture national unanimity or at least broad consensus, which can be translated into additional influence in the Council. This applies especially to issues that are particularly salient for Finland. While decision-making on routine European legislation in Finland is rather strongly decentralized, with much ministerial autonomy, the overall direction of national EU policy and key policy choices are coordinated within the Cabinet EU Committee and between parties, including the opposition, in the Eduskunta. This domestic consensus-building is at least partially driven by the need to achieve consistency and cohesion when negotiating with other member states and the EU institutions. The search for consensus prevails also in the other two Nordic EU countries, where the overriding goal of national EU policy coordination seems to be 'to create decisions and policies reflecting national consensus or broad compromises. National unity in European affairs, including during the various stages of the decision-making process, is considered vital to the achievement of the best possible policy outcomes.'[11]

Membership in the EU has acted as an important exogenous factor in parliamentarizing decision-making in Finland. Constitutional amendments enacted since the early 1990s have strengthened the role of the government and the Eduskunta in both domestic and foreign policy decision-making. EU matters, the CFSP included, belong almost exclusively to the jurisdiction of the cabinet. The government and particularly the prime minister are firmly in the driving seat, with the president (so far) intervening mainly when questions of the utmost importance for Finland's foreign policy are on the agenda.

The constitutional and political powers of the president have been reduced to such an extent that Finland's government system fits rather uneasily into the category of semi-presidential. The president directs foreign policy, but does so together with the government and through the government's ministerial committee.[12] The president now focuses on promoting foreign trade and on what is left (and that is not much) of so-called traditional foreign-policy matters, that is, Finland's relations with countries outside the EU that are not handled via the Union. Nevertheless, the traditional authority enjoyed by the president in Finnish political culture should not be underestimated. The people seem to favour strong personalized leadership, therefore the system of a dual executive enshrined in the constitution may result in tensions between the government and the president, particularly under conditions of divided government when the president and the prime minister represent different parties.

While an active role for the parliament may obviously slow national EU coordination, due either to divergent preferences or institutional rivalry, the Finnish case indicates that the co-optation of parliamentary views, including the opposition, is important in terms of ensuring a policy consistency that will presumably extend beyond the electoral term. The

Eduskunta has subjected the government to relatively tight scrutiny in EU matters, and this control has improved the overall dialogue between the government and the Eduskunta. The regular appearance of ministers before the Grand Committee forces them to study the issues more thoroughly than might otherwise be the case. There is no doubt that the Finnish model of controlling the government in EU matters works well. Particularly noteworthy is the decentralization of scrutiny and policy formulation to the specialized standing committees, a system that increases the ability of the whole parliament to influence the position of the government. While the executive branch may not always whole-heartedly approve the involvement of ordinary and potentially trouble-some backbenchers, this downward delegation of authority improves the capacity of the whole political system to process European matters, as all or nearly all MPs – and not just those seated in the European Affairs Committee – develop expertise on integration. Through parliamentary scrutiny of EU affairs, national parliaments are now routinely involved in foreign policy decision-making, a policy domain traditionally dominated by the executive branch, the foreign ministry in particular. This applies particularly to Finland, as foreign policy, until the early 1990s, had been exclusively decided by the president. With leadership in foreign policy under the new constitution shared between the government and the president, and with the government in charge of national integration policy, the Eduskunta is in a strong position to influence national integration and foreign policy.

This consensual and pragmatic policy-making style also explains why there has hardly been any conflict, or even tension, between the government and the Eduskunta, on the one hand, and between the government and the opposition, on the other hand. The Eduskunta is a committee-based parliament, and the emphasis is on detailed examination of legislative initiatives in the committees and in the party groups. The system of formulating national integration policy contributes to ideological convergence between political parties and thereby reduces partisan conflict. The ideological moderation necessitated in forming multi-party coalition governments and the corporatist nature of the political system soften ideological conflicts, but the impact of the national EU co-ordination system should not be underestimated, especially as the agendas of the EU and its member states are increasingly interdependent. The goal of 'speaking with one voice' in Brussels is specifically designed to manu-facture national consensus on integration. Significantly, the opposition is accorded a relatively strong role in the formulation of national EU choices, and thus the divide between the government and the opposition that is found in domestic politics does not really extend to integration matters. As the opposition parties are involved in forming national policies, they also simultaneously share the responsibility for the outcome. This reduces the likelihood of the main features of Finnish integration policy being altered after each parliamentary election.

Irrespective of their flexibility and adaptability, the Finnish political elite have not confined themselves only to supporting the major trends in the EU. Even if it is not possible here to investigate in any detail Finland's impact on the various fields of EU policies, some general remarks can be made. The issues that Finland during her EU membership most notably has raised have concerned the ways and principles of EU action. The openness of decision-making, including, among other things, the availability of documents, has formed one of those elements that the Finnish representatives have promoted systematically. This has taken place both in the form of governmental action and in the actions of individual Finns that have held important offices in the EU machinery. Finnish politicians have consistently argued that the EU policy process needs to be made more open and transparent, not least because this would improve national parliamentary scrutiny of integration matters. Heidi Hautala, MEP (the co-chairperson of the Green group in the Parliament after the 1999 elections), has emerged as a vigorous proponent of openness in the EU through the cases in which she has instituted proceedings against the Council of Ministers in the ECJ because she was denied access to EU documents. Because of their character as precedents, the cases have been of great political importance, and they have also received much public attention. Another Finn with a high profile in issues of democracy and openness is the European Ombudsman Jacob Söderman, who was appointed in 1995. Söderman has paid constant attention to the development and enforcement of the openness legislation in the EU. From time to time, the ombudsman's struggle for openness has involved him in disputes with the other EU organs, the European Commission in particular.[13] During the Finnish EU presidency in the latter half of 1999, the modification of the practices of EU decision-making in accordance with the Nordic principles of administration was a consistent goal of Finnish effort. The improvement of the role of national parliaments in the EU has been another important element in the Finnish strategy to increase democracy and openness in the Union.

The Northern Dimension Initiative (NDI) has formed another comprehensive focus of Finland's EU policy. The NDI was originally launched by Prime Minister Paavo Lipponen in Rovaniemi on 15 September 1997, at an international conference on the Barents region, with the clear intention of getting the project on the EU's agenda before the Finnish presidency in 1999. The content of the initiative has been characterized as highly indefinite, with its general goal, however, being the reinforcement of cooperation across the EU's northern borders.[14] The NDI was adopted as official EU policy at the end of 1998. The European Commission then stated that 'within the framework of existing contractual relationships, financial instruments and regional organizations, the Northern Dimension is a concept that can provide added value. It can contribute to the strengthening of the Union's external policies and the reinforcement of the positive interdependence between Russia, the Baltic region and the European Union, notably by achieving further synergies and coherence in these policies and actions.'[15] It is evident that the NDI became a very important project for the Finnish government during the first years of Finland's EU membership. Its main importance can, however, be found in the general role it has played for Finland as a new member state. For Finland, the NDI can be characterized as a very general lesson in membership strategy. It was at the same time a large-scale demonstration of how to use the EU machinery for the advancement of a national political project, and a proof that even the ideas of new and small member states can receive serious consideration at the European level. Arter links the meaning of the NDI with the general role of small states in the EU: 'Getting the NDI adopted as official EU policy by the end of 1998 indicates that small EU states with bright ideas can in the right circumstances exert influence on Union policy-making.'[16] As much as it proved a small state's capacity to exert influence, the NDI proved that Finland has ideas of her own to offer the EU.

THE FUTURE OF FINLAND IN THE EU

Finland's future in the EU seems to depend largely on whether the voters share the positive approach to integration found at the elite level. Indifference towards the EU is widespread, and Finns in general are far less enthusiastic about integration than politicians and key civil servants. Nevertheless, the new specifically anti-EU movements have remained marginal, and it is unlikely that their support will rise in the near future. Opposition to further integration will probably continue to be channelled through individual representatives, particularly MEPs.

Illustrative of the Finnish opinion climate was the lack of any notable popular reaction in 2000 when the European leaders deliberated on the EU's federalist future more explicitly than ever before. The consensus behind national integration policy was not shaken even when Prime Minister Lipponen in his high-profile contribution to the debate took a position that in the Finnish context has to be treated as a federalist one without equal.[17] While not explicitly calling for a federal union, Lipponen supported the idea of drafting a constitution for the EU and saw a clear benefit in the reinforcement of the supranational EU institutions at the expense of the intergovernmental elements of decision-making.

The Finnish political elite, including the government, the Eduskunta, and the main parties, have continued to balance their broad pro-integration statements and policies with a relatively conservative approach to institutional reform. The political elite share a mildly positive attitude towards the gradual federalization of the EU system on the basis of the preliminary agenda adopted for the 2004 IGC by the European Council in Nice.[18] Despite the personal opinion of Lipponen, the Finnish approach is to preserve the overall institutional status quo, with only fairly limited changes in the direction of more supranational decision-making, such as further extension of QMV and the co-decision procedure. For example, in their opinions on the IGC held in 2000, both the government and the Eduskunta were against giving the EP the right to dismiss individual commissioners and against the introduction of supranational EU-wide lists for Euro-elections. The government has repeatedly argued that national parliaments are the primary channel for providing democratic legitimacy to EU decision-making, with the EP complementing the role of national legislatures. The importance attached to the role of national legislatures in the EU reflects the recent parliamentarization of the Finnish political system.

The first eight years of Finland's EU membership has brought Finland to the core of European integration. In contrast to its previous international position, characterized by a reserved attitude towards supranationalism, Finland was the only Nordic country to join the EMU from the beginning. Not even the new pace taken by the deepening defence dimension has made the Finnish leadership hesitate. The policy of non-alignment would without doubt bend, if necessary, in the face of the advancement of the common defence structure. Finland's EU policy is, however, one of those major issues that will be assessed in the general elections scheduled for 2003 and in subsequent negotiations about government composition. If the Centre Party (KESK), which has been in opposition since 1995, wins a key position in the formation of a new government, Finnish EU policy will probably take on a new and more reserved tone. A government led by the KESK would be forced to accommodate in its policy the scepticism of the EU that remains very strong among that party's rural constituency. More critical attitudes towards further integration are also found among all the other main parties. We are not making a political statement against more Euro-sceptical cabinets, but we want to highlight the fact that the commitment to further integration shown by the present government should not be taken for granted outside Finland. Much will depend on the preferences of the party leaders, but, given the fragmented nature of the party system and the need to build ideologically heterogeneous coalition cabinets, the basic substance of Finnish integration policy is unlikely to be radically altered in the near future.

NOTES

1. T. Tiilikainen, *Europe and Finland: Defining the Political Identity of Finland in Western Europe* (Aldershot: Ashgate, 1998). See also M. Jakobson, *Finland in the New Europe* (Westport, CT: Praeger, The Washington Papers/175, 1998).
2. O. Jussila, *Maakunnasta valtioksi* (Helsinki: WSOY, 1987), p. 47.
3. J. Paasivirta, *Suomi ja Eurooppa: Autonomia ja kansainväliset kriisit 1808–1914* (Helsinki: Kirjayhtymä, 1978), pp. 124–5.
4. Jussila, *Maakunnasta valtioksi,* pp. 90–127.
5. U. Kekkonen, *Puheita ja kirjoituksia 2* (Helsinki: Weilin & Göös, 1967), p. 12.
6. T. Tiilikainen, 'Suomen doktriini murtuu – suomalaisen politiikan kulku Paasikiven-Kekkosen realismista kohti yhteisöllisyyden Eurooppaa', *Ulkopolitiikka* 29:4 (1992), pp. 15–22.
7. Characterizations of this kind were, for instance, typical in the assessment of Finland's EU presidency in the international media. See L. Kujala, 'Suomen EU-puheenjohtajuuden julkisuuskuva', in T. Martikainen and T. Tiilikainen (eds) *Suomi EU:n johdossa: Tutkimus Suomen puheenjohtajuudesta 1999* (Helsinki: Helsingin yliopisto, Yleisen valtio-opin laitos, Acta Politica 13, 2000), p. 224.
8. See M. af Malmborg and T. Tiilikainen, 'Comparative Perspective', in B. Huldt, T. Tiilikainen, T. Vaahtoranta and A. Helkama-Rågård (eds) *Finnish and Swedish Security: Comparing National Policies* (Stockholm: Försvarshögskolan and the Programme on the Northern Dimension of the CFSP, 2001), pp. 71–3.
9. At the European level, the government, in order better to protect core national issues, is willing to make concessions and trade-offs in EU decision-making. By showing flexibility and readiness to compromise, the government can expect similar behaviour from other member states when nationally important issues are on the EU agenda. This flexible approach is illustrated by the voting behaviour of member state governments in the Council in 1995–99. Excluding Luxembourg, Finland voted least often against the winning majority. See T. Raunio and M. Wiberg, 'Johdanto: Suomi astuu unioniaikaan', in T. Raunio and M. Wiberg (eds) *EU ja Suomi: Unionijäsenyyden vaikutukset suomalaiseen yhteiskuntaan* (Helsinki: Edita, 2000), pp. 9–23; and T. Raunio and M. Wiberg, 'Parliamentarizing Foreign Policy Decision-Making: Finland in the European Union', *Cooperation and Conflict* 36:1 (2001), pp. 61–86.
10. B. Soetendorp and K. Hanf, 'Conclusion: The Nature of National Adaptation

to European Integration', in K. Hanf and B. Soetendorp (eds) *Adapting to European Integration: Small States and the European Union* (Harlow: Longman, 1998), p. 193.

11. E. Damgaard, 'Conclusion: The Impact of European Integration on Nordic Parliamentary Democracies', in T. Bergman and E. Damgaard (eds) *Delegation and Accountability in European Integration: The Nordic Parliamentary Democracies and the European Union* (London: Frank Cass, 2000), p. 168.

12. D. Arter, *Scandinavian Politics Today* (Manchester: Manchester University Press, 1999), p. 239.

13. The most visible disagreement took place in early 2000, when Söderman criticized the European Commission's proposal for the enforcement of TEU Article 255 on openness. He was accused both by the Commission president, Romano Prodi, and the president of the EP, Nicole Fontaine, of making a criticism that should be a theme for an internal debate between the institutions. See 'Romano Prodi hyökkää rajusti Jacob Södermania vastaan', *Helsingin Sanomat*, 11 March 2000.

14. D. Arter, 'Small State Influence Within the EU: The Case of Finland's "Northern Dimension Initiative"', *Journal of Common Market Studies* 38:5 (2000), p. 678.

15. Ibid., p. 692.

16. Ibid., p. 693.

17. The speech of Paavo Lipponen in the College of Europe, Bruges, Belgium, 10 November 2000. See also P. Lipponen, *Kohti Eurooppaa* (Helsinki: Tammi, 2001). While several leading politicians criticized Lipponen's ideas and (justifiably) argued that his speech did not reflect the official Finnish position, the other parties did not put forward any serious views of their own.

18. Treaty of Nice, Annex IV: Declaration on the Future of the Union.

References

Alanen, P. and Forsberg, T., 'The Evolution of Opinion about Foreign Policy in Finland from the 1960s till the 1980s', *Yearbook of Finnish Foreign Policy 1988–89* (1989), pp. 29–33.

Anckar, D., 'The Finnish European Election of 1996', *Electoral Studies*, 16: 2 (1997), pp. 262–6.

Andréani, G., Bertram, C. and Grant, C., *Europe's Military Revolution* (London: CER, 2001).

Antola, E. and Tuusvuori, O., *Länsi-Euroopan integraatio ja Suomi* (Helsinki: Finnish Institute of International Affairs, 1983).

Apunen, O., *Paasikiven-Kekkosen linja* (Helsinki: Tammi, 1977).

Arter, D., 'The EU Referendum in Finland on 16 October 1994: A Vote for the West, Not for Maastricht', *Journal of Common Market Studies*, 33: 3 (1995), pp. 361–87.

Arter, D., 'Finland', in R. Elgie (ed.), *Semi-Presidentialism in Europe* (Oxford: Oxford University Press, 1999), pp. 48–66.

Arter, D., *Scandinavian Politics Today* (Manchester: Manchester University Press, 1999).

Arter, D., 'Small State Influence Within the EU: The Case of Finland's "Northern Dimension Initiative"', *Journal of Common Market Studies*, 38: 5 (2000), pp. 677–97.

Aspinwall, M., 'Structuring Europe: Power-Sharing Institutions and British Preferences on European Integration', *Political Studies*, 48: 3 (2000), pp. 415–42.

Aylott, N., *Swedish Social Democracy and European Integration: The People's Home on the Market* (Aldershot: Ashgate, 1999).

Bell, D.S. and Lord, C. (eds), *Transnational Parties in the European Union* (Aldershot: Ashgate, 1998).

Bergman, T., 'National Parliaments and EU Affairs Committees: Notes on Empirical Variation and Competing Explanations', *Journal of European Public Policy*, 4: 3 (1997), pp. 373–87.

Bergman, T., 'The European Union as the Next Step of Delegation and Accountability', *European Journal of Political Research*, 37: 3 (2000), pp. 415–29.

References

Bergman, T. and Damgaard, E. (eds), *Delegation and Accountability in European Integration: The Nordic Parliamentary Democracies and the European Union* (London: Frank Cass, 2000), published also as a Special Issue of *Journal of Legislative Studies*, 6, 1 (2000).

von Beyme, K., 'Niedergang der Parlamente: Internationale Politik und nationale Entscheidungshoheit', *Internationale Politik*, 53: 4 (1998), pp. 21–30.

Biscop, S., 'The UK's Change of Course: A New Chance for the ESDI', *European Foreign Affairs Review*, 4 (1999), pp. 253–67.

Boedeker, M. and Uusikylä, P., 'Interaction Between the Government and Parliament in Scrutiny of EU Decision-Making; Finnish Experiences and General Problems', in *National Parliaments and the EU – Stock-Taking for the Post-Amsterdam Era* (Helsinki: Eduskunnan kanslian julkaisu 1/2000), pp. 27–42.

Borg, S., 'Kansalaisten suhde politiikkaan murroksessa', in P. Suhonen (ed.), *Yleinen mielipide 1997* (Helsinki: Tammi, 1997), pp. 99–118.

Borg, S. (ed.), *Puolueet 1990-luvulla: Näkökulmia suomalaiseen puoluetoimintaan* (Turku: Turun yliopisto, Valtio-opillisia tutkimuksia n:o 53, 1997).

Borg, S., 'Puolueet, ehdokkaat ja äänestäjien valinnat', in P. Pesonen (ed.), *Suomen europarlamenttivaalit* (Tampere: Tampere University Press, 2000), pp. 124–47.

Borg, S. and Sänkiaho, R. (eds), *The Finnish Voter* (Tampere: The Finnish Political Science Association, 1995).

Borg, S., Pehkonen, J. and Raunio, T., 'Äänestämässä käynti ja äänestä-mättömyys', in P. Pesonen (ed.), *Suomen europarlamenttivaalit* (Tampere: Tampere University Press, 2000), pp. 106–23.

Börzel, T.A., 'Towards Convergence in Europe? Institutional Adaptation to Europeanization in Germany and Spain', *Journal of Common Market Studies*, 37: 4 (1999), pp. 573–96.

Bulmer, S. and Burch, M., 'The "Europeanisation" of Central Government: The UK and Germany in Historical Institutionalist Perspective', in G. Schneider and M. Aspinwall (eds), *The Rules of Integration: Institutionalist Approaches to the Study of Europe* (Manchester: Manchester University Press, 2001), 73–96.

Bulmer, S. and Lequesne, C., 'New Perspectives on EU-Member State Relationships', paper presented at the ECSA Biennial Conference, 31 May–2 June 2001, Madison, Wisconsin.

Cardozo, R., 'The Project for a Political Community', in R. Pryce (ed.), *The Dynamics of European Union* (London: Routledge, 1989), pp. 49–77.

Caul, M.L. and Gray, M.M., 'From Platform Declarations to Policy Outcomes: Changing Party Profiles and Partisan Influence over Policy', in R.J. Dalton and M.P. Wattenberg (eds), *Parties Without Partisans: Political Change in Advanced Industrial Democracies* (Oxford: Oxford University Press, 2000), pp. 208–37.

Cole, A. and Drake, H., 'The Europeanization of the French Polity: Continuity, Change and Adaptation', *Journal of European Public Policy*, 7: 1 (2000), pp. 26–43.

Damgaard, E., 'Conclusion: The Impact of European Integration on Nordic Parliamentary Democracies', in T. Bergman and E. Damgaard (eds), *Delegation and Accountability in European Integration: The Nordic Parliamentary Democracies and the European Union* (London: Frank Cass, 2000), pp. 151–69.

van der Eijk, C. and Franklin, M.N. (eds), *Choosing Europe: The European Electorate and National Politics in the Face of Union* (Ann Arbor, MI: University of Michigan Press, 1996).

Ekengren, M. and Sundelius, B., 'Sweden: The State Joins the European Union', in K. Hanf and B. Soetendorp (eds), *Adapting to European Integration: Small States and the European Union* (Harlow: Longman, 1998), pp. 131–48.

Elinkeinoelämän valtuuskunta, *Suomalaisten EU-kannanotot* (Helsinki: EVA, 1994).

Elinkeinoelämän valtuuskunta, *Suomalaisten EU-kannanotot 1998* (Helsinki: EVA, 1998).

Esaiasson, P. and Heidar, K. (eds), *Beyond Westminster and Congress: The Nordic Experience* (Columbus, OH: Ohio State University Press, 2000).

Falkner, G., 'How Pervasive Are Euro-Politics? Effects of EU Membership on a New Member State', *Journal of Common Market Studies*, 38: 2 (2000), pp. 223–50.

Falkner, G. and Müller, W.C. (eds), *Österreich im europäischen Mehrebenensystem: Konsequenzen der EU-Mitgliedschaft für Politiknetzwerke und Entscheidungsprozesse* (Wien: Signum, 1998).

Forsberg, T., 'Finland and the Kosovo Crisis: At the Crossroads of Europeanism and Neutrality', *Northern Dimensions* (2000), pp. 41–9.

Forsberg, T., 'Ulkopolitiikka: Puolueettomasta pohjoismaasta tavalliseksi eurooppalaiseksi', in T. Raunio and M. Wiberg (eds), *EU ja Suomi: Unionijäsenyyden vaikutukset suomalaiseen yhteiskuntaan* (Helsinki: Edita, 2000), pp. 263–77.

Franklin, M., 'European Elections and the European Voter', in J. Richardson (ed.), *European Union: Power and Policy-Making* (London: Routledge, 2001), pp. 197–213.

Franklin, M., Marsh, M. and McLaren, L., 'Uncorking the Bottle: Popular Opposition to European Unification in the Wake of Maastricht', *Journal of Common Market Studies*, 32: 4 (1994), pp. 455–72.

Gabel, M., 'European Integration, Voters and National Politics', *West European Politics*, 23: 4 (2000), pp. 52–72.

Gaffney, J. (ed.), *Political Parties and the European Union* (London: Routledge, 1996).

Gourlay, C. and Remacle, E., 'The 1996 IGC: The Actors and their

Interaction', in K. Eliassen (ed.), *Foreign and Security Policy in the European Union* (London: Sage, 1998), pp. 59–93.

Green Cowles, M., Caporaso, J. and Risse, T. (eds), *Transforming Europe: Europeanization and Domestic Change* (Ithaca, NY: Cornell University Press, 2001).

Gstöhl, S., 'The Nordic Countries and the European Economic Area (EEA)', in L. Miles (ed.), *The European Union and the Nordic Countries* (London: Routledge, 1996), pp. 47–62.

Guyomarch, A., Machin, H. and Ritchie, E., *France in the European Union* (Basingstoke: Macmillan, 1998).

van Ham, P., 'The EU and WEU: From Cooperation to Common Defence?', in G. Edwards and A. Pijpers (eds), *The Politics of European Treaty Reform: The 1996 Intergovernmental Conference and Beyond* (London: Pinter, 1997), pp. 306–25.

Hanf, K. and Soetendorp, B., 'Small States and the Europeanization of Public Policy', in K. Hanf and B. Soetendorp (eds), *Adapting to European Integration: Small States and the European Union* (Harlow: Longman, 1998), pp. 1–13.

Heidar, K. and Koole, R. (eds), *Parliamentary Party Groups in European Democracies: Political Parties Behind Closed Doors* (London: Routledge, 2000).

Heidar, K. and Svåsand, L. (eds), *Partier uten grenser?* (Otta: Tano Aschehoug, 1997).

Helms, L., 'Parliamentary Party Groups and Their Parties: A Comparative Assessment', *Journal of Legislative Studies*, 6: 1 (2000), pp. 104–20.

Héritier, A., Kerwer, D., Knill, C., Lehmkuhl, D., Teutsch, M. and Douillet, A.-C., *Differential Europe: The European Union Impact on National Policymaking* (Lanham, MD: Rowman & Littlefield, 2001).

Hine, D., 'Factionalism in West European Parties: A Framework for Analysis', *West European Politics*, 5: 1 (1982), pp. 36–53.

Hix, S., 'Dimensions and Alignments in European Union Politics: Cognitive Constraints and Partisan Responses', *European Journal of Political Research*, 35: 1 (1999), pp. 69–106.

Hix, S., *The Political System of the European Union* (Basingstoke: Macmillan, 1999).

Hix, S. and Goetz, K., 'Introduction: European Integration and National Political Systems', *West European Politics*, 23: 4 (2000), pp. 1–26.

Hix, S. and Lord, C., *Political Parties in the European Union* (Basingstoke: Macmillan, 1997).

Holkeri, H., 'Suomi hakee tietään', *Ulkopoliittisia lausuntoja ja asiakirjoja 1990* (Helsinki: Ministry of Foreign Affairs, 1990), pp. 15–16.

Hooghe, L. and Marks, G., *Multi-Level Governance and European Integration* (Lanham, MD: Rowman & Littlefield, 2001).

Huber, J. and Inglehart, R., 'Expert Interpretations of Party Space and Party

Locations in 42 Societies', *Party Politics*, 1: 1 (1995), pp. 73–111.

Ingebritsen, C., 'Coming Out of the Cold: Nordic Responses to European Union', in A.W. Cafruny and C. Lankowski (eds), *Europe's Ambiguous Unity: Conflict and Consensus in the Post-Maastricht Era* (Boulder, CO: Lynne Rienner, 1997), pp. 239–56.

Ingebritsen, C., *The Nordic States and European Unity* (Ithaca, NY and London: Cornell University Press, 1998).

Ingebritsen, C. and Larson, S., 'Interest and Identity: Finland, Norway and European Union', *Cooperation and Conflict*, 32: 2 (1997), pp. 207–22.

Jääskinen, N., 'Eduskunta: Aktiivinen sopeutuja', in T. Raunio and M. Wiberg (eds), *EU ja Suomi: Unionijäsenyyden vaikutukset suomalaiseen yhteiskuntaan* (Helsinki: Edita, 2000), pp. 114–34.

Jääskinen, N. and Kivisaari, T., 'Parliamentary Scrutiny of European Union Affairs in Finland', in M. Wiberg (ed.), *Trying to Make Democracy Work: The Nordic Parliaments and the European Union* (Stockholm: Gidlunds, 1997), pp. 29–47.

Jahn, D. 'Der Einfluss von Cleavage-Strukturen auf die Standpunkte der skandinavischen Parteien über den Beitritt zur Europäischen Union', *Politische Vierteljahresschrift*, 40: 4 (1999), pp. 565–90.

Jahn, D. and Storsved, A.-S. 'Legitimacy through Referendum? The Nearly Successful Domino-Strategy of the EU Referendum in Austria, Finland, Sweden and Norway', *West European Politics*, 18: 4 (1995), pp. 18–37.

Jakobson, M., *Finland in the New Europe* (Westport: Praeger, The Washington Papers/175, 1998).

Jensen, T.K., 'Party Cohesion', in P. Esaiasson and K. Heidar (eds), *Beyond Westminster and Congress: The Nordic Experience* (Columbus, OH: Ohio State University Press, 2000), pp. 210–36.

Johansson, K.M. (ed.), *Sverige i EU* (Stockholm: SNS Förlag, 1999).

Johansson, K.M., 'Tracing the Employment Title in the Amsterdam Treaty: Uncovering Transnational Coalitions', *Journal of European Public Policy*, 6: 1 (1999), pp. 85–101.

Johansson, K.M. and Raunio, T., 'Partisan Responses to Europe: Comparing Finnish and Swedish Political Parties', *European Journal of Political Research*, 39: 2 (2001), pp. 225–49.

Jorgensen, K., 'Possibilities of a "Nordic" Influence on the Development of the CFSP', in M. Jopp and H. Ojanen (eds), *European Security Integration, Implications for Non-Alignment and Alliances* (Helsinki: Finnish Institute of International Affairs and Institüt für Europäische Politik, 1999), pp. 103–36.

Judge, D., 'The Failure of National Parliaments', *West European Politics*, 18: 3 (1995), pp. 79–100.

Jussila, O., *Maakunnasta valtioksi* (Helsinki: WSOY, 1987).

Jussila, O., Hentilä, S. and Nevakivi, J., *From Grand Duchy to Modern State: A Political History of Finland since 1908* (London: Hurst, 1999).

References

Jyränki, A., *Presidentti* (Helsinki: WSOY, 1981).

Kassim, H., 'Conclusion: The National Co-ordination of EU Policy: Confronting the Challenge', in H. Kassim, B.G. Peters and V. Wright (eds), *The National Coordination of EU Policy: The Domestic Level* (Oxford: Oxford University Press, 2000), pp. 235–64.

Kassim, H., Peters, B.G. and Wright, V., 'Introduction', in H. Kassim, B.G. Peters and V. Wright (eds), *The National Coordination of EU Policy: The Domestic Level* (Oxford: Oxford University Press, 2000), pp. 1–21.

Kassim, H., Peters, B.G. and Wright, V. (eds), *The National Coordination of EU Policy: The Domestic Level* (Oxford: Oxford University Press, 2000).

Katz, R.S., 'Representation, the Locus of Democratic Legitimation and the Role of the National Parliaments in the European Union', in R.S. Katz and B. Wessels (eds), *The European Parliament, the National Parliaments, and European Integration* (Oxford: Oxford University Press, 1999), pp. 21–44.

Katz, R.S. and Mair, P. (eds), *How Parties Organize: Change and Adaptation in Party Organizations in Western Democracies* (London: Sage, 1994).

Kekkonen, U., *Puheita ja kirjoituksia 2* (Helsinki: Weilin & Göös, 1967).

Kirchner, E., *Decision-Making in the European Communities* (Manchester: Manchester University Press, 1992).

Kitschelt, H., 'Citizens, Politicians, and Party Cartellization: Political Representation and State Failure in Post-Industrial Democracies', *European Journal of Political Research*, 37: 2 (2000), pp. 149–79.

Kivimäki, T., 'Transnationalisaatio, ryhmäintressit ja Suomen EU-neuvottelut', *Politiikka*, 39: 1 (1997), pp. 30–41.

Knutsen, O., 'Expert Judgements of the Left–Right Location of Political Parties: A Comparative Longitudinal Study', *West European Politics*, 21: 2 (1998), pp. 63–94.

Kohler-Koch, B. and Eising, R. (eds), *The Transformation of Governance in the European Union* (London: Routledge, 1999).

Koivisto, M., *Venäjän aate* (Helsinki: WSOY, 2001).

Korhonen, K., *Meidän on uudesta luotava maa* (Helsinki: Otava, 1994).

Kujala, L., 'Suomen EU-puheenjohtajuuden julkisuuskuva', in T. Martikainen and T. Tiilikainen (eds), *Suomi EU:n johdossa: Tutkimus Suomen puheenjohtajuudesta 1999* (Helsinki: Helsingin yliopisto, Yleisen valtio-opin laitos, Acta Politica 13, 2000), pp. 187–236.

Kuosmanen, A., *Finland's Journey to the European Union* (Maastricht: EIPA, 2001).

Ladrech, R., 'Europeanization of Domestic Politics and Institutions: The Case of France', *Journal of Common Market Studies*, 32: 1 (1994), pp. 69–88.

Ladrech, R., *Social Democracy and the Challenge of European Union* (Boulder, CO: Lynne Rienner, 2000).

Laine, J., 'Suomi ja EY', *Ulkopolitiikka*, 28: 1 (1991), pp. 68–9.

Lampinen, R. and Räsänen, I., 'Eduskunnan asema EU-asioiden valmistelussa', in R. Lampinen, O. Rehn, P. Uusikylä et al., *EU-asioiden*

163

valmistelu Suomessa (Helsinki: Eduskunnan kanslian julkaisu 7/1998), pp. 121–32.

Lampinen, R., Rehn, O., Uusikylä, P. et al., *EU-asioiden valmistelu Suomessa* (Helsinki: Eduskunnan kanslian julkaisu 7/1998).

Lampinen, R., Rehn, O. and Uusikylä, P., 'Loppupäätelmät', in R. Lampinen, O. Rehn, P. Uusikylä et al., *EU-asioiden valmistelu Suomessa* (Helsinki: Eduskunnan kanslian julkaisu 7/1998), pp. 33– 42.

Laursen, F. and Pappas, S.A. (eds), *The Changing Role of Parliaments in the European Union* (Maastricht: EIPA, 1995).

Lijphart, A., *Patterns of Democracy: Government Forms and Performance in Thirty-Six Countries* (New Haven, CT: Yale University Press, 1999).

Linnapuomi, M., 'Täällä Strasbourg, kuuleeko Helsinki? Suomalaiset europarlamentaarikot eurooppalaisen ja kansallisen tason yhteensovittajina', in T. Martikainen and K. Pekonen (eds), *Eurovaalit Suomessa 1996: Vaalihumusta päätöksenteon arkeen* (Helsinki: Helsingin yliopisto: Yleisen valtio-opin laitos, Acta Politica 10, 1999), pp. 228–80.

Lipponen, P., *Kohti Eurooppaa* (Helsinki: Tammi, 2001).

Listhaug, O., Holmberg, S. and Sänkiaho, R., 'Partisanship and EU Choice', in A.T. Jenssen, P. Pesonen and M. Gilljam (eds), *To Join or Not To Join: Three Nordic Referendums on Membership in the European Union* (Oslo: Scandinavian University Press, 1998), pp. 215–34.

Longley, L.D. and Davidson, R.H. (eds), *The New Roles of Parliamentary Committees* (London: Frank Cass, 1998).

Mair, P., *Party System Change: Approaches and Interpretations* (Oxford: Oxford University Press, 1997).

Mair, P., 'The Limited Impact of Europe on National Party Systems', *West European Politics*, 23: 4 (2000), pp. 27–51.

Majone, G., *Regulating Europe* (London: Routledge, 1996).

Majonen, P., 'Kauniita ja rohkeita vai aatteellisia ammattipoliitikkoja? Suomen eurovaalien vaaliteemat ja vaalikampanjointi 1996', in T. Martikainen and K. Pekonen (eds), *Eurovaalit Suomessa 1996: Vaalihumusta päätöksenteon arkeen* (Helsinki: Helsingin yliopisto, Yleisen valtio-opin laitos, Acta Politica 10, 1999), pp. 70–129.

af Malmborg, M. and Tiilikainen, T., 'Comparative Perspective', in B. Huldt, T. Tiilikainen, T. Vaahtoranta and A. Helkama-Rågård (eds), *Finnish and Swedish Security: Comparing National Policies* (Stockholm: Försvarshögskolan and the Programme on the Northern Dimension of the CFSP, 2001), pp. 71–3.

Maor, M. 'The Relationship between Government and Opposition in the Bundestag and House of Commons in the Run-Up to the Maastricht Treaty', *West European Politics*, 21: 3 (1998), pp. 187–207.

Marks, G. and Wilson, C.J., 'The Past in the Present: A Cleavage Theory of Party Response to European Integration', *British Journal of Political Science*, 30: 3 (2000), pp. 433–59.

References

Marsh, M., 'Testing the Second-Order Election Model After Four European Elections', *British Journal of Political Science*, 28: 4 (1998), pp. 591–607.

Martikainen, T. and Pekonen, K. (eds), *Eurovaalit Suomessa 1996: Vaalihumusta päätöksenteon arkeen* (Helsinki: Helsingin yliopisto, Yleisen valtio-opin laitos, Acta Politica 10, 1999).

Martikainen, T. and Tiilikainen, T. (eds), *Suomi EU:n johdossa: Tutkimus Suomen puheenjohtajuudesta 1999* (Helsinki: Helsingin yliopisto, Yleisen valtio-opin laitos, Acta Politica 13, 2000).

Mattila, M., 'From Qualified Majority to Simple Majority: The Effects of the 1992 Change in the Finnish Constitution', *Scandinavian Political Studies*, 20: 4 (1997), pp. 331–45.

Mattila, M., 'Valtioneuvosto: Suomen EU-politiikan määrittelijä', in T. Raunio and M. Wiberg (eds), *EU ja Suomi: Unionijäsenyyden vaikutukset suomalaiseen yhteiskuntaan* (Helsinki: Edita, 2000), pp. 135–50.

Mattson, I. and Strøm, K., 'Parliamentary Committees', in H. Döring (ed.), *Parliaments and Majority Rule in Western Europe* (New York: St. Martin's Press, 1995), pp. 249–307.

Menon, A. 'France', in H. Kassim, B.G. Peters and V. Wright (eds), *The National Coordination of EU Policy: The Domestic Level* (Oxford: Oxford University Press, 2000), pp. 79–98.

Meres-Wuori, O., *Suomen ulko- ja turvallisuuspoliittinen päätöksentekojärjestelmä* (Helsinki: Lakimiesliiton Kustannus, 1998).

Miles, L., 'Sweden and Finland: From EFTA Neutrals to EU Members?', in J. Redmond (ed.), *Prospective Europeans: New Members for the European Union* (Hemel Hempstead: Harvester Wheatsheaf, 1994), pp. 59–85.

Miles, L., 'Conclusion', in L. Miles (ed.), *The European Union and the Nordic Countries* (London: Routledge, 1996), pp. 275–83.

Miles, L. (ed.), *The European Union and the Nordic Countries* (London: Routledge, 1996).

Miles, L., *Sweden and European Integration* (Aldershot: Ashgate, 1997).

Miles, L. (ed.), *Sweden and the European Union Evaluated* (London: Continuum, 2000).

Miles L. and Redmond, J., 'Enlarging the European Union: The Erosion of Federalism?', *Cooperation and Conflict*, 31: 3 (1996), pp. 295–309.

Moravcsik, A., 'Preferences and Power in the European Community: a Liberal Intergovernmentalist Approach', *Journal of Common Market Studies*, 31: 4 (1993), pp. 473–524.

Moravcsik, A., 'Why the European Community Strengthens the State: International Cooperation and Domestic Politics' (*Centre for European Studies Working Paper Series* 52, Harvard University, 1994).

Moravcsik, A., 'Taking Preferences Seriously: A Liberal Theory of International Politics', *International Organization*, 51: 4 (1997), pp. 513–53.

Moravcsik, A., *The Choice for Europe* (Ithaca, NY: Cornell University Press, 1998).

Moravcsik, A., 'A New Statecraft? Supranational Entrepreneurs and International Co-Operation', *International Organization*, 53: 2 (1999), pp. 267–306.

Mouritzen, H., *External Danger and Democracy: Old Nordic Lessons and New European Challenges* (Aldershot: Dartmouth, 1997).

Müller, W.C., 'Austria', in H. Kassim, B.G. Peters and V. Wright (eds), *The National Coordination of EU Policy: The Domestic Level* (Oxford: Oxford University Press, 2000), pp. 210–18.

Müller, W.C., 'Political Parties in Parliamentary Democracies: Making Delegation and Accountability Work', *European Journal of Political Research*, 37: 3 (2000), pp. 309–33.

Müller, W.C. and Strøm, K., 'Conclusion: Coalition Governance in Western Europe', in W.C. Müller and K. Strøm (eds), *Coalition Governments in Western Europe* (Oxford: Oxford University Press, 2000), pp. 559–92.

Norton, P. (ed.), *National Parliaments and the European Union* (London: Frank Cass, 1996).

Norton, P. (ed.), *Parliaments and Governments in Western Europe* (London: Frank Cass, 1998).

Nousiainen, J., 'Finland: The Consolidation of Parliamentary Governance', in W.C. Müller and K. Strøm (eds), *Coalition Governments in Western Europe* (Oxford: Oxford University Press, 2000), pp. 264–99.

Nousiainen, J., 'From Semi-Presidentialism to Parliamentary Government: The Political and Constitutional Development of Finland', in L. Karvonen and K. Ståhlberg (eds), *Festchrift for Dag Anckar on his 60th Birthday on February 12, 2000* (Åbo: Åbo Akademi University Press, 2000), pp. 337–52.

Nousiainen, J., 'Suomalaisen parlamentarismin kolmas kehitysvaihe: konsensuaalinen enemmistöhallinta, vireytyvä eduskunta', *Politiikka*, 42: 2 (2000), pp. 83–96.

Ojanen, H., 'Finnish Non-Alignment: Drills in Flexibility', in H. Ojanen together with G. Herolf and R. Lindahl (eds), *Non-Alignment and European Security Policy* (Helsinki: Finnish Institute of International Affairs and Institüt für Europäische Politik, 2000), pp. 86–154.

Paasivirta, J., *Suomi ja Eurooppa: Autonomia ja kansainväliset kriisit 1808–1914* (Helsinki: Kirjayhtymä, 1978).

Pahre, R., 'Endogenous Domestic Institutions in Two-Level Games and Parliamentary Oversight of the European Union', *Journal of Conflict Resolution*, 41: 1 (1997), pp. 147–74.

Paloheimo, H., 'Kansalaismielipiteiden kehitys Suomessa', in P. Pesonen (ed.), *Suomen EU-kansanäänestys 1994: Raportti äänestäjien kannanotoista* (Helsinki: Ulkoasiainministeriö, Eurooppatiedotus, ja Painatuskeskus, 1994), pp. 41–52.

Paloheimo, H., 'Pohjoismaiden EU-kansanäänestykset: puolueiden peruslinjat ja kansalaisten mielipiteet Suomessa, Ruotsissa ja Norjassa', *Politiikka*, 37: 2 (1995), pp. 113–27.

Paloheimo, H., 'Divided Executive in Finland: From Semi-Presidential to Parliamentary Democracy', paper presented at the ECPR Joint Sessions of Workshops, Copenhagen, 14–19 April 2000.

Paloheimo, H., 'Vaaliohjelmat ja ehdokkaiden mielipiteet', in P. Pesonen (ed.), *Suomen europarlamenttivaalit* (Tampere: Tampere University Press, 2000), pp. 50–81.

Paloheimo, H., 'Divided Government in Finland: From a Semi-Presidential to a Parliamentary Democracy', in R. Elgie (ed.), *Divided Government in Comparative Perspective* (Oxford: Oxford University Press, 2001), pp. 86–105.

Pedersen, T., 'Denmark', in H. Kassim, B.G. Peters and V. Wright (eds), *The National Coordination of EU Policy: The Domestic Level* (Oxford: Oxford University Press, 2000), pp. 219–34.

Peltonen, P., 'Päätöksenteko Euroopan unionissa – kahdeksan esimerkkitapausta puheenjohtajan näkökulmasta', in T. Martikainen and T. Tiilikainen (eds), *Suomi EU:n johdossa: Tutkimus Suomen puheenjohtajuudesta 1999* (Helsinki: Helsingin yliopisto, Yleisen valtio-opin laitos, Acta Politica 13, 2000), pp. 107–62.

Pesonen, P., 'EU-kannan pohja ja perusteet', in P. Pesonen (ed.), *Suomen EU-kansanäänestys 1994: Raportti äänestäjien kannanotoista* (Helsinki: Ulkoasiainministeriö, Eurooppa-tiedotus, ja Painatuskeskus 1994), pp. 84–95.

Pesonen, P., 'Äänestäjäin EU-päätösten synty', in P. Pesonen (ed.), *Suomen EU-kansanäänestys 1994: Raportti äänestäjien kannanotoista* (Helsinki: Ulkoasiainministeriö, Eurooppa-tiedotus, ja Painatuskeskus, 1994), pp. 74–81.

Pesonen, P. (ed.), *Suomen europarlamenttivaalit* (Tampere: Tampere University Press, 2000).

Petersen, N., 'The Nordic Trio and the Future of the EU', in G. Edwards and A. Pijpers (eds), *The Politics of European Treaty Reform: The 1996 Intergovernmental Conference and Beyond* (London: Pinter, 1997), pp. 159–87.

Petersen, N., 'National Strategies in the Integration Dilemma: An Adaptation Approach', *Journal of Common Market Studies*, 36: 1 (1998), pp. 33–54.

Peterson, J. and Bomberg, E., *Decision-Making in the European Union* (Basingstoke: Macmillan, 1999).

Pinder, J., *The Building of the European Union* (Oxford: Oxford University Press, 1998).

Pollack, M.A., 'The End of Creeping Competence? EU Policy-Making Since Maastricht', *Journal of Common Market Studies*, 38: 3 (2000), pp. 519–38.

Polvinen, T., *Between East and West, Finland in International Politics 1944–1947* (Helsinki: WSOY, 1986).

Pursiainen, C., 'EU-Suomi ja Tshetshenian kaksi sotaa', *Ydin*, 1 (2000), pp. 2–5.

Pursiainen, C., 'Finland's Policy Towards Russia: How To Deal with the Security Dilemma?', in B. Huldt, T. Tiilikainen, T. Vaahtoranta and A. Helkama-Rågård (eds), *Finnish and Swedish Security: Comparing National Policies* (Stockholm: Försvarshögskolan and Programme on the Northern Dimension of the CFSP, 2001), pp. 142–73.

Radaelli, C.M., 'Whither Europeanization? Concept Stretching and Substantive Change', *European Integration Online Papers* 4:8 (2000) (*http://eiop.or.at/eiop/texte/2000-008a.htm*).

Raunio, T., 'Miten käy puolueiden yhtenäisyyden? Euroopan unioni haaste suomalaisille puolueille?', in S. Borg (ed.), *Puolueet 1990-luvulla: Näkökulmia suomalaiseen puoluetoimintaan* (Turku: Turun yliopisto, Valtio-opillisia tutkimuksia n:o 53, 1997), pp. 186–214.

Raunio, T., 'Always One Step Behind? National Legislatures and the European Union', *Government and Opposition*, 34: 2 (1999), pp. 180–202.

Raunio, T., 'Facing the European Challenge: Finnish Parties Adjust to the Integration Process', *West European Politics*, 22: 1 (1999), pp. 138–59.

Raunio, T., 'Kulisseista puoluejohdon valvontaan? Euroedustajien ja kansallisten puolueiden yhteydet', *Politiikka*, 41: 1 (1999), pp. 23–39.

Raunio, T., 'Puolueet : Ideologista lähentymistä yhtenäisyyden kustannuksella', in T. Raunio and M. Wiberg (eds), *EU ja Suomi: Unionijäsenyyden vaikutukset suomalaiseen yhteiskuntaan* (Helsinki: Edita, 2000), pp. 43–65.

Raunio, T., 'Valitsijoiden EU-tavoitteet', in P. Pesonen (ed.), *Suomen europarlamenttivaalit* (Tampere: Tampere University Press, 2000), pp. 82–105.

Raunio, T., 'Finland', in J. Lodge (ed.), *The 1999 Elections to the European Parliament* (Basingstoke: Palgrave, 2001), pp. 100–16.

Raunio, T. and Hix, S., 'Backbenchers Learn To Fight Back: European Integration and Parliamentary Government', *West European Politics*, 23: 4 (2000), pp. 142–68.

Raunio, T. and Wiberg, M., 'Efficiency Through Decentralisation: The Finnish Eduskunta and the European Union', in M. Wiberg (ed.), *Trying to Make Democracy Work: The Nordic Parliaments and the European Union* (Stockholm: Gidlunds, 1997), pp. 48–69.

Raunio, T. and Wiberg, M., 'Building Elite Consensus: Parliamentary Accountability in Finland', *Journal of Legislative Studies*, 6: 1 (2000), pp. 59–80.

Raunio, T. and Wiberg, M., 'Parliaments' Adaptation to the European Union', in P. Esaiasson and K. Heidar (eds), *Beyond Westminster and Congress: The Nordic Experience* (Columbus, OH: Ohio State University Press, 2000), pp. 344–64.

Raunio, T. and Wiberg, M., 'Does Support Lead to Ignorance? National Parliaments and the Legitimacy of EU Governance', Acta Politica, 35: 2 (2000), pp. 146–68.

References

Raunio, T. and Wiberg, M., 'Johdanto: Suomi astuu unioniaikaan', in T. Raunio and M. Wiberg (eds), *EU ja Suomi: Unionijäsenyyden vaikutukset suomalaiseen yhteiskuntaan* (Helsinki: Edita, 2000), pp. 9–23.

Raunio, T. and Wiberg, M., 'Parliamentarizing Foreign Policy Decision-Making: Finland in the European Union', *Cooperation and Conflict*, 36: 1 (2001), pp. 61–86.

Rauramo, J., 'Euroopan parlamentin puolueryhmien koheesio ja koalitionmuodostus 1994–1998', in T. Martikainen and K. Pekonen (eds), *Eurovaalit Suomessa 1996: Vaalihumusta päätöksenteon arkeen* (Helsinki: Helsingin yliopisto, Yleisen valtio-opin laitos, Acta Politica 10, 1999), pp. 281–97.

Ray, L., 'Measuring Party Orientations Towards European Integration: Results from an Expert Survey', *European Journal of Political Research*, 36: 2 (1999), pp. 283–306.

Rehn, O., 'Pienen valtion legitiimi turvallisuusintressi', *Ulkopolitiikka*, 28: 1 (1991), pp. 52–64.

Rehn, O., 'Odottavasta ennakoivaan integraatiopolitiikkaan', in T. Forsberg and T. Vaahtoranta (eds), *Johdatus Suomen ulkopolitiikkaan* (Helsinki: Gaudeamus, 1993), pp. 166–231.

Rehn, O., *Pieni valtio Euroopan unionissa* (Helsinki: Kirjayhtymä, 1996).

Rehn, O., 'EU-asioiden kansallinen koordinaatio ja poliittinen ohjaus', in R. Lampinen, O. Rehn, P. Uusikylä et al., *EU-asioiden valmistelu Suomessa* (Helsinki: Eduskunnan kanslian julkaisu 7/1998), pp. 10–24.

Rometsch, D. and Wessels, W. (eds), *The European Union and Member States: Towards Institutional Fusion?* (Manchester: Manchester University Press, 1996).

Salovaara, J., 'Finnish Integration Policy – from an Economic to a Security Motivation', *Yearbook of Finnish Foreign Policy 1993* (1994), pp. 16–23.

Sandholtz, W., 'Membership Matters: Limits of the Functional Approach to European Institutions', *Journal of Common Market Studies*, 34: 3 (1996), pp. 403–29.

Sandström, C., 'Europeiskt partisamarbete och partiernas idémässiga utveckling', paper presented at the meeting of the Nordic Political Science Association, Uppsala, 19–21 August 1999.

Sänkiaho, R., 'Jako kahteen: ketkä puolesta, ketkä vastaan', in P. Pesonen (ed.), *Suomen EU- kansanäänestys 1994: Raportti äänestäjien kannanotoista* (Helsinki: Ulkoasiainministeriö, Eurooppa-tiedotus, ja Painatuskeskus 1994), pp. 64–73.

Sänkiaho, R., 'Puoluesidonnaisuutta vai sitoutumattomuutta', in Pertti Pesonen (ed.), *Suomen EU-kansanäänestys 1994: Raportti äänestäjien kannanotoista* (Helsinki: Ulkoasiainministeriö, Eurooppatiedotus, ja Painatuskeskus, 1994), pp. 164–73.

Scarrow, S.E., Webb, P. and Farrell, D.M., 'From Social Integration to Electoral Contestation', in R.J. Dalton and M.P. Wattenberg (eds), *Parties*

Without Partisans: Political Change in Advanced Industrial Democracies (Oxford: Oxford University Press, 2000), pp. 129–53.

Schout, A., 'The Presidency as a Juggler: Managing Conflicting Expectations', *Eipascope*, 2 (1998), pp. 2–10.

Sherrington, P., *The Council of Ministers* (London: Pinter, 2000).

Simula, A., 'Suomen EU-puheenjohtajuus hallinnollisten järjestelyjen näkökulmasta', in T. Martikainen and T. Tiilikainen (eds), *Suomi EU:n johdossa: Tutkimus Suomen puheenjohtajuudesta 1999* (Helsinki: Helsingin yliopisto, Yleisen valtio-opin laitos, Acta Politica 13, 2000), pp. 21–50.

Soetendorp, B. and Hanf, K., 'Conclusion: The Nature of National Adaptation to European Integration', in K. Hanf and B. Soetendorp (eds), *Adapting to European Integration: Small States and the European Union* (Harlow: Longman, 1998), pp. 186–94.

Stubb, A., 'The Finnish Presidency', *Journal of Common Market Studies*, Annual Review of the EU 1999/2000, pp. 49–53.

Stubb, A., Kaila, H. and Ranta, T., 'Finland: An Integrationist Member State', in E.E. Zeff and E.B. Pirro (eds), *The European Union and the Member States: Cooperation, Coordination, and Compromise* (Boulder, CO: Lynne Rienner, 2001), pp. 305–16.

Sundberg, J., 'Finland: Nationalized Parties, Professionalized Organizations', in R.S. Katz and P. Mair (eds), *How Parties Organize: Change and Adaptation in Party Organizations in Western Democracies* (London: Sage, 1994), pp. 159–84.

Sundberg, J., 'Organizational Structure of Parties, Candidate Selection and Campaigning', in S. Borg and R. Sänkiaho (eds), *The Finnish Voter* (Tampere: The Finnish Political Science Association, 1995), pp. 45–65.

Sundberg, J., *Partier och partisystem i Finland* (Esbo: Schildts, 1996).

Sundberg, J., 'Compulsory Party Democracy: Finland as a Deviant Case in Scandinavia', *Party Politics*, 3: 1 (1997), pp. 97–117.

Sundberg, J., 'The Enduring Scandinavian Party System', *Scandinavian Political Studies*, 22: 2 (1999), pp. 221–41.

Sundberg, J. and Gylling, C., 'Finland', in R.S. Katz and P. Mair (eds), *Party Organizations: A Data Handbook on Party Organizations in Western Democracies, 1960–90* (London: Sage, 1992), pp. 273–316.

Taggart, P., 'A Touchstone of Dissent: Euroscepticism in Contemporary Western European Party Systems', *European Journal of Political Research*, 33: 3 (1998), pp. 363–88.

Thorhallsson, B., 'The Administrative Working Procedures of Smaller States in the Decision-Making Process of the EU', paper presented at the ECPR Joint Sessions of Workshops, Copenhagen, 14–19 April 2000.

Thorhallsson, B., *The Role of Small States in the European Union* (Aldershot: Ashgate, 2000).

References

Tiilikainen, T., 'Suomen doktriini murtuu – suomalaisen politiikan kulku Paasikiven-Kekkosen realismista kohti yhteisöllisyyden Eurooppaa', *Ulkopolitiikka*, 29: 4 (1992), pp. 15–22.

Tiilikainen, T., *Europe and Finland: Defining the Political Identity of Finland in Western Europe* (Aldershot: Ashgate, 1998).

Tiilikainen, T., 'The Finnish Neutrality – Its New Forms and Future', in L. Goetschel (ed.), *Small States Inside and Outside the European Union* (Boston, MA: Kluwer, 1998), pp. 169–79.

Tiilikainen, T., 'Suomi johtajana EU:n ulkosuhteissa', in T. Martikainen and T. Tiilikainen (eds), *Suomi EU:n johdossa: Tutkimus Suomen puheenjohtajuudesta 1999* (Helsinki: Helsingin yliopisto, Yleisen valtio-opin laitos, Acta Politica 13, 2000), pp. 163–86.

Törnudd, K., 'Ties That Bind to the Recent Past; Debating Security Policy in Finland Within the Context of Membership in the European Union', *Cooperation and Conflict*, 31: 1 (1996), pp. 37–68.

Tuomioja, E., 'Konsensus tärkeää pienelle maalle', *Hallinto*, 4 (1998), pp. 4–7.

Väyrynen, R., 'Finland and the European Community: Changing Elite Bargains', *Cooperation and Conflict*, 28: 1 (1993), pp. 31–46.

Verbeke, J. and van de Voorde, W., 'The Presidency of the European Union: Some Reflections on Current Practice and Recent Evolutions', *Studia Diplomatica*, 47: 3 (1994), pp. 29–40.

Vesa, U., 'Suomen YK-politiikan pitkät linjat', *Ulkopolitiikka*, 37: 3 (2000), pp. 18–28.

Wallace, H., 'The Presidency: Tasks and Evolution', in C.O. Nuallain (ed.), *The Presidency of the European Council of Ministers* (London: Croom Helm, 1985), pp. 1–22.

Weiler, J.H.H., *The Constitution of Europe* (Cambridge: Cambridge University Press, 1999).

Wessels, W. and Rometsch, D., 'Conclusion: European Union and National Institutions', in D. Rometsch and W. Wessels (eds), *The European Union and Member States: Towards Institutional Fusion?* (Manchester: Manchester University Press, 1996), pp. 328–65.

Wiberg, M. (ed.), *The Public Purse and Political Parties: Public Financing of Political Parties in Nordic Countries* (Jyväskylä: The Finnish Political Science Association, 1991).

Wiberg, M. (ed.), *Parliamentary Control in the Nordic Countries: Forms of Questioning and Behavioural Trends* (Jyväskylä: The Finnish Political Science Association, 1994).

Wiberg, M., 'The Partyness of the Finnish Eduskunta', in K. Heidar and R. Koole (eds), *Parliamentary Party Groups in European Democracies: Political Parties behind Closed Doors* (London: Routledge, 2000), pp. 161–76.

Wiberg, M. and Raunio, T., 'Strong Parliament of a Small EU Member State:

The Finnish Parliament's Adaptation to the EU', *Journal of Legislative Studies*, 2: 4 (1996), pp. 302–21.

Wiberg, M. and Raunio, T., 'Where's the Power: Controlling Voting Outcomes in the Nordic Parliaments 1945–1995', in G.-E. Isaksson (ed.), *Inblickar i Nordisk Parlamentarism* (Åbo: Meddelanden från Ekonomisk-Statsvetenskapliga Fakulteten vid Åbo Akademi, Ser. A:470, 1997), pp. 245–59.

Wright, V., 'The National Co-Ordination of European Policy-Making: Negotiating the Quagmire', in J. Richardson (ed.), *European Union: Power and Policy-Making* (London: Routledge, 1996), pp. 148–69.

Zilliacus, K.O.K., '"New Politics" in Finland: The Greens and the Left Wing in the 1990s', *West European Politics*, 24: 1 (2001), pp. 27–54.

Index

Index

For Product Safety Concerns and Information please contact our EU
representative GPSR@taylorandfrancis.com
Taylor & Francis Verlag GmbH, Kaufingerstraße 24, 80331 München, Germany

www.ingramcontent.com/pod-product-compliance
Ingram Content Group UK Ltd.
Pitfield, Milton Keynes, MK11 3LW, UK
UKHW021439080625
459435UK00011B/306